# LONDON'S SHADOWS

# London's Shadows
*The Dark Side of the Victorian City*

Drew Gray

BLOOMSBURY

LONDON · NEW DELHI · NEW YORK · SYDNEY

**Bloomsbury Academic**

An imprint of Bloomsbury Publishing Plc

| 50 Bedford Square | 175 Fifth Avenue |
|---|---|
| London | New York |
| WC1B 3DP | NY 10010 |
| UK | USA |

**www.bloomsbury.com**

First published 2010
This paperback edition first published 2013

**British Library Cataloguing-in-Publication Data**
A catalogue record for this book is available from the British Library.

ISBN: HB: 978-1-8472-5242-5
PB: 978-1-4411-4720-2

Typeset by Pindar NZ, Auckland, New Zealand

# Contents

# Acknowledgements

This project has grown out of my work with third-year undergraduates at the University of Northampton and so I would like to express my thanks to the many students that have stimulated debates, argued about the identity of 'Jack' and listened to my lectures over the past six years. I hope they enjoy this book. In particular I would like to thank Lucy, Rachael and Katie for enlivening the classes in 2009. As ever my colleagues at Northampton have all been very supportive while I have tried to complete this volume and find the time for my teaching duties – their understanding of my occasional lapses are most appreciated.

Aside from the welcome feedback from my editor, Michael Greenwood, I want to express my thanks to my mother, Diana Falkiner, who read my drafts and corrected many of my errors. Finally, and most of all, I would like to thank Jill Spencer for reading my work and helping me shape my ideas, but most importantly for letting me into her life and for believing in me at all times. This book is for her.

# List of Illustrations

## FIGURES

## TABLES

# Creating the 'Myth' of Jack the Ripper

In August of 1882 a well-meaning female member of the Victorian middle classes wrote a lengthy missive in a periodical magazine urging her sisters to help her and others in bringing reform and inspiration to the poor of East London. 'If only *more* ladies would come forward and help, how much might be done!' she wrote.[1] Margaret Tillard compared the work she and other Victorian women were doing with the life of Christ noting that:

> It is the personal contact, the personal sympathy, the personal interest, as if it were the touch of the Saviour, which is needed. It is not what you give, it is what you do for the poor, which really touches their feelings and binds them to you.[2]

By the 1880s the problems of London's poorest communities had been well documented and were to continue to be the subject of exposés, investigations, parliamentary committees and newspaper articles well into the next century. Margaret Tillard was just one of hundreds who felt compelled, for religious, political or moral reasons, to attempt to mitigate the worst excesses of poverty that blighted some parts of England's capital. London was the heart of empire and it was a damning indictment of the inequality of Victorian Britain that large areas of Europe's most populated city resembled the slums of Calcutta. Contemporary observers compared the denizens of the East End of London with the 'savages' of the Pacific Islands or 'darkest' Africa. For many middle-class Victorians this was a land that God had abandoned, an area ripe for missionary work and charity. Tillard's essay stresses the importance of contact with the people of the East End. She sees the role of her class in almost medieval terms. There is, she states, 'even in these Radical days, a wonderful amount of old feudal feeling amongst us still'. Just as the rural poor looked up to their local squire or lord of the manor so the communities of the East End looked up to their middle-class saviours.

> When they get to know you and your family, there is a pride in you and for you, and a feeling that what belongs to you belongs to them in some way. An instance of

this came before me only the other day. At a concert that was given in an East End district, the people of a certain court would have it that 'their lady's' voice was the best in the room.[3]

Margaret Tillard urges her readers not to simply resort to charitable giving: 'there is a great deal of selfishness in our almsgiving; we give too often, not in the way best for the recipients, but as is the least trouble to ourselves.' In this she was echoing the views of women such as Octavia Hill, the matriarch of the Charity Organization Society (COS) that had established the practice of home visiting in the second half of the nineteenth century. The COS was the forerunner of twentieth-century social work, but it was an organization steeped in Christian doctrine and paternalism. Tillard's wistful reference to feudalism reflects both the Victorian love affair with the middle ages and its rigid class system; a system that was beginning to come under strain but was not to unravel until after the First World War. Tillard and Hill did not envisage a society in which the working classes of the East End would become their equals, nor did they seem to believe that the poor were the victims of a desperately unequal economic system. They themselves were rich women who owed their own comfortable lives to the dowries provided by their parents or to the land and incomes of their husbands. Restricted by the governing principles of 'separate spheres' (which decreed that women were only allowed a domestic role, not a public one) charity work was often the only 'career' open to them.

Tillard, and other 'ladies' like her wanted to bring the message of religious salvation to the homes of the working-class poor. She realized that sometimes this had to be done subtly: those that attempted to preach on the doorstep would often receive short shrift or worse from those living there. Some were almost beyond help – the feckless, the drunk, the criminal – but many others could be carefully steered towards the right path. This sort of missionary work must have brought great comfort to many people and it is easy to sneer at the women of the COS and other organizations from the distance of history, but in looking back at London in the late nineteenth century we are faced with the problem that often it is their voices that predominate. Octavia Hill, Helen Bosanquet and Beatrice Webb have all left behind their opinions about the poor. Charles Booth, Jack London and Henry Mayhew have likewise penned lengthy observations about the state of the poor and the reasons for their miserable lives. Newspaper editors and correspondents to the papers, middle-class and elite writers all, have bequeathed us a hoard of rhetoric and explanation for crime, poverty, vice and disease in the slums of Whitechapel. What we are missing in all of this is the voice of the people of East London themselves. Thus everything we read about the poor comes to us through a filter of middle class and often evangelist ideology. This does not mean we should ignore it but rather it requires that we try and understand that this is merely a partial view of the East End. What the poor themselves felt about the COS ladies who descended upon them is an interesting but unanswerable question.

The East End was the not worst nor the most criminal place to live in London in the 1880s, but it was representative for many Victorians of the depths to which humanity could sink when separated from a close relationship with God and Christian religion. When in 1888 an unknown individual began to brutally murder prostitutes under the noses of the police in the alleys and streets of Whitechapel, some believed that the area had finally reached its nadir of degradation. As a result of the murders, attention was refocused on the social problems facing the population of the East End and the cries that 'something must be done' echoed in the press, parliament and even in the corridors of Windsor and Buckingham Palace. For some people it is the murders themselves that provide the fascination that has endured since then, but in this book I would like to consider the ways in which the killings affected attitudes towards the perceived problems of East London. In doing so I would like to keep in mind middle-class perceptions of poverty and personal responsibility along with both modern and contemporary attempts to manipulate the Ripper murders for political, cultural and social purposes.

## STRUCTURE AND SOURCES

It is over 120 years since the investigation into the series of homicides in East London known as the Whitechapel murders was brought to a close. In that time dozens if not hundreds of suspects have been presented to the public for consideration by a growing number of 'experts' who have been given the name of 'ripperologists'. This in itself is an interesting development in the history of crime and criminology – a subgenre of investigation has emerged from the slaying of five or more women in the late nineteenth century. If you have selected this book because you want to know who Jack the Ripper was then I must advise you that you may well be disappointed by it. I am not a ripperologist and it is not my intention to offer up my own solution to the mystery. Nor is the identity of the murderer the most interesting thing about the case – arguably his anonymity has allowed legions of investigators to delve into the archives in the hope of uncovering something fresh to say about the murders. While there are some excellent histories, notably the work of Donald Rumbelow and Paul Begg in particular, the genre is bedevilled with poorly researched and badly written studies that simply repeat the work of previous histories. Worse still some recent books have attempted to fit the facts of the case, such as they are, to suit their own favourite suspect.

In this opening chapter we will meet some of these 'suspects' and attempt to refute the allegations aimed at them. I am aware that most volumes do this the other way around but then this does not purport to be another Ripper book. Instead this is a book about the London in which the killings took place and will hopefully provide a deeper context for those interested in the murderer and his victims. The Whitechapel murders have so far attracted little real interest from academic historians although there are some notable exceptions. In 1988, Christopher Frayling wrote an important essay and scripted perhaps the most thoughtful television documentary that has been made about the murders. Frayling's article has recently been included in a collection edited by Alexandra Warwick and Martin Willis. While some of the essays have been in circulation for some time (notably one chapter of L. Perry Curtis' most excellent monograph, *Jack the Ripper and the London Press*) there are several new entries and Warwick and Willis are to be warmly congratulated for bringing them to a new audience. In addition, the recent Museum of London Docklands' exhibition produced a well-illustrated volume containing a number of intelligent essays on a range of subjects such as the police, immigrant communities and poverty. However, while there are these few examples the field has largely been left to the ripperologists and amateur historians.[4]

This study has used much of the historiography concerned with crime, the Ripper and London that has been produced over the past 20 or more years and there is a considerable amount of it. Naturally it cannot hope to cover all the work that has been published and so I apologize in advance for any omissions that have been made. Where possible I have tried to return to the original sources for the history of the Whitechapel murders and have used the records of trials at the Old Bailey and of hearings before the Thames Police Court to study the related area of crime and criminality in the period. The chief sources for much of this book have been the contemporary London newspapers that have recently become available via the British Library's internet portal. Newspapers are not without their weaknesses: the presentation of news is often determined by editorial style and the choice of subject by fashion, newsworthiness and contemporary concerns. Despite their protestations to the contrary, newspaper editors are in the business of selling papers. Crime, sexual scandal and sensation are the staple of good copy in the modern newspaper industry and the same was true in the last quarter of the nineteenth century. Thus, we should be warned not to believe everything we read in the newspapers. Despite this caveat the nineteenth-century press does offer us an important window into attitudes towards a whole raft of social issues in the period. Therefore I have used them extensively in this book alongside the reports of parliamentary committees, the works of social reformers, police officials, correspondents to the newspapers and other private individuals.

In this introductory chapter we will look at the Ripper story as the creation of a modern myth, a theme I will return to when considering the role of the press in the late nineteenth century. There is something in the Ripper story that lends itself to the falsification of history – the interplay of popular culture, press reportage and fiction – and what we think of as history. To some extent this has to do with how we envisage the past and how we use history to unravel some of the problems of the present.

I will then go on to look at the suspects in the Ripper case and at how, almost from the moment the first murder occurred, writers have used them to say things about the society in which they were living. In doing so I will start with Frayling's useful thesis that the killer fitted into three archetypes of late Victorian culture: the mad doctor, foreign Jew and the decadent aristocrat. To some extent these tropes have persisted and we will consider why this has been the case. Finally, in discussing those suspected of being the Whitechapel murderer this opening section will offer a critique of the work of some more recent writers who have offered us up both famous and unknown suspects to be tried by the court of public opinion and then executed – as the Ripper would certainly have been had he been caught. In particular I would like to reexamine the work of the American crime writer Patricia Cornwell who had the temerity to declare the case 'closed' when she exposed the painter Walter Sickert as being responsible for the murders. However, those proposing a Royal conspiracy or the founder of the National Archives of Wales, will not escape scrutiny here. This may not be a book about who Jack the Ripper was, but it is certainly partly about who he was not.

Chapter 2 will contextualize murder in the nineteenth century so that the Whitechapel murders can be more properly understood for what they were: extreme examples of sexual homicide almost without precedent in Victorian Britain. However, they were not the first or only examples in Europe, and the work of contemporary and more modern criminologists and psychoanalysts will be used to explore the crimes of the Ripper and those who attacked in similar ways. It will also look at the sorts of murders that made the newspapers in the late Victorian period before going on to examine the file on the Whitechapel murders in some detail. This is necessary for two reasons. First, while many readers may be familiar with the case others may be coming to the story for the first time. Second, so much of what we have learned about the 'Ripper' has been presented in half truths, theories and fiction and so in this section I have returned to the police files and contemporary newspapers to try and reconstruct the pattern of events as closely and accurately as possible. However, it is not the intention of this book to reopen the case and I would refer readers who wish to take an even more in-depth look at the murders to consult the works of Begg and Rumbelow who know so much more than myself.

In Chapter 3 the focus of attention moves away from the murders and to the nature of Whitechapel and how it was envisaged by contemporaries. The Victorians had a problematic relationship with urban environments: to some they represented the sheer magnificence of Victorian culture and economic success while to others they were cesspools of vice and poverty that shamed the Empire. This dichotomy was never more apparent than in the contrasts between East and West London. This chapter will explore these contrasts before going on to examine exactly where and what the East End was and is. Having set out to explore the East End I will then concentrate on its inhabitants, both indigenous and foreign immigrants and the problems that these divergent racial groups experienced. Once again this chapter will be partly concerned with overturning contemporary and more recent myths and stereotypes, to reach a more balanced picture of the East End.

Chapter 4 concentrates on the social problems associated with the East End and with those Victorians who believed it was their mission to bring comfort, relief and civilization to this seemingly neglected area of the Empire. It has been argued that the Ripper murders spotlighted the problems of poor housing conditions and poverty and impelled local authorities to take action to improve the situation. However, as this chapter shows, there had been attempts at reform and improvement long before 'Jack' started his reign of terror. That many of these attempts either failed or simply moved the problem elsewhere was perhaps a reflection of a lack of a unified municipal authority in London. After 1888 the creation of the London County Council went some way to addressing this issue but it was not until the Edwardian and postwar period that real tangible reform began to benefit the poorest inhabitants of East London. This chapter will look at the realities of housing in the district in which the murders took place and at legislation designed to improve it.

Chapter 4 will also examine the underlying philosophies of two of the period's most prominent female philanthropists: Beatrice Webb and Helen Bosanquet. These women, both of whom worked with Octavia Hill in the COS, held strong opinions about the best methods of helping the poor. At times they were in agreement but it is in their disagreements that we can usefully explore the emergence of distinct policies aimed at poverty and dependence that came to affect social reform in the twentieth century and still echo in our current society.

In Chapter 5 we turn our attention to the Victorian press and in particular examine the relationship between the newspapers and other forms of popular culture. From the mid-nineteenth century onwards the newspapers enjoyed a steady growth, encouraged in part by greater literacy and improvements in production techniques. During this period newspapers became cheaper to produce and many more people had access to them. This led to greater numbers of papers and periodicals and increased competition for audiences. In this chapter the development of investigative reporting and the so-called 'new journalism' (as expounded by editors such as the *Pall Mall Gazette*'s William T. Stead) will be analysed. It will also consider the extent to which the press used the Whitechapel murders to create a 'moral panic' for their own purposes. The relationship between the public, popular culture and the newspapers of the late nineteenth century is one of the most fascinating aspects of the Ripper case and, leaving aside Perry Curtis' seminal work, has too often been neglected.

All of the Ripper's victims were street prostitutes and prostitution and its control is the subject of Chapter 6. Using contemporary accounts and more recent historiography this section will attempt to understand Victorian conceptions of, and attitudes towards, prostitution. Using a well-documented newspaper exposé of child prostitution it will also consider the problem of people trafficking in the late 1800s. Much of this sadly makes for comparisons with the present day and the reality of the vice trade in Britain. This chapter will also attempt to look at the women who were forced into prostituting themselves and at how this affected their lives and their families. We cannot consider the problem of prostitution in the Victorian age without looking at the attempts of the authorities to deal with the related issue of venereal disease and its affect on the armed forces. Therefore, this chapter will analyse the Contagious Diseases Acts, the reasons for their implementation, the campaign against them (orchestrated by Josephine Butler) and their eventual repeal in 1884.

This is, of course, a book about crime and criminality, even if the awful events of 1888 are far removed from most murders let alone most criminal activity. In Chapter 7 it is crime and those who committed crime that is the focus of attention. The nineteenth century saw the new social science of criminology develop from its early roots in the eighteenth century and the work of Cesare Lombroso and others drew the attention of the press and public. The notion that a 'criminal class' existed in mid- to late Victorian Britain gained ground and served as a useful tool for those wishing to justify the introduction of more draconian punishments or increased expenditure on professional policing. Thus, Chapter 7 will look at these ideas and how they affected policy-making. It will then explore the nature of crime as it was prosecuted at police courts and the Old Bailey in London using court records and the reporting of events in the newspapers. In this there will be a necessary concentration on property crimes such as burglary and robbery because these were the offences that contemporaries believed were most often committed by the criminal class. However, the work of the police courts was largely involved with policing petty theft, disorderly drunken behaviour and interpersonal violence – this will be covered in some detail here. Finally, Chapter 7 will look at the ways in which those convicted of offences were dealt with. The justice system of the late nineteenth century was dominated by the prison, and commentators and administrators alike debated the most effective and appropriate ways in which to treat those who arrived within the gates of Pentonville and similar institutions. The treatment of prisoners and the state of the prison system is still a matter of intense debate in the twenty-first century and we might remind ourselves that these arguments have been going on for over 200 years.

In Chapter 8 we turn to the police who failed to catch the 'Whitechapel fiend'. The Metropolitan police had suffered a few years of criticism in the wake of a series of events that culminated in the Whitechapel murders. This chapter will look at the way in which the police handled the demonstrations of the unemployed in the 1880s as well as their response to the threat of Irish terrorism during the same period. The story of Fenian outrages has been little told in recent histories and forms an interesting backdrop to the Ripper investigation. Chapter 8 will then consider how effective the police were in trying to catch 'Jack', concluding that they have suffered rather unfairly from some of the brickbats thrown at them both at the time and thereafter.

## THE USUAL SUSPECTS: THE SEARCH FOR THE IDENTITY OF JACK THE RIPPER

For every book written about the Whitechapel murders there is a suspect in the frame. It would seem that most of those who choose to write about the case do so in the hope of persuading the reader that their own pet theory is the correct one. As I stated at the outset, this is not my intention. This desire to solve the mystery of the murderer's identity is understandable, as is the process of refuting each new suggested killer. After all if we actually found out who had killed five or more women in the late summer and autumn of 1888 then who would continue to be interested in the case? Without the mystery the Whitechapel murders become just another tale of sadistic serial killing: interesting but not nearly as compelling.

The Casebook website (perhaps the most useful of all ripperology portals on the internet) has been running a poll of visitors to gauge who is the most popular of all the suspects listed. At the moment the top 20 stands thus:

1. James Maybrick
2. Francis Tumblety
3. Walter Sickert
4. The Royal Conspiracy
5. Joseph Barnett
6. George Chapman
7. Aaron Kosminski
8. The Lodger
9. Montague John Druitt
10. Jill the Ripper
11. W. H. Bury
12. Francis Thompson
13. R. D'Onston Stephenson
14. Michael Ostrog
15. George Hutchinson
16. Prince Albert Victor
17. Dr Thomas Neill Cream
18. James Kelly
19. James Kenneth Stephen
20. Dr Pedachenko[5]

There are more recent additions that have not made the top ten, including a local East End mortuary assistant, Robert Mann, named recently by Dr Mei Trow.[6] Despite the extensive (but not exhaustive) list above new suspects will continue to emerge. This is the nature of ripper studies: the search for a culprit dominates the genre.

As Christopher Frayling observed those selected as possible killers have generally fallen into three types: an 'English milord', mad doctor or foreigner (in particular an immigrant Jew). These suggested suspects are not modern inventions but were in common currency in 1888 and immediately afterwards, and each is a representation of the 'other' in Victorian society.

The contemporary newspapers, the *Pall Mall Gazette* for example, chose the person of Rosslyn D'Onston Stephenson, a self-styled occultist who fitted the image of a decadent English gentleman who killed for pleasure. The image of the depraved aristocrat was a convenient one for the middle-class editor of the *Gazette* to present to a readership recently horrified by the revelations that members of the upper classes were routinely purchasing teenage working-class virgins for as little as £5 a time (as we shall see in Chapter 6). Likewise the Ripper was thought by some to be a middle-class do-gooder, one of the many philanthropists and religious men that had set up camp in the East End to save the area from itself.

The notion that 'Jack' was a doctor arose from the suggestion (by some, but significantly not all, of those who examined the bodies of the victims) that the killer possessed some medical knowledge. This was despite the fact that, as the City of London's own medical expert declared, the killer 'does not even possess the technical knowledge of a butcher or horse slaughterman or any person accustomed to cut up dead animals'.[7] The most recent suspect, the Whitechapel mortuary attendant Robert Mann, is the latest to be linked to the crimes through some tenuous link with medicine. Mann worked alongside professional medical practictioners and thus would have been able to gain a working knowledge of human anatomy. However, this would have applied equally to medical students, countless local slaughtermen and butchers, and presumably anyone who took the time and trouble to consult an anatomy textbook or attend a series of public lectures.

That the Ripper was a foreigner was another theory that engaged contemporary opinion. Perhaps 'Jack' was one of the many foreign sailors who arrived on the London docks from all over the Empire, Europe and beyond. The Portuguese and Spanish were renowned for their use of knives; the more exotic Lascars and Caribs had cultures far removed from civilized Englishmen; the Jews had provided a focus for anti-alienism for centuries and now there were more of them than ever before packed into the workshops and slums of East London. Jews from Eastern Europe also brought with them the contagion of revolutionary socialism and anarchism, so the idea that the Ripper was a mad-eyed Polish revolutionary was not beyond contemporary imagining.

Of course much of this contemporary mud-slinging was initiated by the editors of the London newspapers, keen to provide their readers with a social commentary on the murders and to ensure the story remained uppermost in the public imagination so that increased circulation rates were maintained. However, while we might excuse the late Victorians (who had little understanding of the way in which serial killers operated) their prejudices born of ignorance, can we extend the same allowances to more modern scholars? After all, as Frayling points out, nearly all those who have been put forward as Ripper suspects in the last 120 years still continue to be drawn from the broad typology that he has identified, even when 'there is so much evidence, social *and* psychological, to contradict them'.[8] Thus, we have a plethora of mad doctors: Dr Cream (who supposedly confessed as his hangman launched him 'into eternity'), Dr Tumblety (who escaped the clutches of Scotland Yard by fleeing to the USA) and Dr Williams who helped found the National Library of Wales and apparently bequeathed the bloody knife he used to murder his victims to the archives there.

Neil Cream is an unlikely suspect despite making the top 20 on the Casebook website: his only connection to the murders is his alleged last-minute confession and there is evidence that from 1881 to 1891 he was locked up in an American gaol, although this has not prevented some from suggesting he had a doppelganger who committed the murders while he was incarcerated. Francis Tumblety was put forward as a suspect by Stewart Evans and Paul Gainey.[9] Tumblety was arrested by the police and supposedly charged in connection with the Whitechapel murders. However, it seems unlikely that they truly believed they had their man, given that he was granted bail a few days after Mary Kelly became the Ripper's fifth victim, and he fled the continent under a false name. Stewart Evans' reason for identifying this most unpleasant individual was the emergence of a new piece of evidence in the ongoing Ripper inquiry. This was a letter penned by Chief Inspector Littlechild in 1913 in which Tumblety is named as a 'very likely suspect'. The letter seems authentic and there are several other reasons why Tumblety has remained close to the top of many people's lists of 'Rippers'. However, Tumblety was a known homosexual, indeed it was this that brought him to police attention long before the Whitechapel murders began. From what we now understand of serial killers it would seem unlikely that a homosexual 'lust murderer' would gain any sexual pleasure from mutilating female victims.[10] Littlechild's letter is suitably vague and this allows it to be interpreted in a number of ways. This is a feature of much of the Ripper evidence. Littlechild says, for example, that although Tumblety was 'a "Sycopathia Sexualis"[sic] subject he was not known as a "Sadist" (which the murderer unquestionably was) but his feelings toward women were remarkable and bitter in the extreme, a fact on record'.[11] Littlechild was also writing some 25 years after the murders to a journalist interested in the case. As a result this evidence is not quite as clear or as strong as some might want us to believe: the jury is still out on Francis Tumblety.

Dr (Sir) John Williams is a more recent name to be associated with the murders. When Tony Williams was researching his family history in the National Library of Wales, Aberystwyth, he came across a box which held the doctor's effects including a surgical knife and three slides supposedly containing 'animal matter'.[12] According to this account Dr John Williams worked at the London hospital for a time and murdered the five women in the Ripper case files in his search of a cure for his wife's infertility. This is a most unlikely scenario for a serious medical practitioner and stretches the credibility of Williams as a suspect. According to Tony Williams and Humphrey Price, Dr Williams also performed an abortion on Mary Ann Nichols in 1885 and managed to have an affair with Marie Kelly who he had known from Wales. Overall Tony Williams' case is severely flawed and based almost entirely on conjecture. Williams is not alone in this; many of the scores of Ripper books are poorly researched and would probably not have seen the light of day had they not been about the most elusive serial killer history has so far produced. As Robin Odell notes in an essay published on the Casebook website, 'Making accusations that erode the good name and reputation of long-dead eminent Victorians has become something of a cult in the vast literature that has grown up around Ripperology'.[13] He points out that Dr John Williams is just the latest in a long line that includes Queen Victoria's surgeon Dr William Gull, a man at the centre of one of the most enduring conspiracy theories that surround the case.

Towards the end of the 1970s the idea that the Ripper murders were actually the work of more than one individual emerged in Stephen Knight's book *Jack the Ripper: The Final Solution*. The seed for this had been a BBC Television drama documentary in which Joseph Sickert (the son of the Victorian artist Walter Sickert) alleged that his father had told him the dark truth about the murders. In brief, the conspiracy unfolds thus: Prince Albert Victor Christian Edward (or 'Eddy' to his friends), the grandson of Queen Victoria and therefore possible heir to the throne, became involved with an ordinary working-class girl called Annie Crook who had been introduced to the prince by his friend Walter Sickert. As a result of their dalliance Eddy and Annie had a child (Alice Margaret) and subsequently married in secret. This was of particular concern to the Queen because Annie was not only poor and a commoner – she was a Catholic. This last fact threatened the very fabric of the nation and when the Prime Minister, Lord Salisbury, found out about the affair he ordered that Annie be removed and the pair separated. Salisbury enlisted Sir William Gull's (the royal physician) help in having Annie committed to an asylum where she was forced to undergo an operation that caused her to lose her memory if not her mind. Walter Sickert rescued baby Alice and arranged for her nanny, one Mary Kelly, to look after her and keep her away from the agents of the government and royal family. So Mary took the child to be raised by nuns. Alas Mary was overcome by the enormity of Annie's affair with the Duke of Clarence and broke down. Eventually she fell into prostitution on the streets of Whitechapel where she told anyone that would listen about Eddy's indiscretion and the existence of his love child.

At this point three of her companions, Polly Nichols, Elizabeth Stride and Annie Chapman, recognizing an opportunity to drag themselves out of the gutter, persuaded Mary to use the story to extort money from the government in exchange for not going to the newspapers. Lord Salisbury now persuaded Sir William Gull to silence the women once and for all and he and his cab driver, John Netley, trawled the streets of Whitechapel gradually picking off the women one by one. Unfortunately for her, Catherine (or Kate) Eddowes was a case of mistaken identity as she had used the name Kelly when arrested by the police. When Gull and Netley finally caught up with Mary Kelly – the source of all the trouble – they made sure she would never speak to anyone ever again. In a rather neat twist Knight alleges that as Gull, Salisbury and the head of the Metropolitan Police, Sir Charles Warren, were all Freemasons it was easy to cover up the crimes and put the blame on Montague Druitt (whose body was dragged from the Thames some weeks after the Kelly murder).[14]

The Freemasonry angle allows Knight to get around his lack of any tangible evidence. The network of Freemasons means that it would all have been destroyed. It is a classic conspiracy theory – the lack of evidence is in fact evidence of its veracity. The story also endures because it goes to the heart of Victorian society and touches the Royal Family itself. We want to believe it because it is so incredible, especially in a modern age when the Royals have lost some of their previous glister. It is no surprise that the Royal conspiracy has featured in several films about the murders, including the most recent outing with Johnny Depp and Heather Graham, *From Hell*, inspired by the graphic novel of the same name.[15]

Although the Royal conspiracy is entertaining it has little basis in truth. Indeed truth seems to be almost incidental in some of the books that have claimed to unveil the identity of Jack the Ripper. Having looked at 'killer doctors' we can turn to consider some of the claims made against depraved English gentlemen or those that might fall into a similar category. Montague Druitt, who was one of three suspects named in the infamous McNaughten memorandum, apparently committed suicide soon after the Kelly murder in November 1888. Druitt was a quiet barrister or school teacher who feared he was losing his mind (like his mother before him) and it is alleged, but not proven, that he had lost his position at a private school because he had been caught 'interfering' with one of the boys. If we believe Knight's account, he was fitted up and possibly murdered by the Freemasons. Among the possessions found at his home was a suicide note in which he wrote: 'Since Friday I felt I was going to be like mother, and the best thing for me was to die.' If Inspector McNaughten had not named him, along with Kosminski, 'a poor Polish Jew', and Michael Ostrog, a petty criminal who is quite easily dismissed as a suspect, there would be little reason to suspect him. He is a gentleman and his suicide fits neatly with the end of the murders. But why are we looking for a gentleman at all?

Another Victorian gent has, in recent years, also been accused after his diary surfaced in Liverpool to shed new light on the case in 1991. In his own words James Maybrick recounts the murders in all their gory detail and even left behind a ladies gold watch engraved with the words 'I am Jack – J. Maybrick' complete with the initials of his victims scratched on the back. Surely now researchers had the missing evidence to prove the killer's identity? Unfortunately some have had the temerity to doubt the provenance of the diary and watch. Had it been faked they asked? The person that brought the diary to the attention of the world, Michael Barrett, has admitted it was a forgery and then retracted his confession before again denying its authenticity. After a tremendous amount of investigation it remains unclear whether the diary is genuine or not but even if it is there is no conclusive proof that it was written by the murderer. The diary fits the dramatic narrative of Ripper suspects; after all, Maybrick was himself murdered – poisoned by his wife Florence in one of the most sensational murder stories of 1889. How fitting that he should posthumously confess to an even more sensational crime a century later.

If the Maybrick diary represents one of the worst excesses of ripperology then one final example of a killer gentleman is equally deserving of a serious critique. In 2002 the American crime novelist Patricia Cornwell went to press with her own version of a Ripper whodunit. In *Portrait of a Killer – Jack the Ripper: Case Closed* she argued, using an earlier study as her starting point,[16] that after deploying modern forensic science and large amounts of her own money she had at last unmasked the Whitechapel murderer. This time saw a return to the plot for Walter Sickert, although on this occasion as the central figure rather than a supporting character. Sickert, a fine English painter who enjoyed the atmosphere of the music hall and the company of women of loose morals, had apparently murdered five prostitutes and written gloating messages to the press. In addition he could not resist the impulse to revel in his success at evading the police by painting clues to his alter ego in several of his works of art. Cornwell busied herself in examining the hundreds of 'Ripper letters' received by the London news agencies and in cutting up Sickert's paintings in the hunt for DNA evidence and examples of his handwriting or style of address. Naturally she found no matching DNA as Sickert was cremated, but she found links through the less exact process of mitochondrial DNA (mtDNA) profiling. Cornwell also found that several letters were signed 'Nemo', a nickname Sickert was known to have used. Furthermore Sickert painted a picture entitled 'Jack the Ripper's bedroom', and in 'The Camden Town Murder' Cornwell argued that Sickert had drawn upon visual evidence only available to the Whitechapel killer. Finally, according to Cornwell, Walter Sickert suffered from a fistula on his penis which had left him impotent and with an intense hatred of women. This supposedly explains his desire to cut up five prostitutes in the East End. Thus, there was a small mountain of circumstantial evidence linking Sickert to the letters. However, there is very little evidence that stands up to any scrutiny.

The first problem with this theory is that Sickert clearly enjoyed female company and quite probably fathered at least one bastard child, Joseph. He did, however, frequent the music halls and was fascinated by the Ripper crimes. On one occasion he chased a group of female theatre-goers through the London streets shouting 'I'm Jack!'. This is hardly novel in the rarefied atmosphere of 1888. Most of London was enthralled or appalled by the murders in the East End and Sickert's love of low-life culture places him firmly in the same artistic boat as his French contemporary Toulouse Lautrec. That he drew upon the murders in his paintings is therefore hardly surprising; Lautrec painted prostitutes and dancers, Sickert was no different. As for the Ripper letters and the use of the sobriquet 'Nemo', this was a name that was in common usage during the period meaning 'no-name'. Indeed Charles Dickens' law writer in *Bleak House* signs himself in just the same manner. Cornwell found some matches for mtDNA in some of the letters but this is not an exact science – it is more akin to blood typing – so for Sickert to share some mtDNA with one or more of the letter writers is neither impossible nor a reason to link him to the murders. Regardless of either of these pieces of 'evidence', Cornwell is missing a vital point. It is highly likely that all of the letters are fakes or hoaxes and do not come from the killer at all. The only one that requires a second or third glance is the 'From Hell' letter sent to the chairman of the Whitechapel Vigilance Committee and even this is now widely believed to be a red herring. Notwithstanding this, it should surely have troubled Cornwell that she found no trace of Sickert on this letter at all. The final nail in Cornwell's theory is that Sickert is reported as having been in France with a female lover on at least one of the dates on which the killer struck. She cannot prove he was in London at this time. Her bold declaration of 'case closed' therefore has a very hollow ring to it.[17]

To some extent the very nature of the Ripper murders demands we find a culprit deserving of their particular depravity; that some mundane East London 'Everyman' committed these crimes is simply insufficient for the legions of ripperologists, researchers and interested readers. The perpetual creation of new suspects is symptomatic of our desire for what the Americans would call 'closure'. As a result the five or more victims are slaughtered over and over again as if they were part of a modern computer game as theory after theory is propounded. Cornwell, Feldman (the proponent of the Maybrick diary) and Knight are all guilty of taking a theory and then searching for evidence that supports it. There is nothing wrong with this general approach to writing history, so long as evidence is neither manipulated nor stretched to fit the author's thesis. Worse still, if conflicting evidence is shamelessly misrepresented or ignored then the truth is buried deeper with every new study. Paul Feldman does this by swallowing the hoax diary story, Patricia Cornwell misinterpreted her forensic 'evidence' in her desire to prove that Sickert was the killer, and Stephen Knight fell back on the Freemasonary cover up to paper over the holes in his conspiracy theory. History requires a level of academic rigour that is sadly lacking from many of the Ripper books. Conjecture replaces fact, hearsay is substituted for documentary proof. Needless to say if many of those presented as Ripper suspects were alive today they would have no problem in suing their accusers in the courts and walking away with large financial settlements. Unfortunately for them it is much easier to accuse a dead person than it is to place the same accusation at the feet of a living one. Moreover it is unlikely that a jury would convict any of these suspects on the evidence presented against them.

There are a number of more ordinary Ripper suspects but even these fall within Frayling's broad typology of cultural stereotypes. Aaron Kosminski, David Cohen/Nathan Kaminsky, George Chapman/Severin Klosowski, Jacob Levy and Nikolay Vasiliev are all East Europeans, all Polish (with the exception of Vasiliev) and mostly Jews. The McNaughten memorandum identified a 'poor Polish Jew' as one of the prime suspects and this has led researchers to go looking for likely candidates within Whitechapel's large immigrant population. Once again the distortions of historical research are apparent.

First, Sir Melville McNaughten's 1894 memorandum has perhaps been invested with too much significance. This memo, written by an officer that joined the Ripper inquiry in 1889, was also referred to by Robert Anderson in his memoirs and he seems to have been convinced that the Ripper was a local Jew, an opinion he stuck to after his retirement. The hunt to identify who 'Kosminski' was (McNaughten does not give him a first name and Anderson does not name him at all) has led local historians and ripperologists to scour the archives of the local Poor Law unions and asylums and has turned up a number of plausible characters. However, similar problems beset the Polish Jew candidacy as have plagued the English milord and the mad doctor, records have been lost or destroyed – deliberately or otherwise. Arguably there are enough poor Jews in the East End for us to keep the search for 'Jack' going well into the twenty-first century.

So why are we looking for a Jew? Or a doctor? Or a gentleman? Because they are archetypes, representations of the 'other'; they are not Eastenders but outsiders. They were, and are, convenient scapegoats for a range of contemporary fears and modern misconceptions. They also feed the growing myth making that surrounds the case. Crediting the murders to the Jewish community (both by accusing one of their number and then suggesting that he only evaded trial because Jewish witnesses refused to testify against one of their own) is a clear example of late nineteenth-century xenophobia. The mutilations allow both contemporaries and modern writers to point to the threat posed by 'foreigners who are bent on undermining society in general via covertly ritualized murder'.[18] Thus the murders are elided with anarchism and socialist revolution and firmly associated with Eastern European fanatics sheltering in liberal England and taking advantage of our freedoms. We might note that similar mud is being slung at the modern Muslim community in Britain in the wake of Islamist terrorism in London and elsewhere.

That 'Jack' was Jewish is merely conjecture, that he was insane is less easy to refute. In 1894 the *Sun* suggested that the killer was locked up in Broadmoor prison as a criminal lunatic. In this instance 'Jack' was a member of the London middle-classes-gone-wrong, in other theories he is a mad doctor or a crazed working-class mortuary assistant or slaughterman. He must be mad but there is little real attempt to understand his motivations beyond that. Once again it is convenient to simply dismiss the killer as someone unlike us, someone possessing animalistic, subhuman tendencies, a real-life Mr Hyde. 'Jack' was, like the fictional alter ego of Dr Jekyll, a gothic monster who has been imbued with many of society's fears about itself. The 1880s were a turbulent period in European history, with revolutionary movements abroad and Irish terrorism at home. Britain was in the grip of an economic slump, if not a full-blown depression, the Queen was unpopular, the government even more so. The Empire was under threat from the newly united and expansionist German Reich and the economically powerful United States. As Clive Bloom suggests, 'Jack' came to represent late Victorian fears about the future – he embodied approaching modernity and the 'final frenzied acknowledgment of the coming of the age of materialism'.[19] The victims fit in with this trope. As 'fallen women' they carried both the prejudices of moral crusaders and the guilt of philanthropists. They are both to be pitied and denounced.

The real monster, however, is not 'Jack' but the environment he inhabits. The very streets of East London become synonymous with degraded and neglected humanity. Every image we have of the East End in the nineteenth century is of ragged children, crowded slums and immigrants with blank stares. There is no colour, no life, no sense of community in any of these photographs. In the famous *Punch* cartoon (Figure 1) a spectral figure, a 'phantom' of criminality, drifts through the fetid sewers of the capital brandishing a butcher's knife, undeniably a product of the slums in which he dwells.

THE NEMESIS OF NEGLECT.

" THERE FLOATS A PHANTOM ON THE SLUM'S FOUL AIR,
SHAPING, TO EYES WHICH HAVE THE GIFT OF SEEING,
INTO THE SPECTRE OF THAT LOATHLY LAIR.
FACE IT—FOR VAIN IS FLEEING !
RED-HANDED, RUTHLESS, FURTIVE, UNERECT,
'TIS MURDEROUS CRIME—THE NEMESIS OF NEGLECT !"

**Figure 1** 'The nemesis of neglect', *Punch*, September 1888[20]

We can push the metaphors too hard but in many respects it has become almost impossible to separate the real Whitechapel murderer from the cultural construction that is Jack the Ripper. So we can see that the Whitechapel murder mystery, perhaps uniquely in British crime history, allowed for the creation of a modern mythology that has in many ways obscured whatever truth there was in the Ripper killings. From almost the moment that the first victim's body was discovered in Buck's Row people have been debating the identity of the murderer. Because he was never apprehended, or at least never brought to justice and made to pay for his atrocious deeds, it has been possible to build a composite image of the person responsible that may well bear little resemblance to the reality. Historians are often guilty of interpreting facts in a way that fits their own personal, political or cultural viewpoints – I am not pretending otherwise or simply dismissing the work of the many amateur researchers that have attempted to find out who 'Jack' really was. But I do believe that our ongoing fascination with the Ripper case deserves a study that tries to unravel the reality of the East End of the 1880s from much of the mythology that has surrounded it ever since. In looking at the area, its people and the attempts of the authorities to deal with crime, prostitution, poverty and slum housing, as well as considering this within the context of some of the other pressing issues of the period (such as unemployment, immigration, radical politics and Irish nationalism) this book can provide a useful overview of the East London of the time. At the heart of this is the fact that six prostitutes lost their lives in a most brutal manner between August and November 1888 and this should never be forgotten or misrepresented. However, 'Jack the Ripper' was and is a cultural construction that has been used and misused for over a hundred years. In time I suggest he will have become as much a myth as Sweeney Todd, the demon barber of Fleet Street – the subject of films and scary stories rather than an historical character.

Murder is a most heinous crime and multiple or serial murder remains the rarest form of deviant human behaviour. However, despite or perhaps because of this, it is murder that continues to fascinate readers of novels and true crime books, film-goers and television audiences. Having outlined the structure of this study and introduced the theme of mythologizing the Ripper we can now attempt to contextualize those terrible events within the wider area of homicide and serial killing.

# 2

# Murder and Mayhem in Victorian London: The Whitechapel Murders of 1888 in Context

The Whitechapel murders still have the power to shock a modern audience; in the 120 or so years since the last victim of the Ripper was found – almost unrecognizable as a human being – subsequent generations have experienced world war, genocide, rampant street crime and hundreds of serial killers. While we are neither inured to violence nor can argue that our 'modern' society is less violent or brutal than that in which the victims of Jack the Ripper struggled to survive, there have been vast improvements, not least in our ability to track and catch serial murderers. Nevertheless our newspapers remain full of violent attacks, muggings, rapes and killings. In this chapter we will look at the nature of murder in the Victorian period and in particular look at the extent of murder prosecutions at London's Central Criminal Court, the Old Bailey. There were a number of murders in the Whitechapel area in 1888, both before and after the five murders that have been generally accepted to be the work of 'Jack the Ripper', and how these differed from or were similar to 'Jack's crimes will be explored here.

Serial killing and sexual homicide (for that is how we must view the Ripper attacks) are crimes far beyond the already heinous crime of murder. Both are forms of behaviour that have come under close study by criminologists and psychologists from the late nineteenth century onwards. Therefore, this chapter will offer a brief analysis of current criminological theories as far as they pertain to serial killers. This will hopefully help us to better contextualize the Whitechapel murders. We will then move on to look in some depth at the series of murders of prostitutes in East London in 1888. In doing this work, I will rely primarily on the Metropolitan Police case files held at The National Archives in Kew and in the pages of the British press. It is necessary to point out at this stage that the former does not represent a complete source of information: the police archives have been the victim of pilferage and the pressures of space, and in consequence much information has been lost. As for the newspapers it is always wise to treat reportage with some caution.

Finally, although it is not the aim of this chapter, or indeed this book, to engage in the whodunit school of ripperology, I hope that by thinking a little about the nature of murder and how we as a society deal with it, it may be possible to see how conflicting information, popular culture and prejudice can be combined to create 'folk devils' on whom to lay the blame for brutal murders by sick individuals. As Christopher Frayling has eloquently pointed out, the myth making about the Whitechapel killer began even before the full series of murders had finished and the archetypes of the mad doctor, slumming gentleman and Jewish immigrant have persisted to this day. By looking at the case files we can at least begin to deal with truth rather than fiction. This chapter looks at the murders from the point of view of what the evidence can tell us, not how we might use selective pieces of evidence to fit up a likely suspect.

## MURDER WILL OUT! HOMICIDE IN THE VICTORIAN PERIOD

In 1866 the newspapers carried the story of the murder of a former music-hall singer fallen on hard times, named Peter Mann. Mann had a reputation for drink and violence and had lost his position in the theatre as a result. One Sunday night in June he had been drinking with his brother, his wife Ellen and her father when a quarrel erupted and Mann hit Ellen and 'knocked her down'. Her father intervened and a brawl ensued, during which Mann received a fatal wound. His father-in-law, a 77-year-old Irish labourer, Patrick Harrington, was accused of the murder and was remanded in custody at Thames Police Court. At the Old Bailey on 9 July 1866, Harrington was found guilty of killing Peter Mann but on the intervention of the judge the charge was reduced to manslaughter on account of the provocation of the attack on his daughter. Harrington was sentenced to 12 months' imprisonment.[1] The story was interesting because of the link to the music hall – some readers of the newspapers may well have seen Mann on stage – and because of the unusual intervention by the judge in defence of the accused. Without either of these elements the story was hardly newsworthy in a period when murder and indeed domestic violence was not uncommon. Throughout Victoria's long reign there were more than 2,500 trials for unlawful killing (meaning murder or manslaughter) heard before the Old Bailey courtroom, 453 of these in the decade in which the Ripper murders took place. Of the 453 between 1880 and 1890, almost 36 per cent were murder trials (162) and 58 per cent resulted in guilty verdicts, with almost a quarter of defendants being sent to the gallows.

In 1888 itself, four men were sentenced to death for committing murder:

Henry Bowles for the murder of his wife, Hannah; James White for killing his wife, Catherine; William Pierrepoint for the murder of Sidney Pierrepoint, his youngest son; and Levi Bartlett for murdering his wife, Elizabeth. All the cases have one common denominator – the victim and the accused were related by blood or by marriage. Modern criminology has shown us that most murder victims are killed by someone close to them: a spouse, lover or acquaintance – stranger murder is extremely rare. Therefore, the story of Peter Mann's murder and the evidence from the four men convicted of homicide in 1888 confirms a pattern across the nineteenth and twentieth centuries. Some murders, however, were much less straightforward – at least in the way in which they were carried out or in how the perpetrators attempted to cover up their crimes. The following is a case in point.

In September 1875, a cab carrying Henry Wainwright (a brush maker) and Alice Day (described as a 'young dressmaker' in the trial record)[2] was stopped by police on the insistence of Alfred Stokes, another brush maker who lived at Baker's Row, Whitechapel. When they searched the couple the police were horrified to find parcels containing human remains. Stokes had become suspicious when Wainwright had asked him to come to his premises in Whitechapel to help him move some parcels and tools. Stokes and Wainwright were employed as managers at Martin's Limited, a firm of brush makers in Whitechapel. Stokes was at first unable to help his colleague as he found that the parcels were too heavy for him. He then noticed a peculiarly unpleasant smell, which Wainwright dismissed as merely 'cat's or dog's dirt'. Stokes was persuaded to carry the parcels up to the street while Wainwright hailed a cab. His suspicions aroused, Stokes took the opportunity of his co-worker's absence to examine one of the packages. 'I felt as if I must do', he told the Old Bailey court, 'I opened it, and the first thing I saw was a human head'.[3] In November 1875 Henry Wainwright and his brother Thomas stood trial at the Old Bailey charged with murder. The victim was Harriet Lane and the brothers were convicted – Henry of her murder and Thomas as an accessory. The papers were fascinated by the arrest and trial of a seemingly uncharacteristic pair of defendants, as the brothers were outwardly respectable traders. Both men denied the crime, with Thomas blaming his sibling and Henry suggesting the killer was some as yet unnamed third party.[4] Henry was executed and Thomas sentenced to seven years of penal servitude. The case was to claim another victim in 1892 when William Wainwright, also a brush maker and the brother of Henry and Thomas, blew his brains out with a revolver in a first class carriage of the North London Railway.[5] Once again the Wainwright murder case was unusual, both for the class of the defendants and the dismembering of the corpse.

Before we turn to the events of the late summer and autumn of 1888 let us pause to consider some of the other murders that took place in East London in that year. In February, a young Russian Jewess was murdered by her husband whom she had abandoned some months before for another man. Her new lover had heard her screams and had arrived in time for her to point in the direction of the escaping killer before she died. Her throat had been cut 'from ear to ear'. A crowd pursued the culprit across Commercial Road until a policeman appeared. On seeing the officer the man 'immediately cut his own throat with a shoemaker's knife' and he 'expired on his way to London Hospital'.[6]

The next murder to draw the attention of the press was the murder of Emma Smith in April. Emma's death has been linked to the Ripper murders – her case notes are contained within the Metropolitan Police files on the Whitechapel killings. However, it seems highly unlikely that Emma was an early victim of the Ripper. Emma Smith, a 45-year-old prostitute who had enjoyed better times in her youth, almost survived the attack that killed her. She had managed to crawl home at which point her landlady, Mary Russell, helped her to get to the London Hospital. Smith told Russell that she 'had been shockingly maltreated by a number of men and robbed of all the money she had'. One of the men had been a youth of 19. Smith had been seen by another witness at 12.15 a.m. talking to a man near Farrant Street. It would seem that this was a dangerous place for women to loiter late at night (a 'fearfully rough quarter' was how she described it) as this witness (who is not named in the newspaper report of the inquest) had 'herself been struck in the mouth a few minutes before by some young men'.[7] At half past one Smith was making her way down Whitechapel Road when she noticed a group of men ahead. She crossed the road to avoid them but they followed her into Osbourne Lane and about 300 yards from her home in George Street they attacked and 'outraged' (raped) her. Smith was also robbed of all her money.

According to the reports 'a blunt instrument had been inserted into her vagina with great force and had ruptured the perineum'.[8] She died in hospital of peritonitis as a result of her wounds. Smith, an alcoholic who 'acted like a madwoman' when she was drunk, seems to have been the victim of a random gang attack by a group of likely drunken men who were perhaps unaware (or unconcerned) that they had inflicted fatal wounds on their victim.[9] The coroner, Dr Wynne Baxter, stated that 'such a dastardly assault he had never heard of, and it was impossible to imagine a more brutal case'.[10] Baxter's imagination was about to be stretched to the limit. Emma Smith's murder does fit the pattern of the later 'Ripper' in one clear way: all five (or six) women murdered in the summer and autumn of 1888 were street prostitutes in their forties (with the exception of Mary Kelly who was in her twenties) who had been married, lost their families and legal occupations through addiction to drink and had ended up in poverty and degradation as a result. Drink had its part to play in the next East London murder to fill the column inches of the London press in 1888.

In August a dock labourer was brought before the Thames Police Court accused of trying to kill his wife and her brother. Richard Patterson had stabbed his wife, Annie, four times with a carving knife when John Barry intervened to save his sister from further injury. Patterson then turned on him and 'stabbed him in eight places'. The wounded pair were taken to London Hospital and made a full recovery; in the meantime Patterson made himself scarce. At the hearing it became clear that Patterson had been drinking and this clearly fuelled the argument that resulted in the violence.[11] On the previous night Patterson had apparently attacked his wife with a paraffin lamp that had struck her head and required a plaster. At his trial it emerged that Patterson had been teetotal for several months but had started drinking heavily that evening, and while Annie was not drunk she was far from sober herself. The pressures of marriage at this time often resulted in domestic violence and this would seem to be a fairly typical example of a marriage breaking down; Barry testified that Annie's husband was affectionate 'except when he was drinking'.[12]

Even as the Ripper murders were dominating the headlines another 'ghastly discovery' was made in the capital. Contractors working on the new police headquarters on the Thames Embankment found the trunk of a woman in a cellar on the site. The trunk was quickly associated with other body parts found a few weeks earlier, fished out of the Thames near Lambeth and at Pimlico.[13] The doctor examining the parts at the mortuary on Ebury Street believed that it would not be hard to match the limbs found there with the new discovery in Westminster as it was likely that both belonged to a woman of 'no small stature'. The *Birmingham Daily Post*, took the opportunity of the ongoing Ripper enquiry to once again point out the ineptitude of the Metropolitan Police: 'They have no clue, and there seems very little possibility of their obtaining one, in which case publicity would be the best detective; but this they appear to ignore'.[14] So far the authorities had a torso and two arms and the Central News Agency speculated that the victim was a woman in her late twenties or early thirties and, fascinatingly for their readership, she 'belonged to the middle, or possibly even the upper, grade of society'.[15] This revelation followed an examination of the clothing that the torso had been wrapped in, which proved to be made of black broché silk, quite unlike the material of the cheap dresses worn by the Ripper's victims. At the post-mortem a third arm – found in front of the blind school in Lambeth – was ruled out as belonging to the main body. In any other year the mysterious appearance of a dismembered body in the Thames would have kept the newspapers busy for weeks but in October 1888 they were wrapped up in a much bigger media event. Before we look in detail at the police file on the Whitechapel murders we will consider modern theories of serial murder and sexual homicide.

## THE RIPPER IN CONTEXT: SERIAL KILLERS IN CRIMINOLOGICAL RESEARCH

The Ripper murders were different to what we might refer to as 'conventional' murders because they were both serial and sexual in nature. Sexual murder is a form of paraphilia (defined as sexually deviant or abhorrent behaviour, it is taken from the Greek – literally *abnormal love*)[16] and in the late nineteenth century was termed 'lust murder' by Richard von Krafft-Ebing in his 1893 study, *Psychopathia Sexualis*.[17] In this work Krafft-Ebing noted that:

> Just as maniacal exaltation easily passes to furibund destructiveness, exaltation of the sexual emotion often induces an impulse to expend itself in senseless and apparently harmful acts . . . Through such cases of infliction of pain, during the most intense emotion of lust, we approach the cases in which a real injury, wound, or death, is inflicted on the victim. In these cases, the impulse to cruelty, which may accompany the emotion of lust, becomes unbounded in a psychopathic individual; and at the same time, owing to defect of moral feeling, all normal inhibitory ideas are absent or weakened.[18]

His late nineteenth-century analysis is echoed by more recent criminological studies which have stated that the 'lust murderer harbors deep-seated, erotically charged fantasies in which his attacks and slayings sate, although incompletely and temporarily, the need for more sexual violence'. Such killers usually mutilate their victims, targeting the genitalia in particular.[19] Lust murder, or more properly *erotophonophilia*, arguably requires three or more killings with a 'cooling off' period in between victims 'indicating the premeditation of each sexual offense'.[20]

However modern criminologists and law enforcement agencies choose to define it, the Ripper murders clearly involved some level of sexual perversion. The Ripper killings also appear to have been an example of *picquerism*, which can be defined as a desire to cut and stab the flesh of the victim, in particular the breasts and genitals.[21] This was one of the key elements that raised the Whitechapel murders above the normal staple of Victorian crime and its reporting. The second element was the serial nature of the murders

– somewhere between five and nine in the space of four months to two years (depending upon how many murders we ascribe to the same individual).

Criminologists have also recently identified two different, but overlapping (in terms of their behaviour) types of lust murderer; the organized non-social killer and the disorganized asocial type. The former exists within society and manipulates or abuses others to satisfy his sexual appetite. He is aware that what he is doing is wrong but has little or no regard for other people. Typically he is cunning and leaves few non-deliberate clues for the police at the scene of his crimes. Such killers revisit the scene of their crime, both to satisfy their lusts (by reliving the murder), and to see how the investigation is proceeding. His victims are usually strangers, are often of a similar type (such as age, occupation, lifestyle, or even hair colour). Being socially able he may engage his victims in conversation, to the degree that he could lure them into a place of his choosing.[22] According to some writers such killers are not visibly suspicious, or at least do not draw overt attention to themselves by their appearance or behaviour. In short, the organized non-social killer is not easy to distinguish – importantly he does not look like a monster.

The second or asocial type of killer is much less cognizant of his actions. He is likely to be unable to relate to others and will typically be a loner, or outcast, and is often sexually incompetent. His murders are more often frantic and less well planned. It is possible that, as a result of the randomness of his attacks, the victim could be either a stranger or someone he knows and the age or type of victims is much less important here. This type of killer is most likely to attempt to mutilate or disfigure his victim (both for sexual excitement and to try to conceal the identity of the murdered person).[23] He will also revisit the scene but will not involve himself in the police investigation. This person is a more classic 'fit' for the Whitechapel murderer because of the mutilations but he would also have found it much harder to evade arrest, even in the dark alleys and courts of the East End. It may be the case that 'Jack' was a composite of both personality types and so we will keep these conflicting profiles of sexual killers in mind as we look at the actions of the Whitechapel murderer as they may help us understand the sort of person that may have perpetrated these crimes. While it is not the purpose of this book to identify a contemporary protagonist in the Ripper murders it is useful to reflect on the sort of person that carried them out – this in itself helps us to undermine or reject many of the names that have been put forward as Ripper suspects in the past 100 or so years.

However we differentiate between types of lust murders we need to be clear that, unlike many other murderers who act on the spur of the moment or 'in a fit of passion', sadistic murderers *intend* to kill their victims. This might seem straightforward and obvious but most murder is not as baldly intentional as it may appear on the surface. Sadistic killers 'kill with rage, but with rage that is often remarkably controlled – that is, aware of risks and, hence, effective'.[24] In Italy, 1879, a murderer who displayed this sadistic rage – and whose *modus operandi* is similar to that of 'Jack' – was arrested, tried and imprisoned. Vincenz Verzini (b. 1849) murdered or attempted to murder three women and mutilated their corpses. Verzini confessed and in doing so we can gather some idea of his motivation. According to Krafft-Ebing the 'commission of them gave him an indescribably pleasant (lustful) feeling, which was accompanied by erection and ejaculation . . . It was entirely the same to him, with reference to these sensations, whether the women were old, young, ugly, or beautiful'. Verzini did not rape his victims but he did display what criminologists have termed vampiric tendencies, in that he drank the blood of the women he killed.[25] He also 'carried pieces of the clothing and intestines some distance, because it gave him great pleasure to smell and touch them'.[26]

Since the Whitechapel murderer was never caught we can only speculate as to his personal motivation but even at the time the police were aware that some form of perverted sexuality was involved. Sir Robert Anderson noted in his memoirs: 'One did not need to be a Sherlock Holmes to discover that the criminal was a sexual maniac of a virulent type'.[27] Was 'Jack' another Verzini? It is certainly possible that he was motivated by the same desires. Another killer studied by Krafft-Ebing echoes some of the mutilations and the type of victims that were to be associated with the Ripper killings. Gruyo, aged 41 at his trial, murdered six street prostitutes over a ten-year period in the late nineteenth century. 'After the strangling he tore out their intestines and kidneys *per vaginam*. Some of his victims he violated before killing, others he did not.'[28] Recent research has argued that sadistic sexual murderers are generally young men, between 20 and 30 years of age.[29] Gruyo would have been in his early thirties when he started killing. Interestingly, most of the witness statements relating to the Whitechapel killer suggest he was in his early to mid-thirties. It is extremely difficult to generalize about serial killers but research has suggested that the motors of serial violence are present in individuals from childhood, sometimes manifesting themselves in acts of cruelty to siblings, peers and animals. The sadistic sexual nature of the Ripper killers was one factor that marked them out from the normal diet of murder stories in the Victorian press; the other was that there were several of them over a three-month period. This was new for the Victorian public and made the killings much more frightening and titillating as a result.

Arguably 'Jack' was not the first serial killer, after all, Burke and Hare, the body-snatchers of Edinburgh, killed 16 people in 1828. According to Philippe

Chassaigne the first serial killer was a Frenchman named Martin Dumollard. While in his forties, Dumollard went to Lyons and lured young women into quiet areas of the city and attempted to rape and kill them. He denied murder but was convicted of killing three women (several escaped him and it is probable he killed more) and was executed in 1862. In Spain, between 1870 and 1879, a man named Garayo murdered six women, committing necrophilia on the corpses, while in Italy Callisto Grandi butchered four young boys aged between 4 and 9 in the space of two years in the mid-1870s. None of these murderers mutilated their victims but all fit Chassaigne's definition of a serial killer. To qualify as a serial murderer in Chassaigne's view a killer has to meet 'at least one of three criteria: the systematic selection of the same type of victim on each occasion, a sexual element in their crime, and sadistic rituals in conducting it'.[30] In the case of the Whitechapel murders we will see that at least two, if not all three, elements were in evidence. So 'Jack' may not have been the first serial killer but he was the first in Britain to fit a profile that modern criminologists would agree separates him from the ranks of what Pieter Spierenburg has termed 'multiple' killers.[31] 'Jack's crimes were not simply multiple murders; they had a pattern and an underlying logic – however perverse.

Another factor that we should consider when analysing the murders of 1888 is geography. One of the more interesting revelations of the modern study of serial killing is the relationship between the killer, his victims and the environment in which the murders occur. The work of David Canter quite clearly demonstrates that in looking to identify a serial murderer we need to pay close attention to the location and pattern of his crimes.[32] Canter demonstrated that killers such as Peter Sutcliffe (the 'Yorkshire Ripper' who murdered 13 women in and around Bradford and Leeds in Northern England in the 1970s and early 1980s) had a discernable pattern to their killing sprees. With the assistance of the police and a research student, Canter plotted the sites of Sutcliffe's murders and the area in which he lived and worked. In doing this Canter was able to show that Sutcliffe had started his series of killings close enough to his home for it to be familiar territory but not so close as to draw attention to himself as a suspect. As he gained in confidence, in Canter's analysis, the murderer was able to range further afield in search of suitable victims (Sutcliffe, with one exception, chose prostitutes to kill – possibly as an homage to his nineteenth-century predecessor: he was found to have studied the Whitechapel murders in detail). It is crucial for the killer to be able to find sufficient 'easy' targets within his killing zone. Naturally for some killers, like Fred West or Dr Shipman, the problem is solved by victims making themselves available in other ways (as guests or patients), but for killers like Sutcliffe (or indeed 'Jack') victims had to be found on the streets.

As Canter studied the geography of the Yorkshire murders he found that a clear pattern, not unlike a spider's web, defined the activities of the killer. At the heart was Sutcliffe's home that he shared with his wife Sonia who was seemingly oblivious to his homicidal nature. Canter was fortunate that Sutcliffe's identity and address was known; the same can not be said for the Whitechapel murderer. However, Canter has attempted to apply the same process of geographical profiling to the 1888 case. If one plots the murder sites of all those listed in the police files (which we shall come to presently) it is immediately apparent that, with one exception (Alice McKenzie – who was not considered to be a Ripper victim by most experts), they are clustered around either side of the Whitechapel Road and Commercial Street. Anyone taking a walking tour of the murder sites will quickly realize the close proximity of all of the places in which the victims' bodies were discovered. This suggests, if we subscribe to Canter's thesis, that the killer either lived or worked somewhere close to the heart of this district. It is not beyond the bounds of possibility that 'Jack' was an outsider; someone who frequently visited Whitechapel but did not live there, but it is unlikely. It is much more plausible to argue that the killer knew the geography of the area very well and so was able to make his escape quickly and without drawing too much attention to himself in the process. This of course assists those researchers (like Mei Trow) who have put forward local characters such as Robert Mann as key suspects in the Ripper case. The Whitechapel murderer, whoever he was, killed fewer women than Sutcliffe and he did not need to stray too far from his base because of the abundance of common prostitutes operating in Whitechapel.

So, we now have the beginnings of a profile of the Whitechapel murderer that we can use in conjunction with the available 'evidence' from the period. It is likely that Jack the Ripper was male, and was either what modern criminologists would term an organized non-social killer or a disorganized asocial one, or some combination thereof. Again, we might expect him to be in his twenties or early thirties and to be physically strong. His motivation was sexual and he was likely to take trophies, to revisit the scenes of his crimes or attempt to recreate them at some later date. Importantly he probably knew the area in which he killed and knew it well enough to avoid capture. Did he know his victims personally? This is a question that has dogged investigators and given rise to some of the conspiracy theories mentioned in the previous chapter. It is likely that if he was a local man and one that frequented the local public houses, shops and streets, then he could have been acquainted with one or more of the women he killed. However, it is more likely that he was a loner, someone who did not integrate well in society, who would have shunned company and the brash entreaties of street whores to buy them a drink or more. The truth about murder and murderers is often much more mundane than the pages of the newspapers would have us believe. The Victorian press chose their murder stories carefully to excite and shock their readership; in the events of the late summer and autumn of 1888 they had a veritable jamboree of murder news to regale their audiences with as we shall see.

## THE WHITECHAPEL MURDERS

For many the story of the Ripper murders is well known. Countless books, television documentaries and films have all described in grisly detail the brutal murders of five East End prostitutes in the late summer and autumn of 1888. Most of these focus on the killings and use them to identify a suspect rather than explain the killings and the society in which they occurred. This search for the killer is as fascinating in what it reveals about the present as it is futile in its objective of unmasking a long dead killer. We will probably never know the truth: most evidence that has survived has long been corrupted by decades of grubby and, occasionally, light fingers while police investigation techniques have developed beyond recognition since the 1880s. It is fair to state that had 'Jack' had struck in the twenty-first century he would have been caught with modern forensics and CSI, just as Stephen Wright was arrested and convicted in Ipswich in 2008. However, as we will see in Chapter 8, the Victorian police had very little technology to assist them in their search for the killer.

The police file on the Whitechapel murders contains the names of nine women: Emma Smith, Martha Tabram, Mary Nichols, Annie Chapman, Elizabeth Stride, Kate Eddowes, Mary Kelly, Alice McKenzie and Frances Coles. However, debates rumble on about the identification of the victims almost as much as about the killer. Only five are accepted as being victims of the Ripper (Nichols, Chapman, Stride, Eddowes and Kelly) although Martha Tabram may well represent his first attempt at 'ripping'.

Emma Smith's murder received little publicity; street violence of this nature was not uncommon in the rougher parts of the capital, even if (as we have seen) her murder was particularly callous and vicious. Coincidentally another resident of George Street, Whitechapel, was the next person to meet with a brutal murder in the summer of 1888. Martha Tabram (or Turner), like Smith before her, was a common street prostitute and on the night she died had been out drinking in The White Swann public house on Whitechapel Road with her friend Mary Ann Connolly. Tabram and Connolly, nicknamed 'Pearly Poll', had attracted the attention of two soldiers and the foursome enjoyed an evening of drinking and flirtation. At a quarter to midnight they split up, Martha going off with one of the men while Poll took her companion to the nearby Angel Alley. At 4.45 a.m. on 7 August, a local man, John Reeves, came across the body of Martha Tabram on the first floor landing of George Yard Buildings, a stone's throw from Whitechapel High Street.[33] The body had been spotted earlier by a cab driver who lived in George Yard but he had taken little notice since it was fairly common for drunks to sleep off the excesses of the night there.[34] Reeves informed the local policeman, PC Thomas Barrett, who told the inquest into Tabram's death that when he found her she was lying on her back, her clothes 'turned up as far as the centre of the body, leaving the lower of the body exposed; the legs were open, and altogether her position was such as to at once suggest in my mind that recent intimacy had taken place'.[35] The constable called for a doctor, Dr Keeling, who established that Tabram had been stabbed no less than 39 times and estimated the time of death at around 2.30 a.m. PC Barrett had spoken to a soldier – a Grenadier Guard – in Wentworth Street close by the murder scene at 2 a.m. The soldier said he was waiting for 'a chum who had gone with a girl'. Barrett visited the Tower of London to see if he could identify the guardsman he had seen. He picked out two men, both of whom could account for their whereabouts that night.[36] The soldiers were also paraded before Mary Connolly but she told the police that the men she and Tabram had picked up had white cap bands. This determined that they were Coldstream Guards rather than Grenadiers and another identity parade was arranged. At this, Connolly did pick out two individuals; one was able to prove he was with his wife that night and the other was registered as being in the barracks. The case against the soldiery seems to have gone cold at this point.

While the attack was extremely brutal, and the killer targeted Tabram's 'breasts, stomach, abdomen and vagina' and despite some suggestions that the murderer had some medical knowledge, nothing exists in police files to suggest that this was something contemporary police officers believed.[37] Was Martha Tabram the Ripper's first victim? Leonard Mathers, author of one of the earliest works on the Ripper murders thought so, as did many contemporaries, but most modern writers are less sure. She may have been killed by more than one man; perhaps the two soldiers were guilty, although this seems unlikely. We now know that serial killers develop their MO (*modus operandi* or method of killing) as they kill and so we might expect the Ripper to make one of more attempts at 'ripping' before he perfected his technique.[38] We cannot be sure but as Paul Begg says, 'the frenzy of the attack took it well beyond the league of "normal" murder'.[39] The coroner said it was 'one of the most dreadful murders any one could imagine. The man must have been a perfect savage to inflict such a number of wounds on a defenceless woman in such a way'.[40]

Tabram was about 37 years old (the police file suggests 35–40) and her body was identified by Henry Tabram, her estranged husband who she had left some 13 years earlier. Tabram had been using the name Emma Turner (that is how her former landlady identified her) and was living with Henry Turner up until about three weeks before she met her death. Tabram and Turner had clearly been in financial difficulty and had left their lodgings in Commercial Road six weeks previously owing rent.[41] Perhaps this had precipitated Martha's move onto the streets and the eventual breakup of the relationship.

Martha Tabram was killed on 7 August 1888 and no one was ever prosecuted for her death. At 3.40 a.m. on Friday, 31 August, Charles Cross was on his way to his work as a carman. As he strolled along Buck's Row (now renamed as Durward Street) he noticed what he thought to be a piece of tarpaulin at the narrow end of the street. When he crossed over he realized it was a body. Cross was soon joined by another worker, Robert Paul, and together they examined the body. Believing that the woman might still be alive they went to find help. As they left the scene PC Neil entered Buck's Row (which was part of his beat) and discovered the woman's body. Using his police lantern, Neil was able to see that her throat had been cut. He called for help and was assisted by another officer who went to fetch a surgeon. When the police surgeon, Dr Llewellyn, arrived he confirmed death and the body was taken to a mortuary in Old Montague Street. There the body was stripped and washed before anyone could make a proper examination despite instructions issued by a police sergeant that no one was to touch the body. The murder scene itself was neither secured nor properly investigated.[42] Dr Llewellyn examined the body again at about 10 a.m. and made his report:

> On the right side of the face was a recent and strongly-marked bruise ... which might have been caused by a blow from a fist or by pressure of the thumb. There were two cuts in the throat, one four inches long and the other eight, and both reaching to the vertebrae, which had also been penetrated. The wounds must have been inflicted with a strong-bladed knife, moderately sharp, and used with great violence. It appeared to have been held in the left hand of the person who had used it. No blood at all was found on the front of the woman's clothes. On the abdomen were some severe cuts and stabs ... the murderer must have had some rough anatomical knowledge, for he seemed to have attacked all the vital parts.[43]

Much has been made of the phrase 'some rough anatomical knowledge' by contemporaries and later writers, but it is far from conclusive. Dr Llewellyn also stated that it could have taken only four or five minutes to carry out the attack and this was a more significant 'fact' than any suggestion of medical knowledge. The casual treatment of the crime scene was echoed by the easy access afforded to the London press. A journalist from the *East London Observer* visited the mortuary and was shown the body in its coffin. His report set the tone for the reporting of the Ripper murders that was to unfold in the coming weeks and months:

> Opening the lid, he exposed the face of the poor victim. The features were apparently those of a woman about thirty or thirty-five years, whose hair was still dark. The features were small and delicate, the cheek-bones high, the eyes grey, and the partly opened mouth disclosed a set of teeth which were a little discoloured. The expression on the face was a deeply painful one, and was evidently the result of an agonising death. The gash across the neck was situated very slightly above the breastbone; it was at least six inches in length, and over an inch in width, and was clean cut. The hands were still tightly clenched. The lower portion of the body, however, presented the most sickening spectacle of all. Commencing from the lower portion of the abdomen, a terrible gash extended nearly as far as the diaphragm – a gash from which the bowels protruded.[44]

The sensational reporting, with its reference to the mutilations was in sharp contrast to the mechanical description of death given by Dr Llewellyn.

The victim was eventually identified as Mary Ann Nichols (also known as 'Polly Ann'). Polly was a 42-year-old prostitute who had been in and out of the Lambeth workhouse (where Mary Ann Monk, who identified Polly's corpse, had first met her) having lost her position as servant after being caught stealing. She had been married to William Nichols but the couple had separated nine years earlier 'in consequence of her drunken habits' (as the police report observed).[45] For a while Nichols had supported her with an allowance of 5s a week but this stopped in 1882 when he discovered she was prostituting herself. From May till July 1888 she had found work as a domestic servant but had lost it again when she absconded, stealing some clothes. In August 1888, Mary Ann roomed in a lodging house at 55 Flower and Dean Street, prior to that she had digs in a common lodging house at 18 Thrawl Street. On the night of the murder, a little the worse for drink, and very proud of her new black straw bonnet, she was on her way to earn enough money to pay her rent for the night. At 12.30 a.m. she was seen leaving the Frying Pan Pub in Brick Lane; she was back at her lodgings at 1.40 a.m. still short of the necessary cash but told the deputy warden there to keep her room free for her as she 'would soon get the money'.[46] At half past two a fellow resident at the lodging house found her 'dead drunk' standing on the corner of Osborn Street and Whitechapel Road and tried to persuade her to go home. Instead Polly made off in the direction of Buck's Row, about half a mile away. No one saw her alive after that.

The hand-to-mouth existence of some East End residents is clearly shown by Polly's tragic death. Her pitiful possessions also indicate her poverty. Aside from her new bonnet she had what she was standing up in, and these clothes had seen better days and included a dress and underwear that she had been given at the workhouse.[47]

At first locals suspected that the murder was the work of one of the gangs that preyed on prostitutes. The Nichol's gang, named for the street they infested, were notorious for extracting 'protection' money from the area's 'unfortunates'. But Inspector Abberline, the detective in charge of operations from Leman Street, was sure it was the work of one man. The newspapers began to link Polly's death with that of Martha Tabram. They also speculated wildly on the nature and personality of the killer. It was clear, the *Northern Echo* stated, that the murders were the work of one individual, in all probability a 'ferocious maniac'. He was

a homicidal lunatic possessed apparently of the supernatural cunning and force by which such unfortunate beings are sometimes characterised – a human tiger with no more moral responsibility than that huge and ferocious cat, his thirst for blood whetted with three successful crimes, is at large, according to this idea, in the midst of such a teeming horde of humanity as Whitechapel!'[48]

This coalescing of the murderer with the inhuman or non-human helped to create a mythology around the figure of 'Jack' and linked his crimes to those of Spring Heeled Jack, the London Monster and Sweeney Todd – all semi-mythical bogeymen in London's history that will be discussed in Chapter 4. It is not unusual for serial murderers to be credited with superhuman or alien powers; indeed this helps to set them apart from humanity and allows us to see them as different from us rather than as a part of our community. We like to do this with criminals and in particular with killers despite the fact that few animals kill for pleasure and none do so for political purposes in the way that humans do. In a sense serial killers are entirely and uniquely human, killing as they do to gratify their desires and lusts rather than for food or to defend territory from other animals. As a consequence of this early speculation about the mental health of the murderer, a local lunatic, Henry James, had fallen under suspicion following Mary Ann's death but was soon absolved of responsibility by the coroner.

The inquest was held at the Working Lads' Institute as Whitechapel did not have its own coroner's court, nor had it a town hall or vestry hall or even a purpose built mortuary, all which again indicate the relative poverty of the neighbourhood since most West End parishes had courts and even in St Georges' in the East and Poplar there were parochial buildings that could be and were used when necessary. Certainly the area needed a mortuary since a previous one had been demolished to make way for a new street but the compensation paid to the local authorities by the MBW (Metropolitan Board of Works) had not been spent on providing a new one.[49] At the inquest the foreman told the coroner that in his opinion, 'the government ought to offer a reward – and a big one. If it had been a rich person that was murdered there would have been a reward of £1,000 offered but just because it is a poor "unfortunate" there is hardly any notice taken'. The coroner disagreed, both with the idea of the reward and with the sentiments expressed: 'For some time past the offering of rewards has been discontinued, no distinction being made between rich and poor', he argued. The foreman would not be put off and announced that a reward was being put together, and he himself was donating £25.[50] The idea of a reward and the belief that no one outside of Whitechapel cared if poor women were being murdered persisted throughout the investigation.

The second, or possibly third, victim – depending on how one views the murder of Martha Tabram – was Annie Chapman. 'Dark' Annie, as she was also known, had been married to a coachman and had three children, but following the death of her eldest child Emily from meningitis, her marriage collapsed. It is very possible that this was simply the last straw for her husband; Annie's character and her alcoholism had undoubtedly undermined the relationship some time before. Her husband continued to support her after their separation in 1884 but his death in December 1886 forced Annie to resort to prostitution alongside some part-time work selling matches or flowers on the streets and some piece-work in crocheting. Annie was dying from a terminal disease of the lungs and brain and in early September had admitted herself to the casual ward of the workhouse. On 7 September she had again complained of feeling ill to her friend, Amelia Farmer, but said, 'It's no use my giving way. I must pull myself together and go out and get some money or I shall have no lodgings.'[51] It was a fatal decision.

At 5.30 the next morning (8 September), Elizabeth Long was on her way to Spitalfields Market and noticed a man and woman on the street close to number 29 Hanbury Street. The woman she identified as Annie Chapman but she did not know the man. However, she offered a loose description of an individual who looked 'foreign' and was 'dark':

> He had a brown deerstalker hat and I think he had a dark coat on. But I'm not quite sure about that. I couldn't say what age he was but he looked over forty and he looked a little taller than the woman. He looked like a foreigner. He had a shabby genteel appearance. I could hear them talking loudly. He said to her, 'Will you?' She said 'Yes'. They were still standing there as I passed. I didn't look back.[52]

Mrs Long may well have seen Annie's killer because the next person to see Annie was John Davis. At 6 a.m. he came down from his third floor room to the hallway that ran the length of the house in Hanbury Street. Going out into the yard he found the dead body of a woman in a recess between the steps of the house and an old rotten fence. He ran back to Hanbury Street and called out to two passers by: 'Men! Come here! Here's a sight. A woman must have been murdered!'[53] The police were alerted and Annie's body taken to the mortuary. Outside the house a large crowd began to gather, curious voyeurs to an unfolding horror. The papers reported that:

> Not even during the riots and fog of February 1886, have I seen London so thoroughly excited as it is to-night.[sic] The Whitechapel fiend murdered his fourth victim this morning and still continues undetected, unseen, and unknown. There is a panic in Whitechapel which will instantly extend to other districts should he change his locality, as the four murders are in everybody's mouth. The papers are full of them and nothing else is talked of.[54]

The press were clearly linking Annie's murder with those of Tabram and Smith as well as Polly Nichols. When the inquest into Annie Chapman's death opened on 10 September the press went to town on the inadequacies of the police. Across the Atlantic the detective department was described as 'utterly hopeless' and the press stated that 'the police have no clue. The London police and detective force is probably the stupidest in the world'.[55] Most of the derision was aimed at Sir Charles Warren, the Chief Commissioner who was accused of militarizing the police rather than training detectives. Some of this criticism was well deserved and we will return to it in Chapter 8. A letter in *The Times* criticized the actions of the police and mortuary officials in the immediate wake of Annie's death. In the letter writer's view it was a contempt of the coroner's court to wash the body since 'there would probably have appeared on the body some finger mark, which would have been very useful'. The correspondent, who probably had too much faith in the usefulness or otherwise of fingerprint evidence in 1888, also stated that the killer was probably 'a person making research from motives of science or curiosity', an opinion that has persisted in attempts to track down the identity of the murderer.[56]

The inquest was also told that the poor woman's body had suffered mutilations similar to those found on the previous victim. However, the chief medical witness – Dr George Bagster Phillips – was reluctant to be explicit about these. He told the coroner 'I think I had better not go into further detail of these mutilations which can only be painful to the feelings of the jury and the public'. Dr Phillips suggested that the murder weapon must have been a 'very sharp knife with a thin narrow blade at least six to eight inches in length, probably longer'. He dismissed the idea that a bayonet could have done the work but conceded that it could have been a surgical instrument with the caveat that 'ordinary surgical cases might not contain such an instrument'. Crucially he then went on to tell the court that the 'whole of the body was not present. The absent portions are from the abdomen. The way in which these portions were extracted showed anatomical knowledge'.[57] Once again the link with the medical profession, however tenuous, was made. It has proved a hard connection to break and has lent weight to the theories surrounding Sir William Gull, Tumblety and Cream and, more recently, Dr Williams.

The inquest was adjourned for two weeks before Phillips was pressed to explain what he meant by his observation that part of the body was missing. While the press did not report this part of the evidence an article in *The Lancet* on 29 September 1888 revealed the extent of the murderer's actions and why Phillips believed a medical man may have been responsible.

> The abdomen had been entirely laid open ... the intestines, severed from their mesenteric attachments, had been lifted out of the body, and placed by the shoulder of the corpse; while from the pelvis the uterus and its appendages, with the upper portion of the vagina and the posterior two-thirds of the bladder, had been entirely removed. No trace of these parts could be found, and the incisions were cleanly cut [. . .] obviously the work was that of an expert – of one, at least, who had such knowledge of anatomical or pathological examinations as to be enabled to secure the pelvic organs with one sweep of a knife.[58]

This murder took place when it was light, probably at about 5.30 in the morning; there were also plenty of people about – Spitalfields Market had opened at five o'clock. In the opinion of the police surgeon it took the murderer 15 minutes to complete his work. He then had to make his escape, possibly with hands covered in blood (there was no evidence that he stopped to wash his hands at the tap in the yard), carrying not only the murder weapons but also part of Annie with him. Did no one see him, or did he not stand out in any way? The first scenario is unlikely, with so many people living in this busy area of Whitechapel, so we must conclude that the murderer blended in with his surroundings and had a very secure knowledge of the local geography as David Canter has suggested. Annie had taken her killer into the yard behind 29 Hanbury Street, a site familiar to local prostitutes and used by many people. No one would have been surprised to hear voices in the early hours but there was a chance to catch 'Jack' on this occasion. Before John Davis discovered Annie's dead body another man had gone out into the yard next door to answer the call of nature. He heard a cry and the sound of something heavy hitting the fence. He ignored it and went back inside, if he had but peered over the boundary he may well have been able to identify the Ripper. One of the features of the Ripper murders is the luck that the killer seemed to possess – on several occasions he came extremely close to being discovered committing his crimes.

The next three weeks were characterized by mounting panic with the failure of the police to catch the killer. Inhabitants of Whitechapel banded together into self-defence and vigilante groups. Suspected individuals were hounded in the streets, notably an unsavoury character called John Piser or 'Leather Apron'. Piser was a Jew who was known to prey on prostitutes, beating them and even threatening to 'rip them' with the long butcher's knife he carried. The papers identified him as the murderer and he went into hiding. When he was eventually discovered

**Figure 2** 'Is he the Whitechapel murderer?', *The Illustrated Police News*' front page coverage of Annie Chapman's murder was typical of the sensationalist reporting of the Whitechapel murders.[59]

he was taken into custody as much for his own safety as that of the local whores. At the station he was searched and, as the newspapers reported, he owned a strange assortment of possessions but none that singled him out as a killer. He had 'a heap of rags, comprising pieces of dress fabrics, old and dirty linen, two purses of a kind usually used by women, two or three pocket handkerchiefs ... two small tin boxes, a small cardboard box, a small leather strap, which might serve the purpose of a garterstring, and one spring onion'.[60] He was described as 5 ft. 7 in., 'slightly built' and 'dressed shabbily', he wore a beard and moustache and a cloth skullcap 'which did not improve his appearance' in the opinion of *The Times* reporter.[61] Piser, while a cruel and violent man, was not a killer (or at least not the serial killer that was at large in 1888) and had an alibi that satisfied the police. Inspector Abberline was convinced he had nothing to do with the murders. The treatment of Piser was symptomatic of the panic that gripped the East End. Lynch mobs prowled the streets, and dubious looking characters and those carrying Gladstone bags or similar (in other words, those that looked like 'medical men') were set upon and chased through the streets.

On 1 October, the Central News Agency announced that they had received a letter (dated 25 September) supposedly written by the killer. At first it was treated as a prank or sick joke but in the light of events that day (and the receipt of a second note in the same handwriting) the police were forced to take it more seriously.

Dear Boss,

I keep on hearing the police have caught me, but they won't fix me just yet. I have laughed when they look so clever and talk about being on the right track. That joke about Leather Apron gave me rare fits. I am down on whores, and I shan't quit ripping them till I do get buckled. Grand work the last job was. I gave the lady no time to squeal. How can they catch me now? I love my work. I want to start again. You will soon hear of me with my funny little games. I saved some of the proper red stuff in a ginger beer bottle over the last job. I did write with it, but it went thick like glue, and I can't use it. Red ink is fit enough, ha, ha, ha! The next job I do I shall clip the lady's ears and send them back to the police officers just for jolly. Wouldn't you keep this letter back till I do a bit more work; then give it out straight. My knife is so nice and sharp, I want to get to work right away, if I get the chance. Good luck,

Yours truly,

*Jack the ripper*

Don't mind me giving the trade name. Wasn't good enough to post this before I got all the red ink off my hands, curse it. They say I'm a doctor. Ha! Ha! Ha!

It was followed by a postcard dated 1 October that read:

I was not codding, dear old Boss, when I gave you the tip. You'll hear about Saucy Jack's work tomorrow. Double event this time. Number One squealed a bit. Couldn't finish straight off. Had no time to get ears for police. Thanks for keeping last letter back till I got to work again.

### Jack the Ripper

The press now had a name for the murderer and what a name! If a journalist was responsible (as seems likely) it was an inspired intervention. Whether these two communications were genuine or not has exercised ripperologists ever since. A third letter signed by the Ripper was received several days later but was widely believed to be a clever hoax. Hundreds of Ripper letters were sent to the police over the course of the crisis and beyond, almost all of them are now widely accepted to be fakes. The public engagement with the Whitechapel murders in this way is one of the most fascinating, if disturbing, aspects of the case. False trails have featured in several serial murders since 1888, some being laid by the killers while others have been set down by attention seekers or mischief makers.[62] Whatever the real identity of the letter writer, the 'double event' he referred to did take place.

At 1 a.m. on 30 September, the body of Elizabeth Stride, known as 'Long Liz', was found in Berner Street (now Henriques Street), Whitechapel. Berner Street was a 'tolerably respectable street' just off Commercial Street. It was poorly lit but had recently seen the addition of a new Board School. Opposite the school was a building occupied by several Jewish families that was also home to the International and Educational Club, which held regular meetings on all manner of 'improving' subjects. On the night of the 29th its members were enjoying a discussion entitled 'Judaism and Socialism'.[63] The club's steward, Lewis Diemschutz, had been out that evening and when he returned to the yard with his barrow from Crystal Palace, his pony shied at an object in the yard. On striking a match he was able to make out the body of a woman. At first he feared it was his wife, passed out drunk from carousing while he had been at work, and he ignored it. But on closer examination he realized that the woman's throat had been cut – probably only moments before. In the opinion of Dr Phillips, who examined her at 1.16 a.m., she had been 'seized by the shoulders and placed on the ground and that the perpetrator of the deed was on her right side when he inflicted the cut'.[64] The body was still warm and the doctor believed she had probably been attacked at about 12.45–12.55 a.m. and so Diemschutz must have come very close to disturbing the killer. We can be quite clear about this because, once again, there were witnesses who saw Liz just before her death. Indeed the killer may well have had to hide himself when Diemschutz arrived unannounced.

On the night of Stride's murder Israel Schwartz turned into Berner Street from Commercial Road at 12.45 a.m. When he reached the gateway to Dutfield's yard (where Liz's body was discovered) he saw a man stop and speak to a woman. The man then attacked her and threw her down. On seeing Schwartz the attacker shouted at him, calling out 'Lipski!' (The word 'Lipski' was derogatory slang for a Jew, referring as it did to a Jewish murderer hanged in 1887.) There was another person in the street at the time, a man in a hat who was lighting a pipe. According to Inspector Abberline, who interviewed him, Schwartz spoke little or no English. The man that shouted at him evidently alarmed him and he ran off, only for the 'pipe' man to follow him.[65] Abberline was not clear from his interview with this witness whether the two men were working together or if the man with the pipe was equally unnerved by the attack on the woman and just ran away in the same direction as Schwartz. No other witnesses could be found in Berner Street despite house to house enquiries.

Schwartz later identified Stride's body as that of the woman he had seen in the gateway. The man he described was about 30 years old, 5 ft. 5 in. tall, with a fair complexion, small brown moustache and brown hair, and was dressed in dark clothes with a black cap that had a peak. The other man was taller, about 5 ft. 11 in. and had a brown moustache and wide brim felt hat. Schwartz did not give evidence at the inquest, and it is not clear why. What *is* likely is that he saw the killer, but whether it was the man attacking the woman or the man watching while smoking his pipe, or two men working together we cannot be sure. Again the killer had escaped arrest by a whisker and his luck held.

Elizabeth Stride's story was a similar one to the other Ripper victims. Despite her claim that her family had been drowned in a well-documented shipping tragedy (the loss of the *Princess Alice* that she told people she had survived) her tale was more mundane. Stride was a Swedish woman who had married an Englishman in 1869. The couple separated in 1884 because of Liz's drinking and her husband died two years later. Another curious piece of evidence emerged from the police inquiry. On the night of her death Liz had bought some grapes from Matthew Packer's shop at 44 Berner Street. Packer had shut up shop at 12.30 that night since it was raining and 'it was no good for me to keep open'.[66]

Neither he nor his wife saw anything suspicious that night. At the mortuary Packer identified Stride as the woman he had served and said that she had been joined by a man shortly afterwards. This was at about midnight.[67]

Liz's body had not been mutilated leading some researchers to suggest that she was not a Ripper victim. The third letter the Central News Agency had received also denied that she was killed by the same hand. However, it seems likely that the simple reason for a change in the killer's actions was occasioned by the arrival of Diemschutz's pony and barrow. Realizing he was about to be discovered, the killer fled, leaving his work unfinished. This of course echoes what the second letter stated: 'Number One squealed a bit. Couldn't finish straight off. Had no time to get ears for police.' However, it is more plausible that this letter was another hoax and perhaps written after the event by someone (in the press pack or even the police) who had some knowledge of the events of that night. Whatever the reality was, the real killer, unsatisfied by his failure to carry out his ritualized killing by the untimely arrival of Diemschutz's pony and barrow, set off again and crossed from Whitechapel into the jurisdiction of the City of London Police to kill again.

While the Metropolitan Police under Abberline were investigating the Berner Street killing, another woman was attacked across the City border in Mitre Square. Catherine Eddowes was, like the other victims, a casual prostitute in her forties. If the killer had been diverted from his purpose by Diemschutz then he more than made up for it in Mitre Square. PC Watkins of the City force entered Mitre Square at 1.45 a.m. – trudging across the cobbles that exist to this day. Mitre Square was surrounded by buildings on all sides, including lodging houses that served as homes to a number of people including a City of London police officer. PC Watkins had crossed the square 15 minutes earlier and had found it deserted. Now he discovered Kate's mutilated corpse. Her throat had been cut in the same manner as the other canonical victims but when Dr Sequeria and Dr Gordon Brown, the City police surgeons, arrived they found that the killer had incised a V under each eye and had cut the tip off her nose. He had also removed one of her kidneys and her uterus. She was lying on her back and her intestines had been 'torn from the body, and some of them lodged in the wound on the side of her neck'.[68] Once again the police surgeon's report alluded to medical knowledge but suggested that the actions could have been those of 'a hunter, a butcher, a slaughter man, as well as a student in surgery or a properly qualified surgeon'.[69] Kate's pockets had been rifled through and turned out, suggesting the killer was perhaps looking for something or wanted it to appear like a robbery. But why would he bother? Her possessions, like the other victims, were minimal and pathetic: Kate had a small cardboard box that held two pawn tickets (in the name of Jane Kelly and Emily Burrell, both giving false addresses), it is unlikely

she had any money for the murderer to steal but it is possible he took away some
personal effects as trophies.

Once again there were witnesses who had seen Kate in the moments before
she died. At 1.35 a.m., just 10 minutes before PC Watkins found her dead
body, Kate was seen talking to a man who was described as being 'aged about
30, 5ft 7in or 5ft 8in, tall with a fair complexion and a fair moustache'. He was
dressed in a 'pepper-and-salt loose jacket, red neckerchief and grey cloth cap
with a peak'.[70] There is a theory that the Ripper was a sailor, or sailors – probably Portuguese. On 30 August 1888, the Portuguese vessel, the *City of Oporto*
docked in the Pool of London; the vessel left on 4 September, Polly Nichols
was killed on 31 August. On 7 September the *City of Cork* arrived, sailing
again on 11 September, Annie Chapman was murdered on the 8 September.
On 27 September the *City of Cork* docked again for five days and the 'double
event' occurred on 30 September. Finally when the last victim, Mary Kelly, was
slaughtered on 9 November the *City of Cork* had been in London for one day.
Two men, Manuel Cruz Xavier and José Laurenco could have been responsible
for the deaths, but apparently not acting together. This, however, seems unlikely
given the ease with which the killer negotiated the streets of Whitechapel and
evaded capture: it would suggest he was familiar with the layout of the streets
and alleys, something that is unlikely to have been the case with Portuguese
sailors however frequently they visited London. Once again the desire to pin the
murders on an outsider has perhaps obscured reality. Whatever the truth, the
killer certainly displayed some raw cunning that night. Walter Dew, who was a
young detective in 1888 and went on to become the 'man that caught Crippen'
in 1911, recorded in his memoirs that, 'Even now I am completely mystified as
to how the terrible events of that night could have happened. What courage
the man must have had, and what cunning to walk into so carefully prepared a
trap and to get out again without anyone having the slightest suspicion that he
was abroad'.[71]

Paul Begg argues that the description of the man seen with Eddowes is close
enough to that of the man seen by Israel Schwartz for them to be one and the
same and this is a much more persuasive observation – he had indeed crossed the
City boundary from Berner Street. The witness, Joseph Lawende (another local
Jew), could not be sure of the man but he was able to recognize Kate from her
clothes. The timings of the murder and the various witness reports are inform-
ative: the square was empty at 1.30 a.m. and Kate was alive at 1.35 a.m. Just ten
minutes later she was dead and the killer had removed two of her organs and
escaped. The mysterious killer now left the police a series of clues, deliberately
or otherwise.

That he had come into the City from Whitechapel was clear but we also know that he then moved off back in the direction of the streets around Spitalfields because a scrap of bloodstained cloth was found in Goulston Street just before 3 a.m. by PC Long. The police constable had passed the spot at 2.15 a.m. and had reported seeing nothing unusual in the street at that time. According to the police report, the piece of apron 'corresponded exactly with the part missing from the body of the murdered woman'.[72] This was therefore part of Kate's apron and tangible evidence for the detectives. Above the piece of cloth, written in chalk, were the words 'The Juwes are men who will not be blamed for nothing'.[73] This curious message has exercised historians ever since and was almost immediately erased on the orders of Sir Charles Warren, the Metropolitan Police commissioner, for fear of it inflaming local prejudices against the Jewish community. Whether it was written by the killer is open to speculation but we can at least be sure that he dropped the bloody rag in his flight – that the writing appeared there as well may be coincidental. It has been noted since that the writing was in such a position on the wall that it would have to have been written in daylight. The author had chosen to write his message in chalk on the painted part of the entrance so that it was clear; he or she could not have done this in the dark, making the link with the killer much less likely. As with so many aspects of this case we will never know for certain.

We do know a little more about Kate Eddowes. Eddowes hailed from Bermondsey and had been married but was long separated from her husband Thomas Conway, whose initials she had tattooed on her arm. Again, as with the other victims, the breakdown in the relationship was probably a result of Eddowes' alcoholism. Her current partner or common law husband was John Kelly and he lodged at 55 Flower and Dean Street. Earlier that evening Eddowes had been arrested by police for running up and down Aldgate High Street while 'drunk and incapable' and impersonating a fire engine! At the police station she had given the name of 'Kelly', which as we have seen has led the 'Royal conspiracy' theorists to suggest that this explains the killer's decision to murder her in his search for Mary Kelly. If they are right then Eddowes was particularly unlucky in her choice of partner. However, this seems – as with most of the rest of the theory – rather far fetched. Eddowes gave her name as Kelly either because that was how she was known or perhaps to protect herself against repeat prosecutions if she came before the Thames Police Court Magistrate Mr Lushington, who took a dim view of drunkenness. She need not have worried as on this occasion the policeman on duty clearly did not want to bother with the paperwork and Kate was released just after midnight when she had sobered up a little. It almost goes without saying that if police procedure had been to hold drunks over night and take them before a magistrate the next morning, Eddowes would have lived at least a little longer.

The 'double event' caused yet more outrage and panic in the Whitechapel community. On the Sunday following the murders the streets were crammed with sightseers desperate to get a look at the murder scenes. The *Pall Mall Gazette* described the situation in colourful prose:

> On approaching the scene of the murders yesterday morning it was easy to see, no nearer than a mile away, that something unusual was in the air. Along all the main thoroughfares a constant stream of passengers, all impelled by the same motive of horrified curiosity, was rolling towards the district. The scanty details which had then transpired were eagerly passed from mouth to mouth. There was but one topic of conversation. The few acres of streets and houses between Mitre-square and Berner-street seemed to be a goal for which all London was making.
>
> ... From Commercial-road, Berner-street seemed a sea of heads from end to end ... At nightfall the stream ran the other way. There seemed an exodus of disreputability from the East. Along the two great avenues leading westward the miserable creatures who apparently have most to fear from the mysterious criminal seemed to be migrating to a safer and better-lit quarter of the metropolis. The noisy groups fleeing before the approaching terrors of night were conspicuous among the better-dressed wayfarers in Holborn and the Strand.[74]

This immediate voyeurism was to be repeated outside Dorset Street following Mary Kelly's murder and is a reminder that 'Ripper fever' is not a modern invention. Tours of the murder sites began in 1888, and opposite the London Hospital a wax works exhibition entertained shocked passers by with its reconstructions of the murder sites. As the crowds grew along Commercial Street costermongers were quick to set up stalls to sell them snacks of fruit and nuts and one enterprising retailer even opened a small shop in Mitre Square itself.[75]

The panic grew in intensity and was raised to fever pitch when the chairman of the local vigilance committee was sent a bloodstained letter that contained part of a human kidney. The note had a definite style that was different from the other two letters, which either suggests a different hand or a deliberate attempt to disguise authorship, and its provenance is discussed in Chapter 3. It was addressed to the chairman of the committee, George Lusk, as coming 'From Hell' and was signed 'catch me when you can'. Whether this was a deliberate attempt at obfuscation or the confident taunt of a psychotic killer the letter is believed to be the only one of hundreds received by the police and news agencies that is at all likely to be genuine. If it is genuine then we might note that there is no signature and certainly no reference to either 'Saucy Jack' or 'Jack the Ripper'. The police and press also received several suggestions from members of the public as to how they might catch the murderer. As the *Gazette's* correspondent pointed out some of these were 'positively idiotic' but they also reflect the unusual level of public engagement with the crimes. The police were advised to use 'baby-faced pugilists' who could disguise themselves as women and then trap the unwitting assassin: 'Twenty game men of this class in women's clothing loitering about Whitechapel would have much more chance than any number of heavy-footed policemen'. Another suggested the killer was a deranged army doctor suffering from a 'Jekyll and Hyde'-style personality disorder while once again an escaped lunatic, this time from Leavensden, was also put forward as the likely culprit. As we shall see when we look at the Police's attempts to catch 'Jack' the sheer volume of public intervention in the case may well have made it harder to track down the real killer.[76]

As far as most experts are concerned the Whitechapel murders came to an end in November 1888 with the final murder being even more brutal than those that preceded it. Mary Kelly's body was discovered by Thomas Bowyer when he visited Kelly's room at 13 Miller's Court to try and extract some of the rent money that she owed to his boss and her landlord John McCarthy. McCarthy owned several properties in the area and had connections with at least one other of the murdered women.[77] He had rented 26 Dorset Street to Kelly and her boyfriend Joseph Barnett in January of 1888 possibly because he knew the couple and wanted them to live close to him at 27, where he kept a small shop. Since 26 Dorset Street opened onto an alley called Miller's Court he had renamed the property accordingly.[78] Kelly had fallen into arrears to the tune of about 30s, which represented almost two months rent so it is understandable that McCarthy was keen to get something from her. However, when Thomas Bowyer arrived at number 13 he found the door locked. After getting no response to his knocking he peered through a hole in the window that had been broken during a row that Kelly and Barnett had had because she had been allowing a friend of hers to sleep in the room. Bowyer later recollected that 'the sight we saw I cannot drive away from my mind, it looked more like the work of a devil than a man'.[79] In horror at what he had seen he rushed back to get McCarthy.

When he arrived McCarthy saw Mary's dead body lying naked on the bed with blood everywhere. Presumably to avoid a local panic (or to protect his own property from voyeurs and souvenir hunters) he dispatched Bowyer to fetch the police with an admonishment to keep what he had seen to himself. Dr Phillips arrived at 11.15 p.m. and saw the body through the window, Inspector Abberline turned up at half past and a photographer recorded the scene (possibly the first instance of crime scene photography in British police history). The examination of the body was delayed while bloodhounds (to be employed in a vain attempt to track the killer) were called for but never arrived. Eventually the door was forced open and the first police officer to see the extent of the damage to Kelly was Walter Dew. He described it as the 'most gruesome memory of the whole of my police career'.[80]

The post-mortem makes for grim reading as Kelly's body was terribly mutilated – almost unrecognizable, which has led some to speculate that it may not have been Kelly at all. Her body had been taken apart: her chest had been opened up and her heart removed (and was not found in the room), her breast lay on the bedside table and her reproductive organs had been taken out. Blood and human tissue were splattered about the room, suggesting a frenzied attack rather than a calm surgical procedure. Dew thought it was the work of a lunatic: 'the man at times must have been quite mad. There can be no other explanation for those wicked mutilations. It may have been sex mania, blood lust, or some other form of insanity, but madness there certainly was.'[81]

At just 25 years of age Kelly was the youngest victim and was considered to be a 'good looking young woman, of fair and fresh-coloured complexion'.[82] She had a son, a boy aged 6 or 7 according to the papers, who lived with her but thankfully was not with her that night. Presumably Kelly had friends that were used to looking after her boy when she was working. Kelly seems to have been very down at the time of her death and this was not unusual; the utter humiliation of prostitution caused many of London's 'unfortunates' to take their own lives and on the night of her death Kelly supposedly told one acquaintance that if she could get no money she would 'do away with herself'.[83] Interestingly, Kelly has been described as a frightened woman. At the inquest into her murder her boyfriend Joseph Barnett (himself a suspect in some minds) remarked that she had expressed this fear to him several times and that he had read newspapers to her about the killings. In his memoirs Walter Dew wrote that, 'There was no woman in the whole of Whitechapel more frightened of Jack the Ripper than Marie Kelly'.[84] This has obviously spurred the conspiracy theories surrounding the Duke of Clarence and the Royal Family but there are other interesting things to note about Kelly's murder and its aftermath.

On 12 November George Hutchinson walked into the local police station to make a statement. He had met and spoken to Kelly at 2 a.m. on the morning of 9 November when she asked him for money. Hutchinson had none to give and Kelly wandered off and he saw another man approach her. He 'tapped her on the shoulder and said something to her' whereupon they 'both burst out laughing'. The man was carrying a small parcel with a strap around it. Hutchinson followed them into Miller's Court and overheard snatches of their conversation (or said he did; his evidence has a rather constructed feel to it – as if he is describing a composite of newspaper speculations). She said 'alright' and the man replied 'alright my dear you will be comfortable'. Hutchinson watched them until they disappeared from view then he waited for three quarters of an hour and then left. Why did he hang around? The man he saw was about 31 to 35 years old and 5 ft. to 5 ft. 6 in. tall, so once again not dissimilar to previous witness statements. Again, how far this reflects what Hutchinson saw or what he wanted the police to think it is hard to say. In his report Abberline noted that Hutchinson was apparently surprised to see 'a man so well dressed in her company'.[85] The description was quite particular, noting the buttons on his coat and a 'very thick gold chain' that he was wearing. Hutchinson also suggested the man looked Jewish. This enabled *The Illustrated Police News* to print a detailed, if stereotypical, picture of the suspect. The inquest into Mary Kelly's death was held at Shoreditch Town Hall and opened on the 12th before concluding a day later with the coroner needing little persuasion that it was a case of murder. Little information was made public for fear of hampering the investigation and this starved the press of news. As a result newspaper interest swiftly faded away following Kelly's death. Two days prior to Kelly's murder the government had offered a pardon to any accomplice of the Whitechapel murder and on the same day Sir Charles Warren resigned.

This is the point at which most writers agree that the killings ceased. There were several more arrests and a number of men were chased through the streets with shouts of 'lynch him' because they were mistaken for the Ripper. One was well known to the London Hospital, perhaps suggesting he was suffering from a mild form of mental illness.[86] He was accosted because he had been seen near to where Martha Tabram had been murdered and had frightened a female passer by. Another suspect sporting a blackened face claimed to be 'Jack the Ripper' and was jumped on by two local men, one a former soldier, and a crowd soon surrounded him and started abusing the man who had to be rescued by the police. At Leman Street Police Station he asserted that he was a doctor at the London Hospital; again it may be that he was suffering from some form of mental illness. The police soon released him.[87] On 13 November the police arrested Thomas Murphy at the Holborn workhouse. Murphy gave a poor account of himself and his movements and looked as if he was or had been a sailor – another rough fit with some of the, albeit conflicting, witness statements.[88] For several years the shadow of the Whitechapel killer loomed over the streets of East London. Unsolved murders were invariably attributed to 'Saucy Jack' but there were only two events in which he could conceivably have been involved. These were the deaths of Alice McKenzie and Frances Coles.

Alice McKenzie was a 40-year-old prostitute who was killed in Castle Alley near Wentworth Street. The alley was known to locals but it was not the sort of place a stranger would go unless he had been taken there before; again this suggests a local man with local knowledge. McKenzie was murdered and her body attacked but not mutilated to the same degree as the other victims. Dr Bagster Phillips examined her in a makeshift mortuary – a shed in Pavillion Yard – that, in the opinion of *The Times*, 'tended greatly to the thwarting of justice having such a place to perform such examinations in'.[89] Almost a year after the killer spree had begun in Whitechapel, and despite the huge interest and spotlight that had been thrown upon the district, no dedicated mortuary or coroner's court had been established. Whitechapel, it would seem, simply did not warrant any real money being spent on it. Once again the streets were crowded with interested onlookers and worried locals. McKenzie's death, in July 1889, prompted the police to step up patrols in the area but there were no more killings that year. McKenzie's killer had evaded capture by a whisker since, as at Mitre Square, a policeman passed the spot just 6 minutes before she was found. This might explain why her body was not as savagely hacked about as some of the previous victims. The police report on Bagster Phillip's examination certainly drew links between Alice's wounds and the earlier killings:

> I see in this murder evidence of similar design to the former Whitechapel murders viz: sudden onslaught on the prostrate woman, the throat skilfully and resolutely cut with subsequent mutilation indicating sexual thoughts and a desire to mutilate the abdomen and sexual organs. I am of the opinion that the murder was perpetrated by the same person who committed the former series of Whitechapel murders.[90]

The coroner shifted the emphasis onto the prostitutes of the area suggesting that if they stayed off the streets the killer would have no one to murder, an obvious but unhelpful observation.[91] According to the witnesses that identified her body at the mortuary, Alice had lived with a man called John McCormack and had been in the neighbourhood for at least 14 years, living at 52 Gun Street, a common lodging house. Alice, like the previous victims, was prone to drinking heavily and on the night she died she had not paid the deputy for her bed. Alice had picked up a client on the evening of 16 July at the Cambridge Music Hall where she had been with George Dixon, a blind boy who she took back to Gun Street before going off with the stranger. However, this was at just after 7 p.m. and the police clearly did not think that Alice's punter had anything to do with her death. Initially the police questioned a man called Isaac Lewis who was off 'to get something for my supper' but he was not really suspected. Then on 19 July a man named William Brodie presented himself at Leman Street and confessed to the murder. Brodie had been convicted of burglary in 1877 and had served 13 years. He told the police that he was responsible for nine murders in Whitechapel but that 'none of them had troubled him except the last one, that was why he had given himself up'.[92]

There is no record of a William Brodie appearing at Old Bailey in the 1870s but a William *Broder* (aged 20) was sentenced to 14 years (the amount Brodie claimed) for stealing an overcoat and other goods. In the previous case Broder had met a man, Frederick Hebden, at the Alhambra Palace and accompanied him back to his chambers near Leicester Square. Hebden expressed surprise to find Broder in bed with him in the morning – was this a homosexual liason, was Broder a male prostitute? Broder asked Hebden for money, and became aggressive when Hebden refused, threatening 'he would smash me and my place up'.[93] Eventually Hebden was forced to hand over a variety of items and write a note authorizing Broder to pawn a carriage clock – he was clearly very frightened that Broder was out of control and extremely violent as he had been that morning. The manager at the printing workshop where William Brodie's brothers were employed described Brodie as a 'reckless character addicted to drink' and it is not impossible that Broder and Brodie were one and the same person.[94] According to his landlady and her daughter, Brodie was generally quiet and well behaved but 'when in drink he is very curious in his manners and says some quaint things'.[95] Brodie claimed to have been to South Africa to work in the diamond mines and when this claim was examined it proved he had sailed on 6 September 1888 and so could not have been responsible for the murders in that year. He was also found to have confessed to a murder in Kimberly and so it would seem that he was a rather disturbed individual who was simply wasting police time. Once he had been discharged for murder they arrested him for fraud.[96]

The trail had gone cold again but the police increased the numbers of detectives and plainclothes officers in the area in case Alice McKenzie's murder really did mean the killer was operating again. Was McKenzie the Ripper's sixth (or seventh) victim? We cannot rule out the possibility that, as with Liz Stride, the killer was interrupted in his work and that is why her mutilations were less severe. However, it could also be the work of a copycat killer or even someone who knew McKenzie and wanted her dead and saw a way in which to make it look like the work of the Ripper. Like so much of this case the more one uncovers the less clear the overall picture becomes.

On Friday, 13 February 1891, PC Ernest Thompson found Frances Coles lying in a roadway under a railway arch. Her throat had been cut and before a doctor could arrive she expired. A man named Sadler was eventually prosecuted for her murder and some believed they had 'Jack' at last, but the case against Sadler collapsed when he was able to establish an alibi. Frances' killer, like the other women before her, was never caught. This is where the case files into the Whitechapel murders are closed.

## CONCLUSION

So what have we learnt about Whitechapel murders based upon the evidence (such as it is) surviving from the police archives and the pages of the press? The killer remains masked and will probably never be revealed to everyone's satisfaction. Modern criminology would support a theory that the murderer was, if operating alone, either a non-social or disorganized asocial killer: both have elements that fit the persona of 'Jack'. We also need to consider David Canter's geographical profiling as all of the victims shared a very similar locale. This may be purely coincidental of course, and it is not beyond the bounds of possibility that a 'slummer' or other person was travelling into the district because he knew he would find a suitable target for his rage and lust. But it would be more plausible to believe that someone who evaded the law and left so few clues and was seen by so few people knew the area he operated in and had somewhere close by to escape to. This would make 'Jack' a local man and also someone who could blend into his surroundings with some ease; a nondescript individual of little or no importance. That he assumed centre stage with his devastating purge of Whitechapel's 'unfortunates' must have caused him a frisson of excitement: perhaps that is one of the reasons he killed.

The murders were beyond anything Victorian society had experienced before, both in their intensity and in the way that they unfolded in the press, week by week. The press and the public became involved in this case in an unprecedented manner, which merely served both to add to the panic and obfuscate the police's attempt to catch the villain. Murders were often newsworthy but in 1888 even the discovery of a headless torso paled in comparison with 'Jack's antics. The press are the subject of a later chapter of this book but without them it is possible that the Whitechapel murders might not have become the international sensation that they did. Certainly the myth making that has surrounded the killings have raised this case above all previous murders in British history and we need to be very careful about how we think about the murders.

Having now established the context for the Whitechapel murders both within Victorian murder reportage and more recent criminal profiling we will now turn to the area in which the killings occurred, Whitechapel, and more broadly, the

East End of London. If the Ripper has been the subject of myth making then so has this area of the capital. Unpacking the truth about the East End is just as problematic as identifying the culprit behind the mask of 'Jack the Ripper'.

# 3

# East Meets West: The Contrasting Nature of Victorian London and the Mixed Community of the East End

Towards the end of the 1850s the great Victorian essayist and champion of British art and culture John Ruskin summed up the fears of many Victorians at what they saw as the slow suffocation of rural England at the hands of industry:

> The whole of the island . . . set as thick with chimneys as the masts stand in the docks of Liverpool; that there shall be no meadows in it; no trees; no gardens; only a little corn grown upon the house tops, reaped and thrashed by steam, that you do not even have room for roads, but travel either over the roofs of your mills, on viaducts; or under the floors, in tunnels; that, the smoke have rendered the light of the sun unserviceable, you work always by the light of your own gas: that no acre of English ground shall be without its shaft and its engine . . .
>
> *Two Parks* (1859)

By the 1870s Ruskin's dislike of industry and, in particular, the omnipresent railways that carved great swathes through the verdant countryside, had brought him to embrace the back-to-the-land movement with his fellow travellers Edward Carpenter and William Morris. Ruskin believed that open fields and all the flora of nature were 'essential to the healthy spiritual life of man' and furthermore argued that agricultural labour was somehow superior to the industrial labour that so many British workmen had been forced into performing.[1]

In this chapter we will look at this dichotomy at the heart of Victorian culture and at how competing views of country and town manifested themselves within the ages of the nineteenth-century press and periodicals. The long shadow created by the growing towns and cities threatened to destroy the traditional pastoral image of 'merrie England'. While the new industrial centres of the Midlands and north clearly defined much of this threat, it was in London that the real danger to civilization had reared its ugly head. Having explored general attitudes towards the city this chapter will therefore focus on London, and in particular on the East End of London and the fears that surrounded it. It will consider how we define and understand this complex area of the capital and the people that lived in it. The East End has been represented and misrepresented for several centuries and uncovering its real nature is not an easy task. Nonetheless this chapter will attempt to discover the real Eastender (whoever he or she may be). In doing so it will look at the various migrants that have made the east side of London their home and at the problems they encountered there. This will be the story of the Irish and the Jews, but it will not neglect the indigenous people of Bethnal Green and Tower Hamlets, the Cockneys, costermongers and pearly kings and queens and the feisty match girls who recorded one of the most memorable and formative industrial relations victories of the late Victorian era.

## COPING WITH CHANGE: VICTORIAN VIEWS OF THE COUNTRYSIDE AND TOWN

The Victorians, perhaps more than any previous generation, were having to come to terms with the changing environment around them. The 1830s and 1840s had seen acceleration in the industrializing process that had begun in the previous century. While we should be cautious of depicting mid-nineteenth-century Britain as predominantly industrial (for it was far from that), the rate of change was arguably dramatic. A falling death rate ensured steady population growth despite a falling birth rate. In addition internal migrants flocked to the growing towns and cities from all over the United Kingdom, and they came to London in particular.[2] Britain's population doubled between 1801 and 1851, from some 9 million souls to more than 18 million. While for most of the eighteenth century the rate of population growth had been 0.46 per cent, in the period to 1911 it averaged some 10 per cent.[3] According to a royal commission report of 1841 an 'entirely new population [had] been produced'. Where once 'there was not a single hut of a shepherd, the lofty steam engine chimneys of a colliery now send their columns of smoke into the sky'.[4] In the period 1801 to 1911 the proportion of the British populace that lived in urban areas rose from 20 per cent to 80 per cent.[5]

The popular literature of the day reflected this change in the rural landscape; *Merry & Wise* published a short story called 'Pits and Furnaces, or life in the Black Country' where three children comment upon the strange activities of a group of men in a field near their home. 'Papa!' exclaimed Fanny, 'what do you think they are going to do? I hope they will not spoil that green field: there are so few

others near our house'. Her father explains that they are looking for coal and this
excites the imagination of Fanny's brothers who realize they can 'watch them
very easily, and shall see it all from the beginning', thus neatly juxtaposing the
Victorians' competing attitudes towards progress and conservation.[6] The story
unfolds as the boys explore the developing site, taking home samples for analysis
and demonstrating the Victorians' love of science. Fanny, representing a female
stereotype associated with continuity by way of contrast to the more dynamic
aspect exhibited by her brothers, questions her mother about the origin of coal.
She learns, as does the intended reader, that coal comes from the great forests that
once covered the land before men (specifically *English* men) cultivated the soil.
Yet all the efforts of ancient and 'modern' men are placed within the context of
religion in shaping human society. As Mrs Hope tells her daughter Fanny, 'most
wonderful of all that God should so arrange it that the decay and destruction of
the plants of past ages should prove such a source of comfort and wealth to the
present race of beings – thus linking us with times long gone by, and encouraging
us to trust Him for the future'.[7] Religion and science, those two contrasting and
competing bastions of Victorian society, are thus neatly entwined in this story
of progressive industrialization.

The contrasts between town and country appear in other popular publications of the day. In Jane Boswell Moore's 'The Black Pony', Charlie and Phil go
to live with their grandfather where, 'instead of the dull streets they had become
accustomed to' were 'pleasant green fields, with high grass and corn'.[8] Much later
in the century the Rev R. F. Horton complained that there 'are vast tracts of this
green and pleasant land where the grass and flowers have ceased to grow, and
the trees which survive are stunted and warped'.[9] That the Victorians were well
aware of their somewhat ambiguous relationship with rural and urban living is
demonstrated by this interactive poem published in 1874:

It has often been urged, and with some reason, that pastoral poetry must fail to be
properly appreciated by dwellers in towns; while on the other hand . . . urban verse
must be unintelligible to the rustic. In the following poem we have striven to meet
the requirements of both classes of readers.

> When the day is dying,
> And the {soot/dew} is falling;
> When the winds are sighing,
> And the {Pots is/rooks are} calling;
> When the shadows lengthen
> Neath the {lamps'/stars'} bright spots,

And the outlines strengthen
Of the {chimney pots/distant cots};
When the {newsboys'/shepherds'} voices
Echo through the {square/air};
And the {clerk/flock} rejoices
Homeward to repair;
Robert to his Mary
Hastens {on the sly/through the rye};
Gliding {down the airy/through the dairy};
Joy – {And rabbit pie/His love is nigh}![10]

Doggerel it may be but the emphasis is firmly placed on the differences between urban and rural life with a sense that the former is less pure, but perhaps more interesting. The manufactured nature of the urban environment and the natural-ness of the rural reflect Cowper's idiom that 'God made the country, man made the town'. However, we should not read Cowper too simplistically: 'If man made the town, then the town demonstrates both his state of original sin and his capacity for the greatest of human achievements'.[11] Thus Cowper reflected the ambivalent position the countryside had in contemporary discourses, 'sometimes seen as the abode of joy and tranquillity, more often regarded as dull'.[12] Beatrix Potter had also highlighted the differences between urban and rural life in her *Tale of Johnny Town-Mouse* (1918). As P. J. Waller has noted, in Potter's tales the 'town is mannered and alarming to Timmy [the country mouse], the country dull and dirty to Johnny'.[13] Potter herself lived in London before later moving to the Lake District. The cities of England held a fascination for those that lived outside them, a fascination made all the more real by the rapid advance of the railways, which meant that almost anyone anywhere in Britain could experience urbanity for the cost of a few shillings.

The Victorian economy was built upon progressive and successful industrial growth in which knowledge and skills were crucial. Towns and cities were, by the mid-nineteenth century, well ahead of the countryside in this respect. The availability of labour (and importantly cheap labour), along with the clustering of workshops and suppliers with access to transport networks and the large numbers of available customers drove business growth in the urban environ-ment. So it is perhaps odd that Victorians were so concerned with the growth of towns and the implications this had for their society. After all, it was extremely successful in terms of the wealth it created. Certainly many contemporaries were very positive about the city and Victorian urbanites were proud of their towns and built impressive architectural monuments to demonstrate this. We need only cast our gaze at the town halls, squares, statues and other buildings that survive from the Victorian era or at the wealth of guide books, engravings, paintings and maps that 'celebrated and explored the towns' of Britain in the nineteenth century.[14] We can tell what the Victorians felt about their urban environments when they festooned these buildings with words such as 'progress', 'growth' and 'improvement'. These were powerful expressions of urban pride.

In the early years of the nineteenth century new arrivals in the growing towns and cities felt little sense of neighbourhood, having exchanged the close-knit community of village life for the anonymity of urban living. However, as transport networks expanded and towns grew in size new identities were created and competition developed: village rivalries expanded into town and even regional competitiveness. This rivalry was fuelled by economics and trade, the growth of organized sports such as football and rugby and, after 1880, by the emphasis placed on civic pride by compulsory education.[15] Thus, while England was becoming a predominantly urban culture as the last decades of the nineteenth century approached it retained its strong links to the countryside and to nature. Ruskin's gloomy vision of the future was coupled with his own obsession with all things medieval and both reflect the Victorian discomfort with industrialization and urbanization.[16]

All of which brings us back to the concerns so often expressed at the time that the towns and cities of Britain were somehow detrimental to the health of the nation. Even today it might be fair to say that Britain has an anti-urban sentiment in its culture with our eulogizing of the countryside and our attempts to restrict urban sprawl even in the face of a massive housing shortage. We see ourselves as living in a 'green and pleasant land' despite the fact that most of us live and work in cities and towns and enjoy the benefits that they bring. Two modern institutions devoted to the preservation of our rural heritage had their origins in the late Victorian and Edwardian eras. The Campaign to Protect Rural England (CPRE) was established in 1926 and today calls for a closer engagement with a protected and sustainable countryside. The CPRE was preceded by the National Trust, which was founded in 1895 by three Victorian philanthropists: Octavia Hill, Sir Robert Hunter and Canon Hardwicke Drummond Rawnsley, all of whom were concerned about industrialization and unchecked development and set up the trust to conserve Britain's countryside, coastline and buildings. The preservation or conservation of England has therefore been closely linked to notions of national identity for over a century. Today the city carries most of our fears about modern society and thus echoes with our Victorian past. For the middle classes of late Victorian London their particular concerns about the dangers of the city were focused on the East End, but this has historically been a difficult area to define and is as much subject to myth making as the Ripper himself.

## DEFINING THE EAST END

Increasingly in the late nineteenth century the city was being identified as 'a place of social danger: from the loss of customary human feelings to the building up of a massive, irrational, explosive force'.[17] Nowhere was this more apparent than in the capital city, London. In London this danger was applied to the east of the metropolis to the area we have come to know as the East End. To some extent, like 'Jack' himself the East End is a product of a complex meshing of perceptions and stereotypes and it becomes increasingly difficult to identify the 'real' East End from that of myth and representation. According to Keating the East End was in many ways a creation of nineteenth-century writers, including novelists, reformers and journalists. 'It was the creation of Edward Denison, Samuel Barnett, Charles Booth, Walter Besant, Arthur Morrison, and Jack the Ripper.'[18] After 1880, according to the contemporary periodical *Nineteenth Century*, the negative association of the East End with poverty and crime was 'rapidly taken up by the new halfpenny press, in the pulpit and the music hall' so that 'it became a concentrated reminder to the public conscience that nothing to be found in the East End should be tolerated in a Christian country'.[19] Since then we have had the additional overlay of the wartime 'Blitz spirit' and the machinations of the residents of Albert Square in the BBC's long running soap opera, *EastEnders*.

For the mid-Victorians the East End was somewhere that only occasionally required their attention. When cholera broke out or when a particularly nasty murder case reached the papers, as it did in 1811 on Ratcliffe Highway, the Victorian middle class shivered in their comfortable homes and held their noses lest they be infected by the pollutant to the east. Indeed it is the smell of the East of London that is most redolent in much of nineteenth-century writing. Thus in visiting the East End in 1841 the future Lord Shaftesbury discovered such 'scenes of filth, discomfort, disease! [such] scenes of moral and mental ill … No pen or paint-brush could describe the thing as it is. One whiff of Cowyard, Blue-Anchor, or Baker's Court, outweighs ten pages of letter press'.[20] Much of the association of the East End with nauseous odours reflects the area's industry and poverty. As London developed, the dirty trades were often located in the East. Here were the slaughterhouses and tanneries, here too many of the homes of the poor – close by the docks where so many Londoners were employed. The area south of Whitechapel High Street was full of butchers and slaughterhouses throughout the nineteenth century. The Poor Law report of 1838 uncovered some of the problems of disease associated with the trade:

> Dwellings thickly crowded with inhabitants stand all around the slaughter-houses [. . .] in the passages, courts, and alleys, on the very opposite side of the street from the houses of which there are no drains into the common sewer, fever of a fatal character has been exceedingly prevalent.[21]

The contrasts between West and East had a long history and were clearly a subject for amusement. In 1840 one periodical reported that in response to the laying out of a park in the East End the 'butchers of Whitechapel have resolved to christen it *Hide*-park, in order not to be behind the West-end in gentility and fashion. Anybody, moreover, who has visited the region in which the slaughter houses are situated, will know that they may easily have a "Rotten-row" of their own'.[22]

Nineteenth-century Eastenders had to live among the dirty trades as they had done since the area had first been occupied. From Saxon times the east side of the capital had been clearly demarcated from the west and centre. The Romans had built their city of Londinium by the banks of the Thames and the Saxon invaders that arrived several hundred years later viewed the crumbling edifices of the Roman empire as the work of gods and giants and chose to set up their much more humble hovels to the west of the river Walbrook, forcing the defeated Romano-British inhabitants out towards the east.[23] Notwithstanding that many of the place names that survive for East London reflect their Saxon origin: Stibba (Stepney), Waeppa (Wapping), Bilda (Bethnal), Deorlof (Dalston) and Haca (Hackney). As Peter Ackroyd has noted, since 'the earliest periods of London history the eastern side has enjoyed a less enviable reputation than that of the west'.[24] This was further emphasized from the eleventh century onwards as the city of Westminster grew into the seat of government and wealth.

Defining the East End is difficult. According to the *Encyclopaedia Britannica* it 'was that part of the walled City near the eastern gate, Aldgate'. Others suggest it starts at 'the point where Whitechapel Road and Commercial Road meet'.[25] Some have defined it socially and not simply geographically so that it takes in Rotherhithe and Bermondsey, and even East Ham and West Ham. We can perhaps settle on an area that is bounded on the east by the River Lea, to the west by the City wall, to the north by Clapton Common and to the south by the Thames. Paul Begg claims that 'the real East End is the community just within and just beyond the eastern gates, primarily Spitalfields and Whitechapel' and this is a useful definition in the context of the 1880s.[26] Alan Palmer restricts the East End to the 'old London Boroughs of Hackney and Tower Hamlets' while acknowledging that the area effectively extends to Hoxton, Shoreditch, West and East Ham and the recently gentrified Docklands.[27] However, the real East End remains elusive, a construction built from nearly two centuries of writing. Much of this writing was negative; indeed we might view the rehabilitation of the East End in the depiction of the plucky cockney smiling-through in the face of repeated German bombings in the Second World War (however divorced from reality this situation might have been).[28] As we shall see in the next chapter, philanthropists and new journalists were quick to point out the squalor of housing conditions in the area around Whitechapel and Spitalfields, and 'slummers' could go and see for themselves 'how the poor lived'. Walter Besant characterized the East End itself as a 'huge cultureless void' into which thousands of desperate working-class people were falling to their doom.[29] Besant declared that:

> Two millions of people, or thereabouts, live in the East End of London. That seems a good-sized population for an utterly unknown town. They have no institutions of their own to speak of, no public buildings of any importance, no municipality, no gentry, no carriages, no soldiers, no picture-galleries, no theatres, no opera – they have nothing. It is the fashion to believe that they are all paupers, which is a foolish and mischievous belief, as we shall presently see. Probably there is no such spectacle in the whole world as that of this immense, neglected, forgotten great city of East London ... Nobody goes east, no one wants to see the place; no one is curious about the way of life in the east. Books on London pass it over; it has little or no history; great men are not buried in its churchyards, which are not even ancient, and crowded by citizens as obscure as those who now breathe the upper airs about them. If anything happens in the east, people at the other end have to stop and think before they can remember where that place may be.[30]

In some respects Besant was wrong of course, the East End had a diverse culture with many places of worship, entertainment and trade and a long history. After 1888 everyone in the world knew where Whitechapel was and in many ways, as was touched on in the introduction to this study, the Ripper murders have obscured the reality of this part of London.

So what lay behind this rhetoric? Manchester had long concerned observers with its rapid expansion from a rural hamlet to the *prima facie* industrial metropolis of the day, populated by a new and demanding working class; one that had carved out rights for themselves. In East London the working classes were seen as passive victims of the dynamic progress of the Victorian age – they were being left behind to become a burden on the rest of society.[31] They had formed a dangerous 'residuum' that needed to be raised up, rescued, reformed and rehabilitated to take their place in the new society that was growing around them. The debates about how this was to be achieved will be tackled in subsequent chapters but for now it is sufficient for us to remember that the construction of a mythic reality for the East End had as much to do with fears about the population of that area as it did about desires to help its inhabitants.

In 1889 Charles Booth published the first of his series of studies of London poverty. This represented an attempt, as he put it, to lift 'the curtain' and reveal the reality of life in the East End. Again, we shall return to Booth later but before we go on to think a little about the reality of the East End and how it was described in the popular press of the day we can finish this section with a quote from Booth:

> East London lay hidden from view behind a curtain on which were painted terrible pictures: Starving children, suffering women, overworked men: horrors of drunkenness and vice; monsters and demons of inhumanity; giants of disease and despair. Did these pictures truly represent what lay behind, or did they bear to the facts a relation similar to that which the pictures outside a booth at some country fair bear to the performance or show within?[32]

We might reflect that in our twenty-first century world of instant media and popular television we are still being fed a constructed image of the East End, one that often bears little relationship to reality.

## THE PEOPLES OF THE ABYSS: THE DIFFERENT COMMUNITIES OF THE EAST END

In a richly illustrated article of 1887 *The Graphic* offered its readership an overview of the people gathering in and around the Thames police office in East Arbour Street, 'sandwiched, as it were, between the two great East End arteries, Whitechapel Road and Commercial Road East'.[33] Among those milling around waiting for their cases to be heard, or for news of loved ones or friends held overnight in the nearby police station, was a cross section of the area's population.

> They are of all aspects, an amphibious and fish-like aspect, a river-side Rogue Riderhood aspect, a Whitechapel thief-like aspect, and a stolid costermonger-like aspect; they are Saturday night faces that one sees not in Begravia. Here are men from the docks and wharves, broad, and burly, and fierce, with wonderful whiskers and fur caps; here are foreigners with rings in their ears and knives at their girdles;

here is our old friend Fagin – and Fagin's old friends en masse, and a whole army of the 'ragged fringe,' poor, poverty-haunted, criminal nondescripts.

The author, F. W. Robinson, paints us a picture of the East End and its peoples complete with all the expected stereotypes (the use of 'Fagin' to represent the Jewish community and the association of foreign sailors with knives) and prejudices. Elsewhere in the pages of the contemporary press we can visit the East End of the nineteenth century, although once again we must be aware that these are representations of the area, channelled through narrow foci for a largely middle-class readership. The *Manchester Times* described the central hub of East London, Spitalfields and Bethnal Green and the weavers that occupied the cleanest parts of the district. By the 1860s, when the paper printed an excerpt from Thomas Archer's *The Pauper, the Thief, and the Convict*, the weavers of Spitalfields (who had done so much to draw immigrants to the area from the seventeenth century onwards) were reduced to a 'very deplorable condition' (in part because of competition from Manchester itself as well as its more traditional rivals, Germany and France). Despite this the weavers enjoyed a few luxuries ('baked potatoes, stewed eels' . . . 'fried fish and whelks' . . . 'all eaten with infinite gusto at a dozen stalls about Brick Lane and Shoreditch') and hoped for something better for their children.[34] The Huguenot influence on Spitalfields was noted by a *Daily News* reporter in 1871 who saw the 'French vivacity in some of the features' of the ragged school children who gathered in rapt attention to see the newly installed Christmas tree in Spicer Street.[35] The French presence in the area is still clearly evident in the streets surrounding Hawksmoor's magnificent Christ Church, Spitalfields, in the shutters that adorn the houses in Wilkes Street and Fournier Street and others. The Huguenot weavers had fled persecution during the French Wars of Religion that had seen a bloody civil war divide Catholics and Protestants. They were not the last European minority to choose Whitechapel as a place of refuge. By 1885 the descendants of the original 15,000 or so silk weavers who had left France in the aftermath of the revocation of the Edict of Nantes in 1685 had dwindled to a rump of perhaps 2,000 at best. These former immigrants had integrated themselves so effectively by the last decades of the century that they felt it necessary to create a Huguenot Society to help maintain their previous heritage.[36]

The Huguenot weavers have left a lasting impression on Spitalfields but it was another ethnic group that dominated for most of the last quarter of the nineteenth century. In 1887 the *Pall Mall Gazette* reported the deaths of 17 people in a public hall on Commercial Street as some 400 theatre-goers struggled to escape from a reported gas leak in the building. The drama in the paper's description of the panic is evident: 'The scene at this time was one of intense excitement. Screams of terror and cries of appeal and advice mingled, while the mass wedged in the doorway struggled and surged.'[37] The list of victims, three of whom remained unidentified at the time the newspaper went to press, tells us a little about the ethnicity of this part of London:[38]

1. Isaac Levy, seventy years, 270, Brunswick buildings
2. Gerty Levy, forty-seven years, 270, Brunswick buildings
3. Solomon Krotofsky, fifteen years, 41, Pelham Street
4. Lewis Krotofsky, thirteen years, 41, Pelham Street
5. Rachel Levy, twenty-two years, 18, Myrtle Street, Commercial Road
6. Reigna Moncadum, forty-five years
7. Unindentified
8. Esther Ellis, sixteen years, 4, Colchester Street
9. Isaac Gubert, twelve years, 3, Chicksand Street
10. Millie Gubert, thirty-six years, 3, Chicksand Street
11. Betsy Aizan, twenty-four years, 143, Hansbury [sic] Street
12. Goa Marks, nine years, 36, Spital Street
13. Janie Goldstein, twenty-four years, 143, Hansbury [sic] Street
14. Esther Rosenfeld, twenty-one years, 5, Regal Place
15. Katie Silverman, twenty-two, 27, Henage Street
16. Unidentified
17. Unidentified

According to the newspaper nearly all those attending were Jews, or 'foreign Jews' as they were described by the *Gazette*. The funerals were held at the Great Synagogue on Duke Street and a subscription list to help the bereaved families was opened by *The Jewish Chronicle*.[39] The *Gazette* described the cultural differences of the Jewish funerals, with just a hint of anti-Semitism in the necessity for a police cordon and the lack of spoken English among some of the survivors who testified at the inquest in front of Dr Wynne Baxter (who was to have a busy autumn in the following year, 1888).[40] The language used reveals long-held prejudices and a reliance upon well-worn stereotypes:

The Jews were out in strong force in the Whitechapel-road, and took a keen and sympathetic interest in the funeral; red-eyed women encased in tawdry finery, women with flabby jowls, faces rouged and powdered, hair towzled [sic] and unkempt, their shapeless figures encased in shabby furs and threadbare velveteens, every hat carrying a nodding plume, of which an undertaker would be proud. The men were even stranger-looking, clad in indescribable garments, from the tattered overcoat of a modern Fagin to the reach-me-down finery of the East-end exquisite.[41]

The author chooses to represent the East End Jew as the descendant of Dickens' Fagin; a character that many in Victorian society would have been familiar with, either through reading *Oliver Twist*, or from seeing Cruickshank's associated engravings. Dickens and Cruikshank, by contrast with Henry Mayhew's more sociological depiction, present Fagin 'not as of a group or class, not martyr or victim, but Mephisophelean tempter of Christians'.[42] Negative representations of Jews proliferate in the nineteenth century as 'foreigners', moneylenders and crooks and these characterizations build upon previous denigrations of Jews in anti-Semitic outbursts from medieval accounts of the Crusades to Shakespeare's characterization of Shylock. Disraeli was described by the Socialist leader H. M. Hyndman (himself an anti-Semite) as a 'Spanish Jew' and so, presumably, unfit to lead an English political party. Even Beatrice Potter, so often sympathetic to the plight of the poor of the East End, was unable to resist falling back on racial slurs in describing East End Jews as grasping, 'profit-seeking' gamblers (as if the pursuit of profit in the golden age of capital was somehow something to be ashamed of).[43] Across the Channel the military and government institutions of France were caught up in a long-running and embarrassing scandal over the wrongful arrest and imprisonment of Alfred Dreyfus for passing secrets to the enemy. Anti-Semitism was rife in late nineteenth-century Europe and London was not immune. Thus, the *Pall Mall Gazette* was, perhaps unwittingly, subscribing to 'racialist representations that defined general cultural images of the Jews for better than a hundred years of English and European culture' since Dickens' novel had first appeared in 1838.[44]

Racial slurs and stereotyping have been a feature of anti-Semitism throughout history and Arnold White, despite his defence of 'common sense' and reasonable persona contributed to this in his depiction of East End Jews as dirty and insanitary. White, who went on to become an advocate of eugenics in the twentieth century, was challenged by Sir Samuel Montagu MP, the member for Tower Hamlets from 1885–1901, on the validity of this viewpoint. White had gathered together a group of Jewish immigrants to give evidence before a select committee and had clearly hand picked his 'team' to demonstrate the poverty of morals and means of the new arrivals. The men White chose were 'greeners', a slang term used to describe new arrivals from Eastern Europe. White had promised them help in returning home or in moving on to the USA in return for perjuring themselves before the parliamentarians.[45] Unfortunately for Arnold White the committee saw through his crude device. Montagu neatly pierced White's façade with detailed information about ritual washing and the availability of public baths for the Jewish community of the East End of which the latter claimed to know little. White was merely propounding a common, and clearly false, criticism of foreigners and the 'other' within society – that they were 'unclean', they did not wash and they smelt bad.[46]

The East End was to experience overt anti-Semitism in the period between the twentieth century's two world wars in the rise of the British Union of Fascists and the subsequent anti-Fascist demonstration at Cable Street. The sense of difference felt by immigrants and their descendants is evident in the recollections of one participant, on his way to the confrontation with Mosley's Blackshirts:[47]

> You pass a Blackshirt selling the Fascist rag. He sees your Jewish face, and shouts, 'Read all about the alien menace.' You clench your teeth and breathe hard. And, you mustn't touch him, you mustn't even say anything, for that would be causing a breach of the peace.[48]

The Jew as 'alien' was a theme that ran through the nineteenth century as thousands of European Jews arrived in the capital fleeing persecution at the hands of the Russian tsars. In 1887 the arrest of Israel Lipski for the murder of Mrs Angel of Batty Street, Whitechapel, (herself a Jew) did little to overcome gentile prejudices. Miriam Angel was poisoned, having nitric acid poured down her throat, and Lipski – who lodged with Miriam and her husband – was discovered hiding under her bed. Lipski had also ingested some of the poison, allegedly to make it appear that he too was a victim of an unknown killer. Although Lipski's motive could only be hinted at (did he intend to perform some 'outrage upon this young woman, or commit a robbery'?), the Old Bailey jury were directed to ignore this minor detail.[49] The 22-year-old Lipski protested his innocence but was convicted and sentenced to death by Justice Stephen, a verdict that had to be explained to him by the court's interpreter as he spoke little English. Lipski eventually confessed to the murder of Miriam Angel but this in itself does not confirm his guilt: two other Jews had been implicated in the murder and Lipski was clearly a man struggling with life as he indicated in his final testament at Newgate gaol.[50] Israel Lipski's name entered the lexicon of negative terms with which to describe Jews, as one witness in the Ripper case was later able to testify.

The Lipski case merely placed another marker on the timeline of anti-Semitism in Britain. In 1886 Arnold White had published his *Problems of a Great City* in which he set out his arguments for restricting the number of poor Jewish immigrants coming to Britain.[51] White also suggested that a tax on foreign immigrants was not unreasonable, with the money raised being used to help others emigrate. While the rhetoric was reasoned and pragmatic, the underlying tone was clearly anti-alien and racist.[52] In the same year a correspondent to the *Pall Mall Gazette* warned that there was a 'Judenhetze [active anti-Semitism] brewing in East London' as a result of the thousands of Jews 'of the lowest type' that had 'planted themselves chiefly at the East End within the past three years, and have a greater responsibility for the distress which prevails there probably than all other causes put together'. The writer declared that foreign Jews 'of no nationality whatever are becoming a pest and a menace to the poor native-born Eastender. They oust him out of all decent habitation and greatly lower the standard of living, as well as the general moral tone'.[53] This view was echoed in a series of reports that the *Gazette* ran under the heading 'How they live'. A needlewoman on the east side of Commercial Road told the paper that, 'Foreigners take the work at lower prices than we can accept. If we refuse a garment a foreigner will take 3d less, taking the whole cutting'. Another woman, whose husband was a bootmaker, when asked what he earned when in full-time work replied that she 'had almost forgotten what that meant'; 'It was the Jews and Germans that cut the work down'. At number 32 a widow complained that, 'The Jews make the prices so bad. They take a lot of work at cheap prices and let it out to "sweaters" in their employ. It is the Jew who gets the benefit. Since Christians have often worked from morning to the next morning'.[54] The paper even found a local Jewish tailor – one who called himself an Englishman because his father had 'been a Londoner before him' – who blamed his current predicament on the influx of foreigners:

> The foreigner is working the English right out. Foreigners beat us by making their entire families of [sic] stitch from daybreak till night, and if a foreigner earns 1s he puts 2d out of it. They are the ruin of the tailoring trade ... How would I remedy that? I think it is the free trade. Every man should stay in his native country. Why should Englishmen be driven to emigrate to make room for foreigners?[55]

The Parliamentary Select Committee investigating emigration and immigration in 1888 was warned by one witness that if the 'present situation' (of Polish Jews working in 'sweated' workshops) continued, 'the ready made clothing trade of the whole of the principal towns will be in the hands of foreigners'.[56]

The negative images of Jews and the latent anti-Semitism that occasionally rose to the surface in a usually tolerant area for immigrants were a product particularly of the large-scale immigration of the late nineteenth century. Jews had, of course, been coming to London in large numbers throughout the century to join communities that had been established in East London for even longer than the Huguenots. It is hard to be precise about the actual numbers of Jews in London in the late nineteenth century. The *Jewish Year Book* estimated that there were just over 100,000 Jews in Britain in 1891. The census data for 1871 suggests that there were 100,638 aliens from Russia, the Russian Pale or Rumania in England and Wales, rising to 247,758 by 1901.[57] But this tells us relatively little about the numbers of Polish and Russian Jews that came to England, many of whom were using London as a temporary staging post on their route to the 'promised land' (or *goldene medina*) of the United States of America.[58] One author claims that 120,000 migrated to England in the years, from 1870 to 1914; another suggests that between April 1881 and June 1882 nearly a quarter of a million left Eastern Europe for America and Great Britain.[59] Charles Booth calculated that in East London itself there were around 45,000 Jews but, as William Fishman notes, this may have been 'an overestimate'. Of these, by far the majority (28,790 according to Booth) were crowded into the streets of Whitechapel.[60]

There were cultural and, to some extent, religious differences between the immigrants of the middle and late nineteenth centuries (although these were often overlooked or not noticed by indigenous Londoners and other contemporary observers like Booth).[61] In the 1860s and 1870s most migrants were arriving from Germany and the Netherlands. In the last decades of the century the travellers were coming further, from Eastern Europe. Spitalfields was home to an established community of Dutch Jews, who had successfully merged with the local population to the extent that they were 'often indistinguishable from their Gentile Cockney neighbours'.[62] Alongside were immigrants from Germany that had arrived from mid-century and who were defined by their industriousness and ambition. Into this melting pot came the so-called 'poor' Jews from the Russian empire, principally Poles. These newcomers created echoes of the communities they had left behind with their own forms of synagogue, dress, language and working practices.

The immigrants had mixed fortunes before and after they reached London but shared similar motivations. In 1869 famine in north-eastern Russia resulted in large numbers of Jews being expelled from the border areas. This was followed by systematic persecution of Jewish communities and the dismantling of their own internal economic system, throwing thousands into poverty. In 1875 and 1876 enforced conscription into the Tsar's armed forces prompted many thousands of Jews to leave. In March 1881 Jews were wrongly accused of the assassination of Tsar Alexander II (one Jewish woman had a minor role in the terrorist cell – *Narodnaya Volya* – that had carried out the killing) prompting pogroms in many Russian towns and cities. This served to persuade still more Jews that their only hope of a peaceful life involved abandoning their homes and communities.[63] As one emigrant explained:

To take myself for an example, I did not leave my native country because I was expelled for political or religious reasons; but nearly every day brought me news of fresh expulsions, or new ukases[63] against the people of my race, and I was asking myself, Where is this going to stop? Whose turn will be next? And I decided to leave the country where I could get neither justice nor mercy. I certainly have not come to live in English fogs for the mere pleasure of it. My case is typical of most Jewish immigrants.[65]

What awaited them in London was a mixed reception. True, London contained lots of fellow congregationalists and while few gentiles spoke the Russian or Polish language most London Jews conversed in a range of tongues, including Yiddish. Immigrants could make themselves understood and they could find kosher food and places to practice their faith. But this aside, the welcome they received was far from all embracing. Native workers were wary of large numbers of semi-skilled craftsmen and labourers flooding the market with cheap labour and deflating wages. Established Anglo-Jewry attempted to dissuade others from joining them in London, warning of the overcrowded housing conditions, hard work for little gain and poor opportunities for prosperity. England would tolerate their religion, it would not persecute them as a race, but neither would it provide them with a good living and comfortable surroundings.

While the Jewish community of the East End had escaped from direct persecution, on ethnic and religious grounds they were often the victims of exploitation and prejudice in their new home. This appears to have been the result of their cultural differences and concerns that they would take the jobs of indigenous workers. The cry of 'Britons first' was commonly heard in the depressed economy of the 1880s. One of the key issues was language: Superintendent Mulvaney of Leman Street Police Station suggested that Scotland Yard might help fund a small group of police officers in learning Yiddish since the local Russian and Polish Jews were frequently putting out bills and 'circulars in this language' and the 'police know nothing of their purport unless the translator is employed to translate them'.[66] The language problem had even made taking the census difficult in 1881 as the superintendent of statistics at the General Register Office told a select committee in 1888.[67] Even between Eastern European Jews language could sometimes be a barrier, or at least serve to distinguish Poles from Russians. The inability of many foreign Jews to speak English forced them to work for those Jewish employers, English born or immigrant, who could understand them. Language was not the only coefficient here: Jewish employers would not force or expect their workers to turn up on Saturdays and so break the Sabbath. As one Christian observer noted in 1867:

It is almost impossible for a Jew to be bound apprentice to a master who is not of the same persuasion; being interdicted from partaking of his food, from working part of every Friday and the whole of every Saturday throughout the year, besides the festivals and periods of mourning, when no Jew can work. This loss of time no Christian master can afford, so there is no possibility of acquiring a trade or of being employed at day-work more than four days and a half per week. No Jews can be employed in Christian factories, shipyards, engine works, or shops.[68]

Jewish immigrants were different because of their faith and religious practices and to a very large extent they were unable to integrate completely with the indigenous community as a result. The ghettos that so many observers deplored were themselves the product of this seemingly irresolvable situation. The new arrivals or 'greeners' were faced with what Fishman describes as a life of 'grinding poverty and unremitting labour'.[69] They found themselves unwelcome in a labour market that was already swamped by foreign workers and deflated by competition from abroad and elsewhere in Britain. The vulnerability of immigrants exposed them to unscrupulous exploitation by their own co-religionists. Jewish workshop owners wilfully broke legislation designed to protect workers' conditions and paid workers at well-below standard rates secure in the knowledge that desperate immigrants were unlikely to complain to the authorities. *The Lancet* commented that,

The employer is master of the situation and can impose any condition. The unfortunate worker greedily accepts starvation wages, and even assists his employer to defy the Factory Act, the Sanitary Act and other laws instituted to protect him, fearing that, by availing himself of our legislature, he may lose the little he is able to earn.[70]

The answer for many was either repatriation or integration (or, for some evangelist Christians, conversion). Integration was favoured by the established Jewish community who, like the Huguenots that had preceded them, had gone to great lengths to blend in with their English neighbours. The mantra chimes with that levelled at the Muslim communities of Britain in the twenty-first century: learn the language, adopt Western dress and embrace popular culture, leave your own culture indoors. The alternative was ostracism, abuse and perhaps violence. Violence towards East End Jews was not uncommon — especially at the height of the Ripper crisis when 'foreigners' were the principal targets of popular anger towards the murders. Some of the anti-Semitic protectionism was more overt

than Arnold White's moderate rhetoric. Margaret Harkness' heroine in her novel
*In Darkest London* rails against the practice of employing Jewish labour: 'I never
take on a foreigner. It's bad enough for us English and I won't make it worse by
giving work to a Jewess'.[71]

In defence of Harkness she was not always critical of the immigrant Jew and
several papers and periodicals, notably *Commonweal*, were quick to present an
alternative view. Harkness was impressed by the depth of faith among London
Jews and by their sense of community – both perhaps qualities that she saw as
lacking within the indigenous working-class population. Others driven by a
socialist critique of the economic system recognized that foreign immigrants
were merely being used as pawns and scapegoats in hard economic times. On
7 May 1888 an article in the *Pall Mall Gazette* entitled the 'Invasion of England'
attacked the immigration of foreign Jews arguing that 'charity should begin at
home' and bemoaning the fact that England had become a haven for the flotsam
and jetsam of Europe. Andrew Scheur writing in *Commonweal* responded by
noting that 'Jew-baiting' was a 'last attempt to bind the native workers against
the real causes of their misery'. The world should be divided not between Jew
and Gentile but between 'the exploiter and the exploited!'[72]

One of the most rational responses to anti-alien sentiments in the press and
elsewhere was printed in the *Gazette* soon after the dire warning about *Judenhetze*
we noted earlier. The minister of the New West End Synagogue wrote a carefully
worded defence of his co-religionists in the East beginning his piece by exposing
the paucity of the anti-alienists' argument:

> It is marvellous to see with what avidity and with what confidence people jump at
> any explanation which throws the blame for their misfortunes upon the foreigner.
> France would not have been beaten in her great struggle had it not been for Prussian
> spies who lined the Boulevards, packed the hotels, lurked in every Government
> office, and hovered around every regiment; and the East-end of London would
> not have been suffering from any distress to-day if it had not been for the influx of
> foreign Jewish refugees . . .

Far from ousting the native dwellers from their homes the Jews of the East End
were living in appalling overcrowded conditions. As for their so-called loose
morals . . .

> any one who will take the trouble to compare the criminal returns in so far as they
> can be referred to Jews and Gentiles, will see with whom the proportionate advantage
> lies; while as regards the purity, sobriety, affectionateness, and mutual helpfulness

of their family life, Jews have not so much to learn from but a great deal to teach their Gentile neighbours.[73]

So the picture that emerges is that of a diverse Jewish community that was in many ways at odds with the environment it found itself in. Immigrants from Eastern Europe had travelled to Britain in the hope of finding passage to the United States, the real goal of European Jewry. Many settled in London because they were unable to journey further; others stayed because they had close kinships in the capital; some found work and prospered. Immigrants were set apart by their language and culture, their religion and dress. These barriers to integration would have applied to some extent to the Huguenot incomers in the seventeenth century but they had largely thrown off these cultural differences and had assimilated with the indigenous population of London's East End. This was also true of Dutch and German Jews that had arrived in Spitalfields and Whitechapel in the eighteenth and early nineteenth centuries.

The antagonism that many migrant Jews experienced was a product of two separate but related factors. To the local working classes, those born and bred in the East End, the arrival of tens of thousands of poor immigrants represented a threat to their jobs and any antipathy they felt towards foreigners is understandable; the 1880s were tough economically and unemployment was increasing. But we need to ask whether the migrants were indeed threatening local jobs and livelihoods and whether this was the primary reason for anti-Semitism in the area. Most Jews found work, if they found it at all, in sweated workshops run by other Jews. They moved into houses already owned or at least occupied by Jews, they bought and sold goods in the Jewish street markets of Brick Lane and Middlesex Street. If they were unfortunate enough to be unable to find work then in the first instance they turned to the local Jewish community for help – not their gentile neighbours. Jewish charities and the Jewish Board of Guardians undertook to assist their co-religionists with relief and sometimes the money to travel on to America. Only when these avenues had been exhausted did the poorest of the immigrants seek help from the parish – they had as little love for the workhouse as did their English-born neighbours. Indeed William Vallance, the generally unsympathetic (unsympathetic to the poor, that is) clerk of the Whitechapel Guardians, reported that very few Jews resorted to the 'house' in his area; he was informed that only a 'dozen Jews have been admitted to the wards [in] nearly 17 years, and it is certainly more than twelve months since the last Jew was admitted'.[74]

If the antagonism felt by some Londoners and the angst and anger expressed in the press could not then be entirely explained by genuine concerns about the impact of foreign Jews on the economy of the East End, what other reasons underlay it? Unfortunately these can only really be understood in the context of widespread anti-Semitism in England and elsewhere in the late nineteenth century. Earlier in the century Britain had displayed a 'grudging tolerance' towards Jews but the waves of immigration from the East created a climate where toleration was in short measure. By 1901 Jews were being blamed for the war in South Africa and Arnold White was able to declare that it was a 'growing rule by foreign Jews that is being set up. The best forms of our national life are in jeopardy'.[75] The Jew, the foreign Jew at least, was a clear representation of the 'other' in Victorian society – this was how he had been depicted throughout the century from Fagin to the Jew of York in *Ivanhoe*. When the suggestion was made that the Whitechapel murderer might be a local Jewish tradesman, John Piser (or 'Leather Apron' as he was known), it sparked violence and demonstrations on the streets. When the police discovered the writing on the wall in Goulston Street in the wake of the 'double event', Sir Charles Warren ordered its removal for fear that the East End might experience a pogrom of its own. As the author of the letter to the *Gazette* in February 1886 had pointed out, when times are hard it is much easier to find a scapegoat without one's community than within it.

In October 1888, amidst all the panic surrounding the murders, Sir Samuel Montagu MP was prompted to write an open letter to the press in which he refuted the allegations made against the local Jewish community and the suggestion that one of them could be the murderer.

In Jewish history there are frequent records that, when epidemics have occurred, or murders have taken place, false accusations have been made against the Jews, inciting the ignorant and criminal class to acts of violence. In this enlightened country, with an educated working class, no such fear need be entertained; but why recall the red spectre of bygone ages, when religious persecution was a matter of course, whichever Christian creed was in power? Few have greater experience than I of the Jews of this and of other countries, and I am able to state with confidence that no similar class of human beings is as free from acts of violence as the Jews of Europe and America. It has generally been admitted that the murderer had considerable practical knowledge of anatomy, and I do not believe that there exists such an individual among the Jews of East London. If the 'handwriting on the wall' was done by the monster himself, can there be any doubt of his intention to throw the pursuers on the wrong track, while showing hostility to the Jews in the vicinity?[76]

For the Jews the problem would seem to be that across the nineteenth and well into the twentieth centuries they have been an easy target for scapegoating.

In Britain, however, we have had other targets for our prejudices and jokes and in the East End another long established community also suffered from poverty, deprivation and lack of work in the last quarter of the nineteenth century. These were the Irish, the internal (and perhaps eternal) migrants of the British Isles. The story of Irish immigration to England is a long one. The Irish in London outnumbered the Jews but did not stand out in the way that the 'dark-bearded men in Russian-Polish dress' did, they were citizens of the United Kingdom rather than incoming foreigners.[77] This did not mean that they passed unnoticed of course, or that they were afforded much more of a welcome than those arriving from Eastern Europe. The Irish had been coming to London for centuries and had been the target of abuse, disparaging comments and jokes for all of that time. Much of this was founded on religious prejudice and intolerance. To observers such as Charles Booth 'neither the Irish nor their [Catholic] faith had much to commend them'.[78] The Irish were often poor and so in addition to their Roman ways they were seen as a drain on the poor rates and frequently fell foul of the settlement laws as parish officers attempted to see them 'passed' out of their responsibility.

After 1815 Irish immigration had increased significantly as more and more Irishmen and women made the relatively short journey across the Irish Sea to look for work in the growing towns and cities of Britain. By 1851, 500,000 Irish had settled in England and Wales; during the famine years of the late 1840s thousands of desperate families arrived each month. This nineteenth-century song illustrates the motivation of those who chose to leave Ireland for the chance of a better life in Victorian London:

> I'll stay no more in Dublin
> To live upon potatoes fare,
> But I'll go up to London.
> Arrah! Pat, won't you come, my dear?
>
> Arrah! come, come away,
> My Irish blade.
> Arrah! come, come away
> 'The Irishman's Ramble to London'[79]

The early Irish settlers in London had gathered around St Giles and Holborn in Elizabethan times, outside of the old City where they had no licence to trade, and then began to colonize Whitechapel in the eighteenth century. As the nineteenth century brought yet more migrants the Irish concentrated in the poorer working-class areas north and south of the river Thames, in places that 'provided both a demand for unskilled labour and a supply of relatively cheap housing'. East London was predominantly Irish in the middle of the nineteenth century.[80] This situation only began to change as the last decades of the century approached: the Irish communities of St Giles had been displaced by the destruction of the infamous rookery, to lay out the broad promenade of Oxford Street and similarly the building of the railways (much of which was carried out with an Irish labour force) drove many more from their old homes.[81] Wherever they moved, however, the Irish recreated their communities; like the Jews from Eastern Europe the London Irish retained their cultural differences, their customs, religion and language. The Irish lodging housekeepers in the East End regularly 'met the Cork steamer to offer new arrivals a bed' for example.[82]

The London Irish also lived in some of the worst conditions of all London's inhabitants, drawing the criticism and condemnation of many of those worthy Victorian philanthropists and social reformers that visited the alleys and courts of the city. Chapter 5 will deal with the social problems associated with housing conditions in London in the 1880s but it is worth reflecting on the views of one visitor to an Irish slum at mid-century:

> Rookeries are bad, but what are they to Irish rookeries? In some cases these courts are choked up with every kind of filth; their approaches wind round by the worst kind of slaughter-houses . . . they are crowded with pigs, with fowls, and with dogs; they are strewn with oyster shells and fish refuse . . . their drainage lies in pools wherever it may by thrown'.[83]

Or we might take the rather impressionistic views of one observer in 1872 who wrote:

> In the neighbourhood of Whitechapel or Bethnal Green is congregated the vast army of Irish toil or Irish misery whom the accursed Land system rooted out of their happy homesteads by the Barrow or the Blackwater, the Foyle or the Shannon, the Liffey or the Slaney – some of them struggling manfully and hopefully against the bitter decrees of destiny – others sinking broken-hearted in the strife – withering like plants of another clime – fading beneath the inclemency of strange skies; and, worse than this, others sinking lower still into that worst and lowest state of all – that lowest deep beneath which even imagination cannot conceive a lower – that sink of moral pollution in which wallow the lowest dregs of English society.[84]

To some extent of course the Irish were the victims both of poverty and a lack of opportunity but also of negative stereotyping. The English working class lived alongside their Irish neighbours in many parts of the capital (including the East End) but it was the immigrants that dwelt in the worst houses and played second fiddle to the indigenous population in the labour market.[85]

The Jewish community of Whitechapel was heavily involved in the 'rag trade' – the production of clothing and shoes – as we have seen, but what of the Irish? Again, the new arrivals to London (and those out of work) relied heavily on the settled population in their attempts to find gainful employment. This was especially difficult in the depressed years of the 1870s and 1880s, and as the ranks of London's immigrant population were swollen by the influx of foreign Jews and poor Irish escaping the latest failure of the potato crop. Those arriving in London had mixed experiences: John Fitzgerald for example left Cork in November 1881 to see if he could find work in the capital 'as he could get no work in Ireland'. At first he had got by sweeping the snow off the pavements but had ended up begging and being arrested for doing so. He was told to seek help from the local Catholic Church and not to 'annoy people by begging' in future.[86]

Undoubtedly there were many success stories among the Irish migrants and Irish-born settlers found employment across the trades of London. As Colin Pooley has noted, 'the experience of acute poverty ascribed in most studies to a small majority of Irish migrants has been used to obscure the fact that many Irish-born gained jobs which required skill and which gave them responsibility, status and financial reward'.[87] The Irish to some extent appear to have dominated on the London Docks and most of the skilled dockers, the stevedores, were Irish.[88] However, employment on the docks was seasonal and subject to considerable fluctuations in trade cycles and the weather. The industry had a surfeit of labour and there were regular gatherings of casuals hoping for a day's or week's work outside the dock gates early each morning. The Irish made excellent dock workers: they had 'strong arms, broad shoulders, and brave hearts that are cheerful and jocund in the midst of toil'. However, the work was extremely hard and it would wear men out after a time. Few dockers could continue beyond their fifties.[89]

The Irish community of Whitechapel also found work in tailoring and shoemaking, where in both trades long hours and poor pay ensured a steady turnover in staff. The Irish that Henry Mayhew talked to in the 1850s were working in the sweated workshops of the East End for very little pay, in just the same conditions that the immigrants from Eastern Europe were to experience a few decades later.[90] Irish women were employed as needleworkers, the men and boys in shoemaking. They also found work in a range of other low-paid industries as one observer noted:

One meets them at every step, young women carrying large bundles of umbrella-frames home to be covered; young women carrying wooden cages full of hats, which yet want the silk and binding . . . and above all female sackmakers . . . These girls have a yellow oily look and are many of them slight and delicate, but they can carry immense loads of sacking on their heads.[91]

Once again the stereotype of the long-suffering poorly paid but plucky and strong Irish migrant is trotted out. This was not the only construction of the Irish in London at this time. There were thousands of Irish servants working in the houses of London's middle and upper classes. Unfortunately Irish servants had a reputation for being cheeky and less able than their English-born counterparts. As a result many migrants found that they were merely offered domestic service roles at the bottom of the employment ladder. Service was a precarious way of earning a living, especially for young women and girls who often found themselves at the mercy of predatory males – both masters and fellow servants. The servant girl that got pregnant through the unwanted attentions of her employer (or his son) had little chance of saving her reputation. Many of London's prostitutes were poor Irish girls (like Mary Kelly – the Ripper's last victim) that had often tried and failed to find or keep a position in a London household.

The clearest differentiation between the Irish workforce in London and that drawn from the English-born majority is in the proportion of migrants that worked as unskilled labourers, however broadly defined. Lees has sampled five areas of London from the 1851 census to show that almost four times as many Irish workers were employed as unskilled labourers than the indigenous London population. There was a similar proportion of lower middle class (shopkeepers, clerks, teachers, small business people etc.) and a very similar pattern emerges for the semi-skilled workers. But the preponderance of unskilled labourers – those often most vulnerable to unemployment or underemployment, and those drawing the lowest wages – goes a long way in explaining the relative poverty of large numbers of the Irish in London (and indeed elsewhere in Britain – studies have shown that in Liverpool, Glasgow and Manchester the Irish diaspora had a similar experience). Thus, while the Irish may not have looked very different to their English-born neighbours – and were not deemed to be 'foreign' by the local population or the authorities – they were in many ways just as marginalized economically and socially as were the later Jewish immigrants to the capital.

Prejudice against the Irish community was rooted, as suggested earlier, in deep-seated anti-Catholicism in England. In 1780 London had been rocked by several days of anti-Catholic rioting as Lord Gordon's demonstration against attempts by parliament to grant Catholic emancipation descended into personal vendetta and mob violence. Throughout the nineteenth century the 'Irish Question' dominated domestic politics and was to split the Liberal party in 1886, when the election was largely fought on that issue alone.[92] The failure of the potato crop in 1845 brought four years of famine to Ireland forcing tens of thousands to emigrate to Britain and America. In 1875 Charles Stewart Parnell was elected to Westminster as the leader of the Irish Nationalist Party placing the issue of Irish Home Rule firmly at the heart of English politics. Parnell, a Protestant landlord, faced the thorny task of uniting Catholic nationalists behind him while at the same time convincing the British government that their best interests were served by granting Ireland some level of independence. His efforts kept Ireland firmly implanted on the political agenda of Great Britain throughout the last quarter of the nineteenth century.

These problems that faced Ireland and its people were exacerbated by returning agricultural depression in the 1870s that led to the widespread eviction of tenant farmers unable to pay their rents. Protests against the forced evictions ranged 'from cattle-maiming to murder' and the number of incidents in 1877 (273) had spiraled to 2,590 by 1880.[93] The underlying opinion within British political circles was that much of the unrest was being fermented and organized by radical republicans who were taking advantage of the weak Irish policing network. In 1881, parliament passed the Irish Coercion Act to deal with all outbreaks of 'terrorist' activity. The extent of Irish terrorism in the nineteenth century will be discussed in some detail in Chapter 5 so it need not detain us here. Neither do we need to explore the issue of Irish Home Rule since it has been covered in great detail in many other histories. It is sufficient to note that Ireland and the Irish dominated British politics in the second half of the nineteenth century, not least because as the vote was gradually extended to reach larger sections of the working classes the competing political parties, Conservatives, Liberals and then, latterly, the new Independent Labour party, all scrambled for their votes. The Irish in London had tended to vote Liberal but began to move towards the Conservatives under the influence of Parnell. Gladstone had failed to get his Home Rule policy through parliament and had split the Liberal party in the process. Politicians like Joseph Chamberlain who opposed Home Rule left to form the Unionists and allied themselves with the Conservatives. At the end of the 1880s Home Rule effectively fell off the political agenda only to be revived in the early Edwardian period when the Liberals once again tried to use it to gain Irish votes.

The Irish in London thus carried with them a plethora of unwelcome stereotypes. They were seen as unskilled and ignorant, useful only for manual work. They were suspect on account of their religion and associated with political violence and fanaticism. But the Irish were also condemned for their raucous popular culture and for their propensity for drunkenness, fighting and general criminality. Between 20 and 28 September 1888, perhaps 12–15 per cent of those charged at the Thames Police Court were clearly of Irish ancestry. Of the men, Henry Hurley, Timothy Malone, Michael Nolan and Michael O'Brien were all fined for being drunk and disorderly and using vile language. Jeremiah McCarthy was prosecuted for an assault and given the option of two weeks' imprisonment or a 10-shilling fine. Michael Murphy and Michael Sullivan were jointly charged with assaulting a policeman, PC Bishop from H division. They were both remanded until the following week but could expect a heavy sentence from Mr Lushington JP, who was known to take a dim view of attacks on police.[94]

Attacks on the police were not uncommon in Victorian London and parts of the capital had effectively become no-go areas for officers. In 1881, four Irish men were convicted at Bow Street Police Court of beating a constable so badly that he could not return to duty for several days; the defendants on that occasion were imprisoned for a month and fined.[95] Irish male violence was also often aimed at wives and partners. Cases of domestic violence, although frequent in the police courts of London and elsewhere, undoubtedly only represent a fraction of the amount of violent abuse that women (and some men) suffered in the nineteenth-century home. One example will serve here to illustrate the problem that women had in controlling the violent behaviour of their husbands. Annette Kelly had been sent out by her husband John to fetch him some 'winkles for his tea'. When she got back the pair had an argument over the change and he hit her in the face. Annette retaliated and the fight escalated with a water jug being thrown and John eventually flooring his wife with a punch to the eye. That was the point at which she decided to go to the police, suggesting that she was prepared to accept a certain level of violence in their four years of marriage. However, she had no real desire to see him punished as a fine or his imprisonment would have impacted adversely on what was already a meagre family budget. Instead she wanted his promise not to repeat the violence again or 'she should leave him'.[96]

James Driscoll, aged 47, was accused of stealing a pair of trousers but discharged by the magistrate while 23-year-old John Murphy was committed to trial for stealing pawn tickets.[97] The case was serious and Murphy, along with another man, John Barrett, took his trial at the Old Bailey on 22 October 1888. The Irishmen had been drinking in the same pub as the victim – a foreign shoemaker called Wolter – at the top of Cable Street and had asked him to buy them beer. He obliged and then left soon after. He had not gone far before four men surrounded him and Murphy grabbed him and held his hand over his mouth so he could not cry out. Wolter's pockets were rifled and the gang made off with his pocket book and money. Wolter shouted 'Thief, thief, my money, my money' before a policeman came rushing to his assistance. Murphy was soon caught and Barrett was picked up a few weeks later when Wolter identified him among a group of men near Leman Street Police Station. Barrett produced a witness who swore that he had been indisposed at the time of the assault, having been in hospital undergoing an operation to remove a tumour from his groin. As a result Barrett was found not guilty while Murphy was sentenced to ten months hard labour.[98]

There were also several Irish women among those charged that week in September 1888. Mary O'Connor was charged with wounding; Catherine Donovan, Elizabeth Donelly and Catherine McGam with being drunk and fighting; and Catherine Murphy with assaulting PC Harrison as he attempted to arrest her. Murphy was given ten days hard labour for her offence while Donelly and McGam were bound over to keep the peace for six months. Mary Ann Bowen was arrested on a charge of disorderly conduct, which probably meant that she had been soliciting as a prostitute and had been picked up by a policeman on patrol.[99] Many of London's whores were poor Irish women who had turned to prostitution in desperation or had been forced into the trade by unscrupulous pimps.However, prostitution was a step too far for some women while for the elderly it was not even an option. In January of 1880 Julia O'Donnell was brought before the lord mayor of London at the Mansion House Justice Room. Julia was aged 60 and had been begging in Fenchurch Street with what appeared to be a baby in her arms. A policeman watched her solicit some loose change from a respectable couple by asking for 'a copper for dear baby's sake'. He approached her and discovered that all she was carrying was a bundle of rags. She denied the charge but was found guilty of obtaining money by false pretences and given seven days' imprisonment.[100]

Another Irish resident of the East End found herself in court before the magistrate because she was also struggling to make ends meet. Kate McCarty was 22 and had left her sickly child at home while she went out to borrow enough money to pay the week's rent. Instead of a loan she had been given a day's work that she presumably felt she could not refuse. Unfortunately for her the doctor who had been treating her one-year-old child for measles had made a house call only to find the baby 'on a bed, exposed to the cold, without fire or anyone to look after it'. He had the child taken to the workhouse and Kate was arrested when she came home at nine o'clock. She had left her sick baby alone for 12 hours but promised not to do so in future and so the magistrate, after reprimanding her, let her go.[101] The desperation that drove a mother to abandon her baby in order to get a precious day's work speaks volumes to the distress that many Irish families experienced in the capital in the late nineteenth century.

In an amusing footnote to these examples of drunken, violent and criminal

Irish men and women is a case from the Southwark Police Court. A man described as 'respectable' and certainly not Irish was arrested for being drunk and disorderly in Borough Market. Thomas Hodges, who told the court he was a schoolmaster, had been found by a patrolling policeman shouting out 'Ireland for ever!' When he approached him Hodges declared, 'I am a supporter of Mr. Parnell. I defy you all!' and refused to go home quietly. In court he was notably repentant and said it must have been all the talk of Home Rule in the press that had led him to make such a display of himself. He was fined 20s, which he paid, and he left the court promising that 'I won't be a Home Ruler again'.[102] The pages of the London press are rich in examples of Irishmen and women coming before the magistracy and higher courts of the capital. It is one stereotype of the Irish in England that they were drunken, violent and criminal. This has led to some speculation that the Ripper himself was a local Irish immigrant as one of the most contentious Ripper letters was allegedly written in an Irish dialect.

On 16 October 1888 the chairman of the Whitechapel Vigilance Committee, George Lusk, received a parcel by post. Inside was a piece of kidney (later identified at the London Hospital as human) and the following letter:

From Hell
Mr Lusk,
Sor
I send you half the Kidne I took from one woman praserved it for you tother piece I fried and ate it was very nise. I may send you the bloody nife that took it out if you will only wate a whil longer
signed
catch me when you can Mishter Lusk

On 19 October the *Pall Mall Gazette* reported the arrival of the parcel and reminded its readers that the fourth victim of the murderer, Catherine Eddowes, had had her left kidney removed. It did not mention the above letter but instead referred to a postcard that George Lusk had received two days earlier.[103] The 'From Hell' missive was soon reported in the London and regional press, all of them carrying a similar description of the contents of the box as well as Lusk's initial belief that it was a nasty hoax. The paper also made the link with the letter and the slaying of Catherine Eddowes. However, none of them suggested that the writer was an Irishman. During the panic surrounding the murders many arrests were made and not all of them in London. The *Manchester Times* reported the release of a man who had been detained in County Derry on suspicion of his involvement in the killings but most of the focus of the investigation appears to have been on the Jewish community and the occasional medical doctor that was chased by local mobs.[104] The use of 'Sor' and 'Mishter' might suggest the writer was either Irish or wished to make it appear that he was Irish and, as at least two ripperologists have noted, the terminology was consistent with contemporary expressions of Irish dialect.[105]

The name Lusk is Celtic in origins, and so it may be that George Lusk originated from Ireland or had Irish ancestry. If the writer of the letter was a hoaxer they may have been deliberately teasing the committee chairman in their choice of inflection. Nevertheless it seems highly likely that all the letters and postcards received by the Whitechapel Vigilance Committee, the police and the newspapers were fake or hoax, written by cranks and attention seekers and so despite the perceived credibility of this missive (because of the kidney it contained) we should also consider it to be a 'red herring'. The police at the time certainly appear to have thought little of it, noting that any medical student was capable of obtaining a kidney that resembled that belonging to a 45-year-old woman with a drink problem. Whatever the truth of the matter the continual pressure of the investigation, and the series of unpleasant letters and postcards, had their effect on George Lusk. On 20 October he resigned, along with the rest of the committee members, citing the 'lack of moral and material support they have experienced during their philanthropic efforts to benefit their fellow citizens'.[106] The suggestion that the writer of the letter was Irish emerged a few days later. *Lloyd's Weekly Newspaper* reported that a man with an Irish accent asked for Mr Lusk's address after seeing a reward notice in the window of a leather workshop in the Mile End Road. Miss Marsh, looking after the shop in the absence of her father, was able to give the man Mr Lusk's address as Alderney Road but she did not know the house number. The parcel, when it arrived, did not have a number on it (presumably the postman knew George Lusk and where he lived).[107] Apart from this, however, there is little to suggest that either the police or local people believed the killer was an Irishman.

London was home to other immigrant communities as well as those from other parts of England, Scotland and Wales. The Irish and Jews were by far the largest groups but there were settlers from China, Italy and Portugal as well as from Africa and India. Britain's position as the world's largest empire ensured that London was a magnet for those seeking new opportunites, adventure or escape from oppression. The reporting of the activities of immigrants often reveals the prevalent prejudices of contemporaries. An extract from *Lloyd's Weekly* is indicative of this stereotyping. The paper reported 'A Chinese funeral in London', noteworthy on this occasion because it was officiated over by an English clergyman. The groom, Sut Poo, was a resident of Limehouse, where most of the

Chinese population of London (and indeed of Britain) lived in the 1880s. This community was fairly small in comparison with the Jews of Whitechapel and Bethnal Green but it was significant. According to the census returns for 1881 there were 665 Chinese-born 'aliens' in England and Wales and a sixth of these lived in London, most on Limehouse Causeway and Pennyfields both situated at the heart of London's Docks.[108]

Unsurprisingly most of the Chinese community here worked as seamen, historically with the East India Company from the eighteenth century onwards. The newspaper described Limehouse as a 'Chinese colony, where many opium dens are known to exist'; it reported that fireworks were set off from the cortege and that there was plenty of food (consumed with chopsticks, naturally) and Chinese gin. The emphasis throughout was on the precise ceremony of the Chinese, something that was frequently noted in any discussion of China and its peoples.[109] Their 'difference' is apparent, as is their exoticism to the English viewer. In a report from the early twentieth century the *Pall Mall Gazette* reflected the view that 'one looks much like another to European eyes'. The reporter referred to the increasing numbers of 'John Chinaman' coming to the capital and willfully makes fun of the hard to pronounce Mandarin names by declaring that this 'gentleman we shall call Wun Lung for want of a better name'.[110] By the 1900s many of those working in Limehouse were operating in laundries (another stereotype for music hall performers and pantomime artists to exploit in the late nineteenth and early twentieth centuries) but remained close to their original settlement and its association with the sea.

Large numbers of what contemporaries referred to as 'Asiatic' sailors worked as crew on British merchant ships throughout the nineteenth century. The British India and the Peninsula and Oriental (P&O) Steam Navigation Company employed something in excess of 17,000 'Asiatics' according to reports in the 1880s. Of these some were Chinese while others are routinely described as 'Lascars'. In some instances this appears to be a generic term for Asian, African and other foreign seamen serving on British ships, while other reports suggest that Lascars were those sailors who came from the Indian subcontinent, in particular from the 'Gulf of Kutch and the fishing villages north and south of Bombay [Mumbai]'.[111] 'Lascar' is also mentioned by contemporaries as the Mohammedan name for a 'seaman' and so could in fact cover a wide range of nationalities and ethnicities. During the panic surrounding the Whitechapel murders the idea that the killer was a Lascar from one of the merchant fleets in the port of London was given initial credibility but with little evidence. The notion that a sailor was the culprit has arisen because several of the witnesses spoke of seeing men with a sailor's cap or 'having the appearance of a sailor', but there is again very little direct evidence that 'Jack' was a nautical man or a 'foreign' one at that.

The desire to blame 'Johnny foreigner' for the outrageous crimes committed by the Whitechapel murderer should not surprise any modern reader; we still look to scapegoat the 'other' for the problems of our own society. London contained many foreign nationals at the time of the murders: Italians in Saffron Hill, Portuguese sailors, Americans working in the travelling Wild West show, as well as Germans, French and other Europeans. Indeed London was a cosmopolitan city at the heart of empire. However, we should not neglect its indigenous local population, and therefore we can close this section by looking at the native Eastender, the Cockney, a character no less the product of prejudice, myth and stereotyping than the East End Jew, Irishman or Chinese.

As we noted earlier, the history of the East End of London has evolved from a blending of fact and fiction, reality and myth, to leave us with an image of an area that is in many ways a construction rather than a reflection of the truth. This is also largely true of the traditional inhabitants of the East End, the London born 'cockneys'. In popular culture the archetypal Cockney was the pearly king or queen, resplendent in their sequin covered suits and oyster feathered hats. They evoke a cheerful bravado, a 'never say die' spirit and a sense of fun. There is a sense that 'pearlies' represent the nineteenth-century East End, an East End that has been lost with the impact of two world wars and the redevelopment of the London Docklands in the late twentieth century. However, the amiable Cockney with his love of the music hall and drinking, his patriotism and mistrust of authority was really a product of the last years of the century – the period immediately after the Ripper murders – and in some ways a last ditch defence of a culture that was in decline.[112]

It would seem that Cockneys have grown out of late nineteenth-century music hall culture. The pearly king is a throwback to a medieval past, a characterization of a 'lord of misrule', representing a challenge to authority (and so helping to ingrain the 'cheeky Cockney' imagery).[113] An alternative view is that the 'pearlies' had their origins in the rough and tumble of the market place where they emerged as 'the uncrowned Kings of their respective communities'.[114] This association with the market is perpetuated within *EastEnders*, the BBC's long-running soap opera that creates a fictitious community in Albert Square centred around a street market that bears little reality to the modern East End. In the early twentieth century the Cockney has been associated with the costermonger, the small trader operating from a barrow on the streets and selling a range of goods or services. But the link between costers and 'pearlies', and costers and Cockneys, has its roots in the 1890s and beyond and not wholly in the Victorian period.

Mayhew saw the costers as members of the so-called 'dangerous classes', while the Cockneys of mid-century were focused instead on 'the plebeian smartness of the young journeyman, shop assistant, or lawyer's clerk'.[115] Instead of barrow boy, the Cockney was a 'swell' with money in his pockets and a desire for a good time and fashionable clothes. As one writer to the theatre press remarked: 'Nowadays your attorney's clerk – apparently struck by some "levelling up" theory of democracy – is dissatisfied unless he can dress as well as the son of a duke'.[116] This image of the Cockney was further embedded by the creation of the character of 'Arry by E. J. Milliken in *Punch* from 1877 onwards. 'Arry represented the city dweller, and in one of his first appearances he is writing to his friend Charlie who is stuck in the countryside, urging him to return for 'some sport' in the city.[117] 'Arry was patriotic, conservative and embraced jingoism in the war fever of 1878; he had little time for Gladstone and the Liberals.

'Arry came to represent the stereotype of the Cockney in late Victorian Britain, reaching far beyond the pages of *Punch*. Musical hall adopted him as a character in a very popular song that extolled his characteristics as a virtue, not as the satire that Milliken presumably intended.

> 'Arry likes a jolly good joke
> Quite right, 'Arry.
> 'Arry won't mind the fun that I spoke,
> What say, 'Arry?
> The 'Upper ten' may jeer and say
> What 'cads' the 'Arries are,
> But the 'Arries work and pay their way
> While doing the la-di-da.[118]

As Gareth Stedman Jones has pointed out, 'Arry was the 'symbolic point of tension between civilisation and the masses'. In 'Arry the Cockney we have the realization that the working man that has earned the right to vote under the 1866 Reform Act will not necessarily exercise that right in the way in which the middle classes hoped he would. The genie was out of the bottle and to some extent 'Arry knows this and is prepared to enjoy his new found power within the electoral system. He takes part in demonstrations – even those that involve the socialists to which he holds no allegiance – because he can. His views are ultra conservative as this exchange with his country 'chum' about the rights of women shows:

I've bin to a lecture! Now lectures you know ain't my mark;
Too slow and dry sawdusty mostly, but this was a bit of a lark.

Women's rights and that moonshine, my pippin. Thinks I 'there's a barney on here'
And wherever there is hens on the crow, 'Arry's good for an hinnings, – no fear!
Needn't tell you my views on the subject. The petticoats want keepin' down,
Like niggers and Radicals, CHARLIE; but spouters in bonnet and gown,
While they haven't got votes are amusing. They can reel it off and no kid.
Though I hold their right line is to marry, bile taters, and do as their bid.[119]

By the last decades of the nineteenth century the cockney character that 'Arry represented was a largely negative one and, according to Stedman Jones, was in need of a political and cultural makeover. This was achieved by the coming together of elite and popular culture in the music hall of the 1890s and in the creation of a new stereotype of the Cockney, the hard working costermonger as played by Albert Chevalier. Chevalier used a version of cockney dialect that, while not representing an accurate depiction of coster patter or street slang, gave his audience the sense of cockney speech and made him a more acceptable and engaging presence to the popular theatre-going audience. Chevalier was a less grating character than 'Arry. Easier to embrace and identify with, he was also altogether less threatening to the political classes. Gradually the image of the Cockney changed – from being brash outsiders they were brought back into the fold of the nation. After the upheaval of the London Dock Strike in 1889, and the long-standing fears of a revolutionary residuum, the Cockney emerged in the early twentieth century as a reassuring figure of optimism for early Edwardians. As Stedman Jones notes, this reassuring image was recreated in the 1940s as the Ministry of Information drew upon the 'cockney spirit' 'with its emphasis on "cheerfulness" and the "carry-on spirit", as the dominant motif in its attempt to sustain morale during the Blitz'.[120]

It is very hard to see the real Eastender, the indigenous resident of East London, among all these competing images of foreign migrants and local Cockneys. Most of the population of Whitechapel and Bethnal Green was white and English-born, although London attracted migrants from all over the British Isles. Henry Mayhew and Charles Booth both mapped the community of the East End but these give us views of the inhabitants filtered through a middle-class perspective. The overwhelming image we are left with is that of the poverty of the area and the desperate conditions of its people. This we will address in some detail later and so in finishing this look at the people and geography of the East End we might explore one event in which the real denizens of the east come to the surface in a more positive and proactive way. These were not the flash 'Arry's of *Punch* nor the furtive criminals of Mayhew's *London, Labour, and the London Poor* (1861), but instead the Match Girls who took on Bryant and May and won.

## STRIKING A BLOW FOR THE WORKERS: THE MATCH GIRLS' STRIKE AT BRYANT AND MAY'S

On 23 June 1888, the Fabian socialist Annie Besant published an exposé of conditions at the Bryant and May match factory in the Bow Road, Tower Hamlets. On Friday, 6 July the *Aberdeen Weekly Journal* reported that:

> A strike of match girls in the employment of Messers. Bryant and May has taken place under peculiar circumstances. Mrs. Besant having, in a publication known as the 'Link', given particulars of a system of inflicting fines on the match girls for trivial offences, two girls suspected by the firm of supplying the information on which the article was based were dismissed. The remainder of the female employes [sic] failing to sign a document controverting Mrs Besant's statements, came out on strike yesterday.[121]

The declaration of industrial action was immediately backed by the Women's Protective and Provident League who urged its members and 'its friends' not to buy the company's matches. The walkout on 5 July involved 1,100 or more employees who paraded in the streets for the next two days requiring the police to bring reinforcements into the area in case of trouble. Bryant and May made it quite clear that they would resist any attempt to control the way in which they treated their employees.[122] The dispute was taken up by Annie Besant as part of an ongoing campaign against the practice of 'sweating' (the overcrowding of workshops and the deliberate flouting of the factory acts that we have already seen in relation to immigrant labour in the clothing trade of the area). Besant, along with her ally Charles Bradlaugh MP and others, had consistently called for tighter restrictions to be applied to workshops and the staff employed in them. The House of Lords was undergoing an investigation of the sweating system in the East End, which it eventually published in August 1888. The committee concluded that there were 'grave evils' associated with the practice and recommended that its brief to investigate be extended throughout the country.[123] The practice was defined by a witness to the committee thus:

> The sweating system I take to mean that the work is taken from a merchant by a contractor, who lets it out again to a sub-contractor, and he employs a number of men to do the work.[124]

Charles Booth, however, suggested that the term was more popularly applied to the consequences of this system of middlemen who 'transmit this pressure [from the demands of wholesale suppliers] to those working under them, masters and men suffering alike from the long hours, insanitary conditions, and irregular earnings characteristic of the East End workshop'.[125] Booth was loath to be drawn into condemning a system he was still in the process of exploring himself but he clearly agreed that it represented an abuse of labour relations in that an unfair advantage was being taken of *unskilled* and *unorganized* labour. The key here was the use of the term 'unorganized'. The late Victorian period witnessed the gradual emergence of organized labour trade unions but before 1888 they had had little success in challenging the low wages and poor conditions under which many workers suffered. Arguably the Match Girls' Strike and the Great Dock Strike of the following year did much to change this situation.

The shareholders at Bryant and May met on 31 July at the Cannon Street Hotel to hear Mr Wilberforce Bryant condemn the 'so-called strike' as the work of socialist agitators, ill-informed trade unionists and 'some young men in connection with Toynbee Hall'. He claimed conditions in his factory were excellent and that wages were better than average for the area. He rejected attacks on the payment of dividends to shareholders (which presumably went down well among his audience, who voted themselves 15 per cent per annum) and argued that the falling off of some workers' pay was merely a consequence of a reduction in full-time working during a general decline in the trade and poor weather affecting their ability to earn work picking fruit in the summer.[126] The offer of a mere 15 per cent dividend probably reflected the initial impact the strike had caused along with Besant's exposure of the conditions under which the Match Girls worked. In an article for *The Link* Besant had claimed that Bryant and May had been intending to pay a dividend of 20 per cent (on top of payments of 23 and 25 per cent in previous years) at a time when they were asking their workers to start work at 6.30 a.m. (8 a.m. in the winter) and continue through until 6 p.m., for little pay. The work was hard and injuries not uncommon: one girl was fined for 'letting the web twist round a machine in the endeavor to save her fingers from being cut, and was sharply told to take care of the machine, "never mind your fingers". Another, who carried out the instructions and lost a finger thereby, was left unsupported while she was helpless'.[127] Besant passionately argued the case for the Match Girls who were the seeming victims of unrestrained capitalism, their employer even stopping a shilling from their wages to pay for a statue of Gladstone (of whom he was a fervent admirer) in Bow churchyard.[128] In a later article for the *Gazette* Besant argued for a matchmaker's union made up of male and female workers so that it was 'strong enough to guard its members against abnormal oppression' but recognized that poorly paid workers, as the Match Girls undoubtedly were, could little afford the dues of union membership.

Her vision was of an integrated national and indeed, international, federation of trade unions to give workers real power and influence. Not that she necessarily saw industrial relations as a 'war' between the classes: striking was a last resort, something to be used judiciously, but it 'cannot be wholly given up until capital and labour become friends instead of foes'.[129]

It would be a mistake to view the Match Girl's Strike as one orchestrated and inspired by Annie Besant or her Fabian friends. True, she visited the factory after Clementina Black had alerted her to the poor conditions endured by the workforce and handed out copies of *The Link* as the girls came off shift but it was the workers themselves that took direct action in protest at the sacking of one of the girls who gave information to Besant. A delegation of Match Girls appealed to Besant and her paper directly for help and other newspapers, notably the *Pall Mall Gazette* and the *Daily News*, took up their cause.[130] Subscriptions were raised to support the strike and on Saturday, 14 July the strikers packed into Charrington's Hall to receive a strike payment and a plea from Besant for them to stay 'hold together till they should have compelled their employers to do them justice'. There were rumours that the factory owners were going to bring in workers from Glasgow to break the strike or that the business would be removed to Norway and Sweden. The former was refuted while the meeting was told that inquiries were being made in regard to the latter.[131] The poor pay and long hours were behind the dispute but the publicity surrounding the Match Girls also exposed the health risks that these young women were taking. Matches were made with yellow phosphorous, a highly dangerous chemical. A campaign was launched to protect workers from 'phossy jaw' (necrosis of the jaw) and it was suggested at a public meeting that Bryant and May had 'hoodwinked' the factory inspectorate for some time about conditions within their factory.[132]

Bryant and May were eventually forced to concede and despite their threats to replace them with Scottish labour all the workers were reinstated. The girls were allowed to form a trade union, which they did in August of that year, the Matchmaker's Union, and the factory promised better conditions and increased rates of pay. By all measures of industrial dispute this was a victory for the workers and *Reynolds's News* championed the result:

> A victory of such a complete kind is full of hope for the future ... It will encourage the many others of the poor and helpless classes of workers of both sexes who are ground down under petty exactions, such as have been exposed by this strike, to make their grievances known, and to organise themselves for their removal.[133]

It was a tremendous achievement for the 1,400 or so workers at one East End factory and it undoubtedly inspired others to stand up for their rights in the future.[134] Clearly the support of Besant and *The Link* helped to bring much needed publicity to the strike, as did the intervention of several other London papers including the campaigning *Gazette*. But along with this we should also note the character and attitude of the Match Girls themselves. They had struck before, in 1886, and Clara Collett – researching for Charles Booth – had pointed out the reserves of energy and love of life that the factory workers at Bryant and May's possessed: 'The superabundant energy displayed by the match girls when their work is over, although they have to stand up all day at it, is inexplicable and is in striking contrast to the tired appearance of machinists'.[135] The *Gazette* also remarked on the large numbers of Match Girls who 'stroll along, in parties of from two to ten, or twelve, joking, romping, with each other and the passers by' to the theatre and musical hall, determined to have a 'good time' and enjoy themselves.[136] Annie Besant was clearly inspired by these young women and perhaps it is among the women of the East End that we can look to see the real spirit of the area. The Match Girls' Strike may have a been a relatively small event – indeed it is given surprisingly little coverage either in histories of trade unionism or of late nineteenth-century London – but arguably it had a long echo. The workers who struck in July 1888 were not demanding vast increases in wages, nor were the dockers who went on strike in the following year. Instead they demanded fair treatment, accepting that theirs was a hard job, a dirty job, but that did not mean they could be abused in it. That determination to stand one's ground in the face of oppression, to put up with difficultly but not if it is unfair, might usefully define the inhabitant of the East End, regardless of their ethnic origin.

In a sinister footnote to the dispute, the owners of Bryant and May received a letter from 'John Ripper' on Saturday, 6 October which stated that:

> I hereby notify you that I am going to pay your girls a visit. I hear that they are beginning to say what they will do with me. I am going to see what a few of them have in their stomachs, and I will take it out of them, so that they can have no more to do on the quiet.[137]

The Ripper murdered no Match Girls and he never fell into their clutches. It is quite easy to imagine his fate had they caught up with him.

## CONCLUSION

As we have seen the East End Cockney was as much the product of contemporary construction as the East End was itself. Little of what we understand about the East End comes to us from within the area itself, almost every image we have is presented to us from outside. We are constantly witnessing a magic lantern show about the East End rather than seeing the district and its community for ourselves. We might ask ourselves whether this really matters? We continue to play fast and loose with the past, appropriating bits of history and 'heritage' as they suit our modern purposes. The Ministry of Information's adoption of the cheerful Cockney may have obscured to some extent the reality of the Blitz but it is also built upon a level of truth. The modern East End is a very different place to the one that the victims of Jack the Ripper knew and worked within. 'Banglatown' has echoes of the vibrant international communities of the 1880s and the clothing trade still predominates in the Commercial Road. But the area is changing, it is dynamic – it refuses to sit still, or stay preserved for posterity as the 'East End' in tableau. The immigrant communities of the area have regularly moved on and displaced themselves. The Irish were early settlers, occupying the poorest homes in Spitalfields and Whitechapel before the incomers from Eastern Europe in turn ousted them. As the Jews prospered they in turn moved on, out to the suburbs of North London leaving room for the next wave of Asian immigrants in the postwar period. The old synagogues have become mosques, kosher butchers have become halal and the street traders sell saris and sweet breads rather than *kittels* and salt beef.

In 1957, Michael Young and Peter Willmott published their seminal study of families and family life in London.[138] They chose to focus on the East End and in a challenge to contemporary notions of the 'nuclear' family they uncovered a world in which community and family retained very strong ties with the streets and geography of the East End. The women of the area who, by implication, could not rely on their men folk to bring up and support their families maintained strong female networks of kinship. As the authors have written: 'The extended [East End] family was her trade union, organised in the main by women and for women, its solidarity her protection against being alone'.[139] This is, in some ways, how we now view the East End – channelled as it is through the fictional relationships of the inhabitants of Albert Square – as an area in which some essence of community spirit and extended family ties survives. This is a positive view of East London and it sits alongside that other long-held and equally constructed view of the East End as a dangerous playground for the middle-class 'slummer', full of exotic foreigners, criminals, prostitutes and downtrodden paupers in need of rescue.

As we have seen in this chapter much of the responsibility for representations of both the ingidenous and immigrant populations of the East End can be laid at the door of the popular press. The so-called 'fourth estate' was flexing its muscles in the second half of the nineteenth century and it is arguable that without them the story of the Whitechapel murders and the character of 'Jack the Ripper' would be little more than a distant memory. With this in mind we can now look at the actions and attitudes of the Victorian press in greater detail.

# 4

# Read All About It! Ripper News and Sensation in Victorian Society

nothing can ever get itself accomplished nowadays without sensationalism . . . In politics, in social reform, it is indispensable

So spoke the father of investigative journalism, William Stead, in 1886. Stead, as the editor of the *Pall Mall Gazette*, was in the vanguard of the so-called 'new journalism' that revolutionized the newspaper industry in the last quarter of the nineteenth century. The development of a new and, arguably, 'modern' press had much to do with the importation of new technologies from America and a growing literate and relatively affluent population at home. New journalism can be closely linked to sensation literature, crime reporting and other forms of popular culture such as the music hall and melodrama. The newspaper industry was highly competitive in the late nineteenth century, no more so than in London. This competition drove editors to develop new styles of news presentation to attract readers and advertisers to their products and to search for news items that would keep readers interested enough to follow stories for days or weeks on end. In the Whitechapel murders they had an almost ready-made sensation story to report. 'Jack' provided them with an ongoing news item that ran for several months and an almost mythological villain who harked back to bogeyman figures from the earlier part of the nineteenth century and beyond.

The spotlight of attention that the Ripper murder threw upon the East End allowed the campaigning element of the press to decry the desperate poverty of the district and issue dire warnings about the state of the nation. The failure of the police to capture the killer similarly enabled some sections of the press to use this as a stick with which to beat the government and the commissioner of the Metropolitan Police. In short the Whitechapel murders facilitated the creation of what Stanley Cohen has identified as a 'moral panic' in late Victorian society. In this chapter we will explore the nature and development of the

Victorian press and 'new journalism', and their relationship to sensationalism and contemporary popular culture. In closing we will consider whether in their reporting of the Whitechapel murders the press were responsible for creating a moral panic in late Victorian London.

## THE RISE AND RISE OF THE VICTORIAN PRESS

By the time the Whitechapel murders came to dominate the newsstands of the capital London was served by thirteen morning and nine evening daily newspapers.[1] In addition Sunday papers and weekly journals provided Londoners with a tremendous variety of news, gossip and stories from the Empire and beyond. By the 1880s newspapers catered for a diverse reading public as literacy rates improved and printing costs fell. It was probably this latter development that allowed the massive increase in newspaper sales in the second half of the century. Newspapers had been around for over 300 years but had not become a fixed part of daily life until the late eighteenth century. Newspapers had cut their teeth in the propaganda battles of the English civil war but were subject to government censorship until 1695. Up until 1700 all newspapers had been printed in London but the new century saw the appearance of papers in major provincial centres such as Norwich and Bristol. Experimentation followed quickly and by 1760 some 130 different papers had been inaugurated (although only 35 managed to stay in business) and 200,000 copies were being printed daily – this figure had doubled by 1800. By the late eighteenth century reading a newspaper was an important part of a gentleman's daily activity.

The 1780s saw weekly, thrice weekly and daily newspapers in circulation and by the early years of the new century the political weekly and the Sunday newspaper had appeared. Growth was dramatic, especially in the provinces. However, the provincial press in the eighteenth century had relatively little that was original on their pages. They took their news from London, steered clear of controversy and filled their columns with advertising. However, increased competition in the 1800s led to some changes in these local papers. These provincial papers began to report local issues and were more prepared to use editorials to voice concerns and make political statements. This in turn led to the emergence of some of the more important, and in some cases more radical, papers such as *The Manchester Guardian*.

By 1814 *The Times* had improved its output by utilizing steam power, and faster production was eventually combined with faster distribution after the advent of the railways. This helped the 'respectable' press outstrip and outsell the 'pauper' press (organs such as *The Black Dwarf* which catered for a radical middle and working class that demanded electoral reform). The radical press was still effectively muzzled by government interference and restricted in its readership by the high costs of production and by taxation. However, after the failure (or defeat) of Chartism, politicians became more willing to reduce restrictions on the press in the form of stamp duty.

Historians have characterized the press as an agent of social control in the nineteenth century, inculcating accepted norms of behaviour and standardizing opinions about state institutions. Some contemporaries certainly felt the press could have an important role in society; there was a belief, as expressed by men such as Palmerston and Gladstone, that the press could be force for good by bringing the nation closer together. The new police (created by Peel in 1829 and gradually introduced across England and Wales over the next 25 years) believed it could help cut crime. Educators believed it could increase knowledge in a positive way. As Alan Lee concludes, politically, 'it was argued, a cheap press was an essential component of an educated democracy'.[2] This new confidence in the positive potential influence of print media resulted in tax reform in the 1850s. The duty on advertising was removed in 1853, and this was followed two years later by the exemption of newspapers from stamp duty. Finally production was made cheaper still by the abolition of paper tax in 1861. The result was the birth of a middle-class daily press that was much more affordable to many more consumers. One of the first beneficiaries of this was the *Daily Telegraph*, which had carved out a circulation of 250,000 by the 1880s. The numbers of newspapers soared – from 795 in 1856 to 'well over 2,000 by 1890'.[3]

Removing taxation and government influence from newspapers was one key factor in the expansion of the 'fourth estate' in the nineteenth century but there were other important technological advances in newspaper production that helped extend the reach of journalism during this period. After 1843 the telegraph aided the rapid spread of information and the rotary-action printing machine increased outputs. In 1855 the industry received another injection of technology with the importation of an American invention that relied on rotating type cylinders, the Hoe type revolving machine.[4] By the 1890s the linotype had arrived on Fleet Street allowing the production of 200,000 copies of a paper each hour. Such mass production allowed for cheap prices so that the popular newspaper was 'securely implanted in to the cultural landscape as an essential reference point in the daily lives of millions of people'.[5] The popular press had arrived and would continue to dominate news media until television and eventually the internet challenged its position in the late twentieth and early twenty-first centuries.

As Richard Williams has observed, in 'the course of the nineteenth century the development of the newspaper from a small-scale capitalist enterprise to the capitalist combines of the 1880s and onwards was at every point crucial to the development of different elements of popular culture'.[6] The newspapers brought events like the Ripper murders directly into people's homes, work and leisure places and allowed families to consume the very latest scandals and murders over their breakfast. However, this new development was not universally welcomed and some discordant voices were raised in warning of the consequences of the public appetite for salacious news. One cartoon in *Punch* from 1849 is indicative of a concern that newspapers could have a negative effect on society.

In the cartoon a father reads the newspaper to his wife and family. He recounts the details of a gruesome murder of two children by their father and the rather glib description of the killer and his calm behavior when in custody. The paper is apparently making light of the murder and turning it into entertainment. The walls of the home are covered in images from the popular *penny dreadfuls* which published the short lives of notorious criminals both past and present; there

USEFUL SUNDAY LITERATURE FOR THE MASSES;
OR, MURDER MADE FAMILIAR.

*Father of a Family (reads).* "THE WRETCHED MURDERER IS SUPPOSED TO HAVE CUT THE THROATS OF HIS THREE ELDEST CHILDREN, AND THEN TO HAVE KILLED THE BABY BY BEATING IT REPEATEDLY WITH A POKER. * * * * IN PERSON HE IS OF A RATHER BLOATED APPEARANCE, WITH A BULL NECK, SMALL EYES, BROAD BARDY NOSE, AND COARSE VULGAR MOUTH. HIS DRESS WAS A LIGHT BLUE COAT, WITH BRASS BUTTONS, ELEGANT YELLOW SUMMER VEST, AND PEPPER-AND-SALT TROUSERS. WHEN AT THE STATION HOUSE HE EXPRESSED HIMSELF AS BEING RATHER 'PECKISH,' AND SAID HE SHOULD LIKE A BLACK PUDDING, WHICH, WITH A CUP OF COFFEE, WAS IMMEDIATELY PROCURED FOR HIM."

**Figure 3** 'Useful Sunday literature for the masses', *Punch*, September 1849[7]

is little else in the home, which implies that, in the artist's opinion, rather too much of the family's budget is being spent on such dubious reading material. The father's work tools lie scattered on the floor, as does the family Bible. It is a Sunday and the clear implication is that this family should be at church not idling at home reading the penny press.

By the 1880s the popular press had grown notably by loading its copies with the Sunday papers' traditional mainstay of crime, salacious sensation and gossip. In 1880 *Tit-Bits* was launched in along with *Pearson's Weekly*, both of which offered scraps of information, competitions and jokes. In October 1888, as the Whitechapel murders occupied the column inches of most papers, a new periodical was released. *Pick Me Up!* was launched with the following opening gambit:

> We propose to look mainly in the comic side of life . . . politics we eschew. We have a notion that the party for the time being uppermost will get along just as well without our assistance. Anyhow they must try.

> We don't profess to improve anybody's mind. It takes us all our time to improve ours.

This rather uninspiring publication also carried a poem entitled 'One more unfortunate' which alluded to the downfall and disgrace of a young woman who is 'hunted' (like a butterfly) and who ends up taking her own life by throwing herself into the Thames by Westminster.[8] It managed to treat a difficult subject (many prostitutes committed suicide during this period) in a light-hearted way with doggerel verse and crude line drawings. Unlike the more serious papers, publications such as *Pick Me Up!* were unashamedly dedicated to light entertainment and trivia. However, while the removal of stamp duty and improvements in technology allowed a popular press to develop, there were individuals who still shared the belief with Gladstone and others that the press could be a force for social change and education.

## WILLIAM T. STEAD AND THE NEW JOURNALISM OF THE LATE NINETEENTH CENTURY

While the early nineteenth-century press had sought political influence, that of the second half of the century strove more for profit than political clout. Naturally there were exceptions like *The Times* that, despite its falling circulation from 1860 onwards, persisted with its sober presentation of the news and steadfastly refused to adopt newfangled editorial devices that might have won it a wider audience.

One paper that did choose to innovate was the *Pall Mall Gazette*. The *Gazette* had started life in 1865 under the stewardship of Frederick Greenwood as editor and George Murray Smith as owner. However, when Smith gave up control of the paper to his son-in-law, Henry Yates Thompson, in 1880, Greenwood quickly fell out with the new proprietor over politics. For a while the *Gazette* floundered and Thompson turned to the radical editor of *The Northern Echo*, a Darlington based local paper, to help improve the *Gazette's* circulation and profile. It was a bold and astute move. As editor of *The Northern Echo* William T. Stead had established a reputation for political journalism that had won praise from leading Liberal politicians including Gladstone and Joseph Chamberlain. Within three years of joining the *Gazette* as assistant editor to John Morley, Stead had made the editorship his own. Over the next few years Stead transformed the fortunes of the paper and delivered a series of hard-hitting editorials and features, the most famous of which – the 'Maiden tribute of modern Babylon' – is discussed in Chapter 6.

Stead believed that newspapers had a responsibility to expose the iniquities of politicians and to campaign to improve society in all areas. Thus, over his tenure Stead campaigned (among other things) for an increase in the age of consent; exposed child prostitution at home and overseas; criticized the police for their treatment of protestors in Trafalgar Square and for their inability to catch the Ripper; and slammed the government for the state of the Royal Navy. In May 1886 he set out his vision of the future of journalism and styled himself as a modern-day Oliver Cromwell. He was, like his Roundhead hero, driven by a puritan desire for the truth and to end corruption and immorality wherever it manifested itself. His argument was relatively simple: the fourth estate was a more democratic and therefore more legitimate organ of policy making than was Parliament. Just as Cromwell had overthrown an unrepresentative and unelected king so he sought to enforce the will of the people onto the government of the day:

> The secret of the power of the Press and of the Platform over the House of Commons is the secret by which the Commons controlled the Peers, and the Peers in their turn controlled the King. They are nearer the people. They are the most immediate and most unmistakable exponents of the national mind. Their direct and living contact with the people is the source of their strength. The House of Commons, elected once in six years, may easily cease to be in touch with the people.[9]

Stead was not lacking in self-confidence although he may well have miscalculated the reaction that his procurement of a child prostitute for the 'Maiden tribute' would bring. He served a short period of time in prison as a result and drew the criticism of contemporaries such as the novelist Matthew Arnold and the poet Algernon Swinburne (who sneeringly called the *Pall Mall Gazette* the *Dunghill Gazette*). Stead was probably unmoved by such criticism and apparently detested the city in which he had chosen to work. In particular he thought its newspapers were 'driveling productions ... without weight, influence, or representative character'.[10]

The new journalism that Stead espoused (but did not invent – the genre was well underway by the time Stead established himself at the *Gazette*) was largely aimed at a new audience, the lower middle and working classes, who were buying (or at least reading) the newspapers in greater and greater numbers at this time. At the heart of this new type of journalism was crime reporting. Crime news, especially murder stories, appealed to all readerships regardless of class and the more sensational the murder the better. When Maria Manning's daring attempt to do away with her lover and run off with his railway bonds hit the newsstands the country was gripped. Maria le Roux, a lady's maid on whom Charles Dickens was to base his murderess Hortense in *Bleak House*, had married Frederick Manning but had stayed friends with her other, more wealthy, suitor Patrick O'Connor. O'Connor was brutally murdered, being shot and bludgeoned to death, and his remains buried in the Manning's London home before each made their separate escapes. Both were quickly captured and the trial became a major news story with Maria's angry outburst at the jury when it convicted her one of the highlights. The pair were executed together on 13 November 1849 with the papers describing their last hours and minutes in great detail, particularly Maria's careful choice of clothes. The Mannings' murder case was a great sensation story: it had death, conspiracy, unrequited love and adultery. An evil (foreign) woman and a man she led astray; greed and envy were followed by a manhunt, trial and execution. Maria played her role to perfection. Indeed it was almost flawless as a performance in a melodrama of the period and it was fuelled by the ability of the press to report its every turn. The case demonstrated the ways in which the newspapers exploited crime news as a means to reach an ever-growing reader-ship, of all classes. For example, *Lloyd's Weekly Newspaper,* which had a circulation of 900,000 by 1890, devoted 50 per cent of its content to crime in 1866 and the *Daily Telegraph* likewise owed much of its early popularity to its reporting of criminal activities, murder and trials.

New journalism was also stylistically different from the more traditional form epitomized by *The Times*. The increasing use of the telegraph to deliver news fast, and the dominance of the two key news gathering organizations (The Central News Agency and the Liberal Press Agency) affected the way in which journalism developed. As Rob Sindall has noted there 'was a gain in simplicity and lack of padding, the use of shorter sentences, the over-simplification of complicated issues and the greater distortion caused by increasing use of the emphatic key word'.[11] This style of reporting is very evident in the Whitechapel murders and reflected the fierce competition for sales between the daily, weekly and Sunday papers in London. Much news was still recycled – which in part reflected the dominance of the news agencies – and so the drive to make one's paper distinct was uppermost in editors' minds. *The Star*, launched in 1888, was most fortunate to have such a major news story to capitalize on in its infancy and it achieved dramatic sales figures in October and November of that year.

Thus, in the 1880s journalism underwent a change of direction that built upon earlier moves at mid-century. As Anthony Smith argued, journalism 'became the art of structuring reality, rather than recording it'.[12] The presentation of the news was becoming more important than the news story itself. In this period journalism, for both commercial and reform reasons, began to investigate social issues in a more sensationalist way. The late century saw the emergence of a group of individuals who, along with Stead, pioneered what has been called the 'golden age' of English journalism; these were men such as George Reynolds, Edward Lloyd, Henry W. Lucy of the *Daily News*, Henry Labouchère of *Truth*, the afore-mentioned Frederick Greenwood and Sir William H. Russell of *The Times*. All of the editors and owners that developed and profited from this 'new journalism' benefited from the prevailing desire for sensation in several forms of popular culture. Sensationalism touched the press, literature, society and the stage, and the Victorians devoured it with enthusiasm. In order to place the reporting of the Whitechapel murders in context it is necessary to explore the nature of sensation and the Victorians' relationship to it.

## SENSATION AND THE PRESS: FACT AND FICTION COMBINED IN NINETEENTH-CENTURY POPULAR CULTURE

The word 'sensation' or 'sensational' can be used to mean a number of things in different contexts but here we might simply understand it as a way of exaggerating an event or story to engender a 'startling impression'.[13] The nineteenth century saw an increasing use of sensation in the reporting of crime, society scandals and human disasters. This device was also translated to the stage as London theatre productions became ever more ambitious in their attempts to entertain their audiences. In part this reflected a nineteenth-century interest in innovation.

From the 1860s onwards theatrical directors like Dion Boucicault were devising 'sophisticated new stage mechanics and elaborate three-dimensional scenery' to deliver excitement on the London stage.[14] In *After Dark* (1868) Boucicault staged the most audacious of all sensation scenes in which a character was seen lying helpless on a mock-up of the Metropolitan Line (the underground railway was itself a new 'sensation' having opened only five years earlier) in the path of an oncoming train. As the contemporary review recorded:

> The whistle of the locomotive is heard, and the destruction of the prostrate man seems inevitable; but he is perceived and snatched up at the right moment . . . and then the train sweeps across the stage, raising the audience to a perfect fervour of excitement.[15]

The theatre and the music hall formed a part of a growing popular culture in the nineteenth century, with the latter serving a very wide audience across the capital. Competition ensured directors kept up to date with innovations and changing tastes and fashions: in 1888 the American actor Richard Mansfield brought Robert Louis Stevenson's archetypal sensation novel *Strange Case of Dr Jekyll and Mr Hyde* to an eager and shocked public before the Ripper murders forced him to close the show prematurely for fear of adverse reactions from those that might associate Mr Hyde's actions with those of 'Jack'. Sensation novels and melodrama blended a number of themes such as crime and punishment, sex and violence, human tragedy and heroism, all of which, we might observe, are now the key ingredients for the modern day soap opera.

One of the techniques of the sensation novel was its serial nature. Subscribers and weekly readers could purchase the novel in stages, so that the story unfolded over a period of weeks and months building to its eventual climax, accompanied by powerful images often created by some of the leading artists of the day. Dickens' work was originally published in this form and towards the end of the century Sherlock Holmes' appearance in *The Strand Magazine* perhaps illustrates the apogee of this genre of writing. While some of the sensation novels and short stories published by *Reynolds's Newspaper* and others were fairly poor fare, in Wilkie Collins and Mary Braddon sensation had serious aspirations to literature even if many contemporary purists were loath to agree. George W. M. Reynolds was a notable exponent of the sensation novel as well as being a journalist and the creator of *Reynolds's Newspaper*, which earned a reputation for printing stories others dared not to touch. His novels featured the classic melodrama characters of desperate young women and sadistic villains wrapped up in sugary prose and cheap titillation, as in this example:

Again did the enraptured Harley imprint a thousand kisses upon her flushed and glowing countenance: again and again did he clasp her to his breast – and he could feel her bosom throbbing against his chest like the undulations of a mighty tide ebbing to and fro. Octavia was lost as it were in a new world of ineffable bliss.[16]

However, in Wilkie Collins' works, such as *The Moonstone* or *The Woman in White* the author deployed a much more sophisticated writing style and plot lines. *The Woman in White* became an instant hit and drew on Collins' interest in crime and crime reporting and demonstrated the interconnection between newspapers and fiction. Collins followed the same themes and literary conventions with *The Moonstone*, using several narrators to tell their story so that the reader builds an idea of the plot piece by piece. The critics of sensation novels accused them of concentrating on plot over characterization, but in doing so they were creating the page-turning fiction that still dominates the best-seller charts today.

The press stories of real events were often every bit as gripping as a sensation novel when they were presented in dramatic prose. Witness this description of a steamboat accident in Canada that was reported in *Reynolds's Newspaper* in June 1881. Taking their information from the American press the paper involved its readership in the tragedy by using emotive language and a powerful narrative. Reporting the experience of one survivor, a Mr Montgomery, the journalist (who is unnamed as was often the case in nineteenth-century copy) relates how:

> Mr Montgomery caught hold of an iron rod or bracket of some kind in the awning, and holding to this managed to keep his head above water for some seconds after the collapsed promenade deck beneath his feet had gone into the water. His position at this time was a terrible one. Below the deck which had sunk from under him he knew that scores were perishing, drowning like rats in a hole, while the awning to which he was clinging was rapidly sinking and burying beneath it men, women and children, whose piteous shrieks rent the air on every side.[17]

The loss of the steamboat *Victoria*, near London, Ontario, claimed 238 lives and was made especially newsworthy as the passengers were meant to be enjoying a day out to celebrate Queen Victoria's birthday. *Reynolds's* reporting contrasts with the sober contents of *Reuters Telegram*. *The Illustrated Police News* covered the story on 3 June alongside news of a 'Daring street Robbery', rioting in a Hoxton playhouse, accidents on the Great Northern Railway and the arrival of survivors from an earlier (and unrelated) maritime disaster in April.[18] The *Victoria* had been overloaded with passengers and the ship's master appears to have been the target of blame. *The Graphic* carried an image of the steamboat as it set off on its fatal voyage, clearly crowded with people but on a river that seems calm and unthreatening as if to make the starkest of contrasts with the tragedy that was about to occur.[19] Illustrations were being used more frequently by the press and helped to convey a powerful sense of realizm to the reportage. The delivery of factual reporting with dramatic prose and occasional images give the newspapers of the second half of the nineteenth century a very modern feel.

Similarly the content and themes of popular theatre, in music hall songs and particularly in melodrama, are reflected in much modern television drama and soap opera. Within melodrama gender roles were crudely drawn, men were chivalrous or predatory, while women were passive victims always at the mercy of unscrupulous landlords and lascivious guardians. In melodrama good always triumphs over evil and the hero invariably 'gets the girl'. As for the villains, these men were characterized as 'unnatural', 'cruel' and monstrous beasts wildly different from other 'normal' men. The bestial nature of melodramatic villains was of course paramount in Richard Mansfield's interpretation of Mr Hyde who himself echoed Edgar Allan Poe's ape in *The Murders in the Rue Morgue*. It is a matter of note that the Victorians liked their bogeymen to be inhuman; or to put it another way, as unlike them as possible. Which helps to explain why the Ripper is perceived to be an 'alien', whether foreign or from outside of 'society' is perhaps irrelevant.

THE LATEST MURDER; OR, MAKING THE MOST OF IT!
AND THIS IS THE NEWSPAPER PRESS WE ARE SO PROUD OF! IS IT NOT SICKENING?

**Figure 4** 'The latest murder', *Moonshine*, November 1890. Here the power and perceived lack of responsibility of the press in carrying sensational stories of murder and crime echoes that of the earlier *Punch* cartoon.[20]

London has a longer history of demonic semi-mythical characters within which 'Jack' can be situated. Three (the London Monster, Spring Heeled Jack and Sweeney Todd) are of particular interest in that they all have claims to have existed but have now passed into myth with their stories told and retold until it is very hard to separate fact from fiction. I would argue that the same is becoming true of Jack the Ripper; the abundance of possible suspects, the destruction or renaming of the streets in which his victims died, the purported loss of 'evidence' from police files, the Ripper letters, a number of films and television series, and above all the myth making by both contemporaries and more recent contributors, has muddied the waters to the extent that the truth is now almost completely obscured. Distance has a lot to do with this. History has a tendency to descend into myth the further removed from the events it becomes. Restructuring the past to serve the interests of the present is hardly new – witness Julius Caesar's self-justification in his histories, Shakespeare's demonization of King Richard III or indeed Hollywood's reinterpretation of the Second World War in numerous films that portray American involvement far beyond reality. History is traditionally written by the victors, or the descendants of the victors, but it is also being continually rewritten to serve the needs of the present or to assuage the guilt of the past. Our museums are redesigning their displays to take account of changing sentiments towards colonialism, slavery, the holocaust and other events. School curricula have also been adapted and altered to reinterpret the past and to be inclusive of changing ethnicity within modern Britain. I am not saying that this is a bad thing *per se*, merely that we need to be aware that the mythologizing of the past is a continuum within history writing and that we should be aware of it.

With that caveat in mind we might now turn to the three semi-mythical characters mentioned above, namely the London Monster, Spring Heeled Jack and Sweeney Todd. All three have links in common with the Ripper, all three allegedly terrorized London and the first two at least can – with 'Jack' – be said to have been used by the press to suppress the activities of women. I will return to this point later. So, who were these three 'monsters' and how real are their stories?

## THE LONDON MONSTER, SPRING HEELED JACK AND SWEENEY TODD: SENSATION, OUTRAGE AND MURDER IN NINETEENTH-CENTURY LONDON

In 1789, almost a century before the Ripper struck in East London, several women in the capital reported being attacked by an unpleasant man who followed them in the street, used foul, suggestive and abusive language and then stabbed them in the leg or thigh before calmly walking away. Both the number of attacks and their intensity increased in 1790. By now the attacks had escalated to include attempts to cut hair, clothes and to kick and stab at the buttocks of women. The attacker's final refinement was to conceal a long pin in a nosegay he wore and then offer to let ladies smell it: at which point he stabbed them in the nose. The fiend quickly earned the title 'The Monster' and all London was in uproar about his actions. A reward for the capture of the Monster was offered by a wealthy insurance broker, John Julius Angerstein, who estimated that the Monster had struck over 30 times between May 1788 and April 1790. 'Wanted' posters carrying a description of the culprit were pasted up all over London, these adding to the general air of panic surrounding the attacks. As a result all sorts of people were arrested as Londoners hoped to gain the £50 reward and rid the streets of such a notorious character. None of those detained were identified as the Monster by any of his victims and many were simply the victims of vindictive attacks or greed as their accusers sought to profit from the reward money. The panic was to be a foretaste of that surrounding the Whitechapel murders 100 years later.[21]

Monster-mania gripped London and the press and caricaturists fed the alarm with regular reports of fresh attacks on the city's womenfolk. The inabilities of the Bow Street Runners and Angerstein's campaign to capture the Monster were ridiculed and some women took to wearing protective underwear under their skirts. There were similarities here with reactions to the garrotting panics of 1856 and 1862 which saw Londoners donning neck guards and adopting anti-garrotting tactics suggested by correspondents to the papers and entrepreneurs bent on cashing in on the widespread sense of alarm that the relatively few street robberies had caused.[22] Eventually someone was arrested, charged and convicted of being the Monster. Rhynwick Williams, an artificial flower maker, was brought to trial at the Old Bailey in July 1790. Williams was identified by seven women and initially found guilty, before a retrial in December (where he was able to obtain better legal representation) confirmed his conviction for assault. He spent six years in Newgate Prison. Was Williams the Monster? His key biographer, Jan Bondeson, believes Williams was probably guilty of some attacks and was known to be uncouth and abusive to women that spurned his advances but it would seem unlikely that he carried out all the attacks on women in London. After all, Bondeson lists nearly 60 reported incidents of women being stabbed by the Monster and descriptions of the attacker varied considerably. So it is more probable that copycat 'Monsters', reacting to the press coverage and moral panic, carried out a large number of these assaults which in turn built the phenomenon of the London Monster into a much greater event than it was.[23]

There have been plenty of examples of similar attackers throughout the nineteenth and twentieth centuries and so it is possible to make suggestions or explanations for Williams' behaviour. The most probable is simply that he was an individual who was unable to achieve sexual satisfaction in any other way. In more recent attacks the sexual nature of the crime has been more explicit – it may have been true of Williams but not reported for fear of offending readers. Phantom attackers in Paris, New York and elsewhere were all probably fulfilling a sexual urge that they were unable to satisfy in any normal way. Though less violent than 'Jack' the attacks of the London Monster belong within the same psychological profile.

In what other ways can we read the story of the Monster? The attacks on defenceless women in the capital allowed some men to insist that all women went about accompanied by men or stayed at home, thereby reinforcing paternalistic relationships in a period when enlightenment ideas were promoting democracy, freedom and liberation. Across the Channel the French Revolution was in full swing with its very real threat to the *ancien régime* in wider Europe. As Bondeson has noted:

> Monster-mania can be seen as a paradoxical reaction to this situation: an outburst of show respectability and sensibility against the sexual threat of the man-monsters surrounding the women. The Monster phenomenon identified sexual liberty with bloody violence: his sexual deviancy could be linked to political anarchy. In the act of catching a Monster, and putting him away in jail, the authorities demonstrated their ability to control even aberrant sexual urges, thus re-establishing the sentimental definition of human relationships that many people feared was under threat from the French revolutionaries.[24]

This might be taking things too far but there is, I would suggest, quite a striking similarity with characterizations of the Ripper in the 1880s: a semi-mythical monster that preyed on women (in 'Jack's case those of the poorest class) in a period when bearded revolutionaries such as Marx and Bakunin stalked the capitals of Europe. The Ripper, like the Monster, was to become a representation of a threat to society.

If Rhynwick Williams was the fall guy for fears about a sex fiend on London's streets then the actions of our next case study were even more bizarre and threatening. Spring Heeled Jack, like Jack the Ripper, was never formally brought to justice and has entered folklore almost completely. One February night, in 1838, sisters Lucy and Margaret Scales were walking home from their brother's house in Limehouse at 8.30 p.m. It was already dark as they passed Green Dragon Alley. Suddenly, a cloaked silhouette leapt from the darkness and breathed blue flame into Lucy's face. The laughing figure jumped high over his victim and her sister and landed on the roof of a house. From there he bounded off into the night. Although the attack was shocking it was not without precedent. The previous September a businessman had taken a short cut across Barnes Common in West London (a well-known haunt for highway robbers) when a cloaked figure vaulted the railings of the cemetery as if from a springboard and landed in front of him. The figure had pointed ears, glowing eyes, and a pointed nose. The following night, the strange figure assailed three girls on the common. This time he grabbed at one of them, trying to tear off her clothing. More strange attacks then followed, in Lavender Hill and at Clapham. One victim gave this description of the man who had attacked her:

> He wore a large helmet, and a sort of tight-fitting costume that felt like oilskin. But the cape was like the ones worn by policemen. His hands were cold as ice, and like powerful claws. But the most frightening thing about him was his eyes. They shone like balls of fire.

There were several other reported sightings of the fiend who was dubbed 'Spring Heeled Jack' and some Londoners followed the lead of the Duke of Wellington and armed themselves to patrol the streets at night. Spring Heeled Jack became a popular subject for the penny dreadfuls, and for melodrama, popular musicals and songs. No one was ever positively identified as the devilish attacker although the Marquis of Waterford – a cruel practical joker and prankster who had gone to enormous lengths to bankroll previous, infamous hoaxes – was strongly suspected. Sightings of Jack persisted throughout the century and into the next, and were not confined to London alone: Spring Heeled Jack appeared all over Britain and in Europe. This semi-mythical creature became a bogeyman to frighten children with, as well as being a warning to those women who chose to walk about unaccompanied at night and a phantom that represented all of society's fears about crime and the underworld. Just like the Monster before him, the media had conjured a terror that stalked the streets of the capital of the Empire – no one was safe and the authorities were powerless.[25]

Finally in this section let us turn to the demon barber of Fleet Street, that seemingly archetypal melodrama character, Sweeney Todd. Immortalized in Stephen Sondheim's long-running musical and recently transported onto the big screen played by Johnny Depp, Sweeney Todd appears to be the most elusive of nineteenth-century fiends – more so even that the Ripper. In the musical Todd is a returning felon, wrongfully convicted by a corrupt magistrate, whose wife has died: a classic tragic figure seeking revenge. To get to the judge he sets himself up as a barber (his previous profession) under an assumed name and waits for the lawman to pay him a visit. In the meantime he slakes his thirst for revenge by slaughtering Londoners and destroying the evidence by way of a mechanical chair that sends their dead bodies down to the cellar to be made into pies by his neighbour, Mrs Lovett. This fiendish scheme is eventually discovered and Todd meets his own end along with his partner in crime. In true melodramatic style the judge dies but his daughter marries the only hero of the story, an associate of Todd's who little suspects the monster's true intentions. How much of this is fact? In truth probably very little but tales of a demon barber who preyed upon his customers do appear in the nineteenth century to suggest that Sondheim's musical has an element of truth about it.

The story of Sweeney Todd plays upon a number of fears. There is a great levelling in visiting a barber, especially in the days of the cutthroat razor: after all, one is literally putting one's life in the hands of a servant who, temporarily at least, is possessed of tremendous power. The vulnerability of Todd's victims is echoed by the common prostitutes who willingly acceded to being taken down a dark alley by Jack the Ripper: the level of trust required is not dissimilar. Todd is also an 'avenging angel' driven by a powerful desire for revenge, something that several of the letters to the newspapers claimed 'Jack' to be. The notion that a fiend killer was abroad on London's streets wiping out prostitutes or deciding who deserved to live or die (as in Todd's case) is a powerful metaphor for a broken or corrupted society. Those Victorians who believed that Great Britain, like Rome before it, was an empire that had become fattened and bloated beyond moral repair, would have perhaps seen Sweeney Todd and Jack the Ripper through a similar lens as a purifier.

Sweeney Todd has left most of his true self behind him; what we are left with is myth and legend. The Monster is unknown to most readers and Spring Heeled Jack so bizarre that my students thought I had invented him. One day Jack the Ripper may pass into the realms of fantasy as well, indeed one could argue that he has already achieved mythic status given that even that particular sobriquet was given him by a member of the fourth estate. Thus we come back to the influence of the press on popular culture and indeed the corresponding importance of prevailing cultures on the press' reportage.

So far this chapter has discussed the nature of sensation and sensational journalism in the context of the Victorian press' expansion in the second half of the century. It will now look at the way in which the press manipulated and was manipulated by other agencies in the period, such as government and the police, in its reporting of criminal activities. This again is not something new nor has it ceased in the modern period. The creation of moral panics and their usefulness will now be looked at in some detail to determine whether we can view the reporting of the Whitechapel murders in this way.

## MORAL PANICS AND FOLK DEVILS: THE 'GARROTTER'S LUNCH' EXPLORED

In the summer of 1862 Hugh Pilkington, a member of parliament, was accosted late at night after leaving the House of Commons. Two ruffians attacked him, choking him from behind and hitting him over the head. Having roughed him up they stole his watch and ran off. Pilkington had been the victim of a street (or highway) robbery; what we would identify today as a mugging. However, the incident prompted major consternation in the London press from July onwards and led to some important legislative and operational changes to policing and the wider criminal justice system. The method of attack on the unfortunate MP was not new, there had been similar robberies in the early 1850s and the press described them as 'garrottings'. Presumably the term arose from the attack upon the neck of the victim with an arm or chord or other implement, which made it appear similar to the Spanish method of execution. In the immediate aftermath of the attack on Pilkington the press began to fan the flames of panic. Two days later, on 19 July and without referring to any other specific incidents, *The Spectator* reported that: 'Highway robbery is becoming an institution in London and roads like the Bayswater road are as unsafe as Naples. Case after case has been reported'. *The Observer* then followed this up and talked of 'The wholesale highway robberies that are daily committed'.[26] Having now alerted the public to a spate of robberies or garrotings the press continued to build its story by identifying the sorts of persons they believed to be responsible. *The Observer* described them as 'degenerate, coarse, brutal ruffians' while the *The Guardian* referred to them as 'a race of hardened villains'. Even the usually sober *Times* declared that:

> The garotters and their species have displayed themselves in the true colour of their class as the profound enemies of the human race and their outrages must be suppressed.

The Metropolitan Police swung into action to combat this new threat to people's lives and pockets by deploying extra men on the streets, including plainclothed officers after 10 p.m. Officers were especially instructed to station themselves near to likely garroting sites so as to be able to swiftly arrest any offenders. As a consequence the number of arrests of individuals for being 'suspicious characters and reputed thieves' or as 'persons loitering with intent' increased notably (the latter by 256 and the former by 779) on the previous year's figures. By the end of 1862 there had been 92 recorded robberies with violence on the streets of London, three times the number that had been registered in 1860 and 1861. Were the police using the garroting scare to take known villains off the streets or perhaps using the crisis to demonstrate their effectiveness in controlling criminal behaviour? The two outcomes are not mutually exclusive of course, and the police were under pressure to justify the expenditure needed to fund them: this was still a relatively new force, inaugurated in 1829 and by no means popular with all sections of society. Indeed, the fact that the police arrested some people on suspicion of being garrotters when it seems that all they were guilty of was brawling in public would appear to support an argument that the Met was using the increased public awareness of street crime to pursue its own agenda.

The focus of police investigations and media interest was on those felons that had been released from prison or had returned from transportation on licence. The so-called 'Ticket-of-leave' men were effectively allowed out on parole (to use a more modern term) but under fairly strict regulations. The end of transportation in 1857, after the colonists in Australia had become increasingly uncomfortable about receiving the unwanted criminality of Great Britain and Ireland, caused a crisis of confidence in the criminal justice system in much the same way as the outbreak of war with the American colonists had in 1776. What exactly were we to do with all of our criminals, especially in a period when many believed that a criminal class existed within society, a class of persons that did not subscribe to the work ethic of Victorian society? Ticket-of-leave men were an easy target, leaving prisons such as Pentonville ashen-faced and with little chance of securing respectable employment. They were hounded by police who visited the city's various gaols to list those being set at liberty and those just arrived. As a result of the garroting panic the government passed the Habitual Criminals Act in 1869 which tightened the police grip on released felons further by ensuring that any convicted criminal caught for a second offence had, on release, to undergo seven years of police surveillance and was also subject to rearrest for trivial offences during that period.

The reality of the garroting crisis was that it was far from being the crime spree that police figures and press reports suggested. After Hugh Pilkington fell victim to highway robbers the reporting of incidents seems to have been fairly confused at best. In a sense this was as a result of increased sensitivity of the public to the supposed terror in their midst. This is how 'moral panics', as Stanley Cohen has described them, unfold in the public consciousness.[27] At first a small number of incidents are thrown under the spotlight of the press who then exaggerate either their frequency or their severity. Then, by making the public, the Police and the authorities increasingly aware of a new crime threat the press increases the amount of such crime reported. Often events that were thought of as minor before the panic are blown up into major crimes. Others are literally created by the panic. This was the case in at least one incident from 1862. A man walking home on a foggy night believed he was being followed and feared he was about to be garroted (mugged). Instead of waiting for his pursuer to carry out his heinous crime he turned the tables on him and himself attacked – acting as he saw it in self-defence. However, the man behind him was himself merely walking home in the same direction quite innocently. Both men reported the incident as a garroting attack. Thus, we arrive at a situation where the true number of incidents becomes wildly exaggerated and the public is whipped up into such a frenzy of panic that individuals begin to take drastic action to avoid attacks. In the wake of the garroting panic of 1862 Londoners armed themselves or took advantage of the various anti-garroting devices and armour that canny entrepreneurs were advertising in the press.

Cohen then suggests that the next stage of the panic is for the criminal justice system to enact tougher measures or procedures in response to the perceived crisis. This hopefully calms public fears and the panic subsides; the press will then move on to the next big story and everything returns to normal. However, there are consequences in the form of temporary or permanent changes to the justice system or to individuals caught up in it. In 1862 we have seen that one of the results was an increase in the number of arrests, and this was replicated in the courts by more severe sentences for those found guilty of garroting. Pickpockets, usually dealt with in magistrate courts (which had limited sentencing option – short periods of imprisonment and small fines) were now sent for jury trial where they might receive a much longer custodial sentence. The press called for even tougher sanctions – the return of flogging for felons (characterized in the press as 'the Garrotter's Lunch'), which was sanctioned by legislation in 1863 with the Security Against Violence Act. We have already noted the new restrictions on released prisoners and this was accompanied by the Penal Servitude Act a year later, which took a stricter line on sentencing. Those convicted for a second offence could now expect a minimum of five years penal servitude while the Prison Act 1865 continued the path to severity. As we shall see in Chapter 7, for the first time all gaols in England and Wales, even old local ones, were to have uniformly harsh regimes – separate cells, silent regimes, work on the tread wheel or crank etc. The slogan of the prison authorities was 'Hard Bed, Hard Board, Hard Labour'.

The panic peaked in November 1862; in October there were 12 alleged robberies, in November there were 32. The trial of 23 alleged garrotters at the Old Bailey in November brought the main phase of the panic to a close. By December the sense that many offenders were now in prison and police measures and court actions had dampened anxieties meant it gradually subsided. In early 1863 public and press concern was still high but the crime wave was over, although its consequence echoed throughout penal policy for many years. Thus we can see that the garroting panic had been effectively used by the authorities to implement a much tougher criminal justice regime and to clamp down on criminal behaviour in a climate where fear of crime and a 'criminal class' was on the increase.

Stanley Cohen's original work on moral panics focused on the bank holiday beach fights of the mods and rockers in the 1960s. Historians have applied Cohen's thesis to attacks on elderly New Yorkers in the 1970s as well as the garroting panics of the nineteenth century (in the 1850s and 1860s) and to a series of highway robberies around Colchester in the 1760s.[28] All of these share similar characteristics: a series of incidents that are highlighted by the press; the creation of 'folk devils (whether they be youth gangs, garrotters, or men in white smocks – as around Colchester); the 'panic' causes the authorities to act less leniently towards suspected groups, regardless of the real danger posed by the particular 'crisis'. The question that we might ask ourselves therefore is whether the Jack the Ripper murders constitute a moral panic using Cohen's model.

There was certainly a panic on the streets of Whitechapel, the ripples of which were felt much more widely: even Queen Victoria commented on the failure of the police to catch the killer. The killings produced, or rather built upon, existing fears about outsiders and criminal elements within Victorian society: foreigners, Jews in particular, the mentally ill and doctors were all chased through the streets or presented to the police as suspects to be investigated. Thus, we could argue that the murders had their own folk devils even if these are not as neatly defined as they are in Cohen's paradigm. There were reported sightings of the Ripper and encounters with strange men who frightened those who met them before running off into the night. This is suggestive of a heightened sense of danger caused by a greater sensitivity to the murders brought about by the intense press coverage. The unprecedented public involvement in the police inquiry, well meant or otherwise, was also arguably a manifestation of a similar form of sensitivity that resulted in some Londoners arming themselves or dressing in ridiculous garb to prevent garrote attacks earlier in the century.

However, I feel that overall we are in danger of stretching Cohen's model to breaking point if we wish it to cover the Ripper murders. There were a limited number of well-documented attacks and the press did not need to exaggerate their severity: the killer's actions were well beyond the imagination of the most frenzied journalist. They used the story for their own purposes, principally to sell newspapers and secondly to highlight social issues such as prostitution, poverty and the threat posed by internal unemployment and external immigration. But this was not a classic moral panic in that the events were very real and, apart from the resignation of the Chief Commissioner of the Metropolitan Police (an event that might have been prompted by any number of crises given his unpopularity in some quarters of the media and society) there was very little, if any, change in the process of the criminal justice system.

## CONCLUSION

The Victorian press was a powerful force in the late nineteenth century, much more so than it had been at any period previously. It enjoyed a much wider readership and new technologies had enabled it to disseminate news, to comment and entertain faster and more cheaply than ever before. The style of news also began to change from the 1860s onwards as greater competition and new formats forced newspaper owners to innovate. The last quarter of the century saw the emergence of 'new journalism', a style of writing and presentation that in many ways (the use of headlines and a greater emphasis on investigative reporting) foreshadowed the development of the modern press in the twentieth century. Indeed, it was the success of Alfred Harmsworth's *Answers to Correspondents*, established in 1888, and which achieved a circulation of 250,000, which gave him the necessary funds to launch the *Daily Mail* in 1896. The *Daily Mail* was followed by the *Daily Mirror* in 1903. The era of press barons such as Beaverbrook and Northcliffe was just around the corner.

The newspapers drew upon the associated forms of popular culture of the period, notably melodrama and the emerging sensation novel, to present news as entertainment – a far cry from the tightly set columns of dry information that were the staple fare of earlier newspapers and, to some extent, remained true for *The Times*. In men such as William Stead the age also benefited from editors who believed that the fourth estate had an important role to play in society. Stead was a driven man, in many aspects of his life, fired by a deep religious conviction but perhaps blinded by his sense of righteousness at times. His exposure of child prostitution resulted in a change in the age of consent – a tangible measure of success – but it also ruined his helper, Rebecca Jarrett, and to some degree curtailed Stead's own career in journalism. Stead's own paper, the *Pall Mall Gazette*, maintained a steady critique of the Metropolitan Police and the government throughout the Whitechapel murders. To some extent this was as a result of the actions (or inactions some might argue) in the years immediately preceding the murders. These events, and the desperate poverty of the area that was to some degree highlighted by the attentions of the press investigating the atrocities carried out there, are the subject of the next chapter.

# 5

# The Bitter Cry of Outcast London:[1] *Poverty, Charity and the Fear of Revolution*

In late July 1887 the Commissioner of the Metropolitan Police, Sir Charles Warren, received a number of communications from concerned members of the public and local vestry members. Their intention was to draw Sir Charles' attention to the large numbers of homeless people that had seemingly taken up residence in Trafalgar Square. One correspondent declared that it was, in his opinion, 'about the most terrible sight of open-air human misery to be met with in Europe: and this under the eyes of the wealthiest visitors to London!'[2] A week earlier the vestry of St Martin-in-the-Fields had complained about the 'unseemly conduct of persons sleeping at night in Trafalgar Square', and had asked the Office of Works to 'take such steps as may be necessary in order that the evils complained of may be abated'.[3] The press soon took up the story, with the *Daily News* publishing the vestry's complaint and placing the blame firmly at the door of the police. The *Morning Post*, in late August, carried an interview with a woman who had been charged with being disorderly in Covent Garden. When the defendant was challenged as to where she lived a witness replied: 'Nowhere' – she claimed to sleep in Trafalgar Square. Witness: 'There's hundreds there sleeping on the seats or on the flags.'[4]

It was not just in Trafalgar Square that the homeless gathered: rough sleepers took up births in St James' Park with one young woman even occupying a makeshift tree house. The park was generally cleared at night and the Police were at pains to point out that in both locations they were powerless to act unless a crime was committed. Other park users were outraged at the presence of the 'great unwashed' in one of London's green havens. According to a letter written to *Notes and Proceedings* these 'tramps enjoy al fresco entertainment accompanied by conduct and language of the grossest description, to the scandal of the general public, and the depravement [sic] and detriment of the many children of the cleanly and industrious poor'.[5] The police response, as expressed by Acting Superintendent Beard, was more sympathetic. Aware that the press were scrutinizing police activity Beard informed his superiors that:

any wholesale clearing away of these people would in my opinion lead to a general outpouring against police action ... Many of these people are hardly pressed, if at the close of the day they find themselves penniless they are afraid to enter the casual ward, especially if they have been in it once during the month and thus seek the open spaces of the Metropolis for rest at night. The great majority of them are quite distinct from the rough and give no cause for Police interference.

On the flyleaf of the report is a penciled comment, perhaps from Warren, which reads: 'As this [the *Notes and Proceedings* article] has been answered, no action is required. I am bound to say that however much I may sympathize with the poor people, I am disposed to think that locating them in the streets, and in TS is a mistake which will give us trouble'.[6] At least one of the policemen on duty in Trafalgar Square that summer took exception to the occupation of his patch by the homeless: according to one contemporary observer he 'adopted the practice of sousing the seats there with water "to keep them casuals off"'.[7]

The police were certainly no strangers to trouble in the 1880s and their greatest criminal challenge was less than a year away. That they entered the late summer of 1888 as targets of press criticism – a criticism that grew to a crescendo by the time that Mary Kelly's eviscerated body was discovered – was a result of their mishandling of two important demonstrations in and around Trafalgar Square. This chapter will explore these events and address the social problems that blighted East London in the period. As we can see from the correspondence cited above, there were different views of the poor in late nineteenth-century London. The contrast between the 'cleanly and industrious poor' and the idle and shiftless is a very common one in the rhetoric of Poor Law officials, charity workers, politicians, press and members of the public. The nineteenth century saw the full flowering of social investigation as armies of reformers, 'slummers' and missionaries beat a heroic path to the heart of darkness that was the East End. Thus, this chapter will also analyse the housing conditions they found there, the claims of incest being 'common' and the fear that existed among nice middle-class people that the so-called 'residuum' was ready to throw off its deferential shackles and turn Victorian society on its head. To some degree the activities of philanthropists such as Helen Bosanquet, Octavia Hill and Beatrice Webb can be seen as important landmarks on the long journey to a welfare state. The investigations of men like Charles Booth, Jack London and Andrew Mearns highlighted the extent of misery in the capital of which the actions of political organizations, such as the Social Democratic Foundation, sought to exploit for their own purposes. The state of 'outcast London' was therefore a matter of concern and debate for many different and sometimes discordant voices in late

Victorian Britain, and ultimately contemporaries were seeing the end of one epoch and the gradual birth of the 'modern'.

## THE BITTER CRY AND THE HOMES OF THE POOR: MIDDLE-CLASS VISIONS OF THE UNDERCLASS

In 1883 the Rev Andrew Mearns' exposé of housing problems in London was promoted by the editor of the *Pall Mall Gazette*, William Stead.[8] Mearns brought the attention of his readership to the problems affecting the poorer classes of the capital. The opening lines of *The Bitter Cry of Outcast London* bear scrutiny because they neatly illustrate the fears of the Victorian middle class.

> There is no more hopeful sign in the Christian Church of today than the increased attention which is being given by it to the poor and outcast classes of society. Of these it has never been wholly neglectful, if it had it would have ceased to be Christian. But it has, as yet, only imperfectly realised and fulfilled its mission to the poor. Until recently it has contented itself with sustaining some outside organizations, which have charged themselves with this special function, or what is worse, has left the matter to individuals or to little bands of Christians having no organisation. For the rest it has been satisfied with a superficial and inadequate district visitation, with the more or less indiscriminate distribution of material charities, and with opening a few rooms here and there into which the poorer people have been gathered, and by which a few have been rescued. All this is good in its way and has done good; but by all only the merest edge of the great dark region of poverty, misery, squalor and immorality has been touched.[9]

Andrew Mearns' reference to the perils of 'indiscriminate' charity; of 'rescuing' the poor and to 'immorality' are key themes that run through the rhetoric of those who undertook to study, reform and assist the poor in the last decades of the nineteenth century. The question of poverty and pauperism, and the more specific issue of the housing of the working classes, unveils an ideological battle at the end of the century between those who wished to maintain a 'self-help' position and those who favoured a more interventionist approach. This brought into sharp contrast two of the foremost women of the late Victorian period: Beatrice Webb (née Potter) and Helen Bosanquet (née Dendy). Their story provides a commentary on the battle between collectivism and individualism that was fought out in parliamentary debates, newspaper columns and on the doorsteps of the East End – a conflict that has rumbled on into the twentieth and twenty-first centuries. At the heart of this debate is the question of how society deals with poverty. In 1898 Helen Bosanquet recognised that the middle classes' relationship with the poverty of the working classes was complex. She maintained that a determined commitment to curing the underlying causes of poverty was required if sustainable changes were going to be made to the conditions of the poorest. She cautioned her readership against merely tinkering with the problem of poverty to assuage any guilt they might have at their own wealth and comfort.[10] Beatrice Webb and her husband Sidney, as Fabians and early British socialists, would have agreed with her desire to affect change but not with her methods of doing so: for the Webbs the solutions to the problems of poverty lay in the intervention of the state.

For many of the readers of Mearns' article (which could be purchased for a penny) his revelations must have shocked them to their core. As we have seen Victorian Britain was at its apogee as the century entered its final decades. Middle-class Londoners could be excused their complacency and smugness, even if Britain was experiencing its own 'great depression' between 1873 to 1896.[11] It must have come as a nasty shock to discover that incest was 'common' in the overcrowded tenements where the poor lived. Even if this claim was probably made with a nod to journalistic license, Mearns' intention was to emphasize the consequences that such poor conditions brought with it: 'Immorality' he wrote, 'is but the natural outcome of conditions like these'.[12] In the same year that *The Bitter Cry of Outcast London* appeared, Octavia Hill, the foremost matron of London charity, published a new edition of her *Homes of the London Poor* which drew on her own extensive experience of visiting the poorer classes. Octavia Hill had started her involvement with London's poorest in her early teens, when she had assisted her mother at the Ladies Guild in Russell Place, Holborn. The Guild operated a co-operative crafts workshop involving local children and Octavia soon became familiar with their homes and lives and was horrified at the conditions in which they existed.[13] Inspired in part by her association with John Ruskin but also by her strong belief in the principles of 'self-help' (as propounded by Samuel Smiles), Hill attempted to address the issue of social housing. Ruskin invested in her scheme to build affordable housing for the working classes, and Octavia's career as a social reformer was up and running. The essential element of Hill's philosophy was personal contact with the recipients of her charity. By visiting her tenants, with her growing band of female helpers, to personally collect the rents, Octavia could observe the way they were living and could get to know their problems. As Gillian Darnley notes, 'in effect they were model social workers'.[14]

Let us return to Hill's own writings on the housing issue. She wrote that she wanted to 'free a few poor people from the tyranny and influence of a low class of landlord and landladies; from the corrupting effect of continual forced communication with degraded fellow-lodgers; from the heavy incubus of accumulated dirt: so the poor might have scope to spring, and with it such energy as might help them to help themselves'.[15] In reporting her contact with one male tenant Hill reveals the importance of *reforming* as well as *re-housing* the working classes. On discovering that the tenant would not send his children to school and was allowing an unacceptable level of overcrowding by taking in three additional children, Octavia threatened him with eviction. He requested an interview and expressed the view that since he was not behind with his rent she should let him be. 'The room was his; he took it, and if he paid rent he could do as he liked in it', he argued. Hill countered 'Very well, and the house is mine; I take it, and I must do what I think right in it'. She agreed the extra mouths could stay but insisted that the children were taught to be 'good, and careful, and industrious', warning him that 'If you prefer liberty, and dirt, and mess, take them but if you choose to agree to live under as good a rule as I can make it, you can stay. You have your choice'.[16] The man agreed – the children were sent to school. In the long tradition of charitable giving in England, Hill's approach was paternalistic but it was underpinned by the principles of self-reliance and responsibility.

*The Bitter Cry of Outcast London* and the writings of Octavia Hill were not new commentaries on London's problems. They sat within an ongoing discourse regarding the living conditions, morals and health of the working classes. As we shall see, attempts at solving the problems of poor and inadequate housing and sanitation had been ongoing since the late 1850s. Neither were social investigators, newspapermen or charity workers novel inventions of the 1880s. However, the horrific events of the summer and autumn of 1888 gave renewed impetus to the drive for change, coming as they did hot on the heels of a royal commission a few years earlier.

In 1884, in response to a newspaper campaign orchestrated by the editor of the *Pall Mall Gazette*, William Stead, and the personal intervention of the Prince of Wales, the Liberal administration established a royal commission to examine the housing conditions of the working classes in London.[17] This was not the first, nor was it to be the last occasion on which the honourable members of the Houses of Parliament peered into the homes of the poor of the capital. The problem of poor quality, insanitary and overcrowded lodgings had exercised politicians, social reformers and religious missionaries throughout the second half of the nineteenth century. The Conservative leader, the Marquis of Salisbury, was an active supporter of the commission as was the Prince himself who had visited the poorest areas of London and had himself contributed by speaking in the debate.[18]

The commission's brief was to explore two related questions: first, given that conditions had improved in the previous 30 years, why was there still a problem of chronic overcrowding; and second, to discover why legislation to remedy housing problems was not being enacted. In 1868 a bill sponsored by William Torrens had allowed for the demolition of unfit housing and the re-housing of those made homeless as a result. However, the House of Lords forced amendments to Torrens' bill so that when it became law the requirement to re-house had been omitted and, as a result, Torrens' Act became merely a tool for destruction.[19] Richard Cross' later act (of 1875) had also failed to appreciate the costs involved in implementing his legislation. It had been hoped that clearing away slum housing would bring a concomitant rise in rateable values as areas improved; once it was clear that this was unlikely and that the burden of such clearance schemes would fall on the ratepayer the Metropolitan Board of Works (MBW) and the City of London both backtracked from implementing reforms.[20]

With these previous reforms in mind the commission heard evidence from various parts of the metropolis (including Whitechapel) and more generally from elsewhere in Britain. The findings were sobering. The commission discovered that the inhabitants of Whitechapel cellars who were evicted by sanitary inspectors merely moved to another cellar to continue their troglodyte existence while 'their condemned habitation' was immediately filled by new tenants.[21] The commission was informed of the high relative costs of rented accommodation in London with tenants having to part with anything from a fifth to a half of their incomes in rent. The average weekly rent in Spitalfields was 4s 6d to 6s per week, and that for an unfurnished room. The East End was overcrowded and workers were unable to move to the less congested suburbs because of their need to stay close to their places of work. Casual dock workers had to be able to react to news of work at 6 a.m., others had to start work even earlier (at 3 or 4 a.m.), or when a merchant's vessel came into the Port of London.[22] Costermongers (those selling a range of usually cheap goods from street stalls or barrows) needed to live close to their pitches and supplies.

Centrally located working-class communities also provided better forms of support and cheaper goods than those available outside. Affordable transport schemes were gradually being introduced to encourage families to move away from the centre but these did not come into widespread use until the last decade of the nineteenth century.[23] Other concerns affected some residents of the East End. Jewish immigrants would have found it hard to move out of the centre for all the above reasons but had additional anchors holding them in Whitechapel. As Jerry White has observed, 'For a Jewish family, needing to live within walking distance of a synagogue, a kosher butcher and the ritual baths, there was no alternative to living in the "ghetto" and thus no alternative to overcrowding'.[24]

The housing crisis could not be solved by 'displacement' as James Yelling has noted, instead it required a more holistic approach to the problems of the late nineteenth-century city and these problems were increasing.[25]

In the period between 1851 and 1881 population density in the capital had grown from 7.72 persons per house to 7.85. Now while this in itself was not a dramatic rise it is much more interesting to note that in Bethnal Green and St George's in the East the rises had been steeper (from 6.78 to 7.65 in the former and from 7.87 to 8.16 in the latter).[26] Arguably the situation was worse than this. Census takers were reliant on the honesty 'of those who stood most to gain by underestimating the numbers of occupants' of buildings.[27] Thus, tenants, fearing eviction under sanitary guidelines, and landlords, worried about being prosecuted or stung with increased rates, gave false information and counts were carried out during the day when many householders were out. We need, therefore, to think of reports of overcrowding in London as an *understatement* of the reality.

As slum clearance took place and evictions ensued, the occupants were often caught unprepared – perhaps unwilling – to face the reality of their situation. The commission was told that even when the very poor were given notice 'they never seem to appreciate the fact that their homes are about to be destroyed until the workmen come to pull the roof from over their heads'.[28] In some ways it was the poorest inhabitants that found it easiest to relocate. When the notorious lodging houses of Flower and Dean Street (one of the first targets of Richard Cross' act[29]) were demolished to make way for more respectable artisan model dwellings in the late 1880s, their occupants decamped to Dorset (known locally as 'Dosset') Street and White's Row, across Commercial Road. In turn they ousted the weaker elements who had lived there previously, and the cycle of evictions and upheaval continued.[30]

There are other ways to view the attempts to clean up the East End in the late 1800s. Slum areas were viewed as breeding grounds for crime and immorality as well as diseases such as cholera. Removing the 'nests of disease and crime'[31] by pulling down swathes of decrepit homes would help open up the dark courts of the East End to the view of the police, sanitary inspectors and reformers, and undermine the criminal networks that infested them. As *The Times* put it: 'as we cut nicks through our woods and roads through our forests, so it should be our policy to divide these thick jungles of crime and misery'.[32] The same philosophy underpinned the efforts of Baron Haussmann as he drove 135 km of new boulevards and thoroughfares through the streets of Napoleon III's Paris, with similar consequences for poorer Parisians.

## ENTERING THE ABYSS: HOUSING CONDITIONS IN THE EAST END

> Oh! It really is a werry pretty garden,
> And Chingford to the eastward could be seen;
> Wiv a ladder and some glasses
> You could see the 'Ackney Marshes
> If it wasn't for the houses in between . . .[33]

So ran a popular musical number that reflected both the reality of housing in the district and the coping methods of the inhabitants. In Hanbury Street, the site of Annie Chapman's murder, overcrowding was rife. At number 85 there were nine occupied rooms each of which were home, on average, to seven people. The rector of Spitalfields told the 1884 royal commission that 'in several of these rooms there are adult sons and daughters sleeping together on the floor. In no room in that house is there more than one bedstead'.[34] The single toilet was filthy and residents preferred to use their own chamber pots but these would often remain in the room for long periods before being emptied. This was not the worst of houses; indeed Hanbury Street was 'in the better part' of the parish and its occupants were 'all respectable people'.[35] *The Bitter Cry of Outcast London* had warned its readers of the consequences of such overcrowding: 'That people condemned to exist under such conditions take to drink and fall into sin is surely a matter for little surprise', he wrote.[36] He also warned his readers that 'the family of an honest working man [was] compelled to take refuge in a thieves' kitchen . . . the houses where they live their rooms are frequently side by side, and continual contact with the very worst of those who have come out of our gaols is a matter of necessity'. So, the housing crisis of the 1880s, in the eyes of Mearns and others, forced the poor to live side by side with other 'deviant' types.[37]

This underlying fear, that the 'respectable' members of the working class could be infected by the so-called 'residuum', was a very real one for late Victorian society. Thus, some of the slum clearance schemes of the previous 30 years had been intended to remove notorious rookeries and dens of criminality and vice such as the Old Nichol at the northern end of Brick Lane and other streets around Spitalfields Market.[38] The royal commission tended to confirm Mearns' analysis and Lord Salisbury accepted the need for further housing reforms declaring that 'the more our prosperity increases the more there is the danger that unless remedial measures are taken, the evils of overcrowding will also increase'.[39]

The state of the poor was a worry for many middle-class Victorians who must have viewed the conditions they lived in with rising astonishment. After all, their own lives, in comfortable homes where intimacy was bounded by restrictive social rules that governed the behaviour of adults and children alike, were a long way from those of the working classes. The settled, secure and spacious villas and town houses of the middle classes contrasted sharply with the cramped and Spartan dwellings of the poor. The children of the middle class enjoyed a classical education at school or from governors while the children of the streets attended board schools only sporadically. Many working-class families moved house frequently, 'like fish in a river' as Charles Booth observed.[40] People moved when times were hard and rent difficult to find, often at night to avoid the landlord or his collectors. The musical hall song 'My old man', made popular by Marie Lloyd, describes the migratory nature of some working-class lives.

> we had to move away,
> 'cos the rent we couldn't pay.[41]

The wealthier classes misunderstood this behaviour as 'shiftless' and 'transitory': they worried about the numbers of children running wild in the streets and avoiding the education that was considered to be so essential for the future of nation and Empire (as Octavia Hill had noted, to instill good behaviour and 'industriousness'). It was hard to attend to school without a stable home environment and many children's education must have suffered as a result. Indeed it is hard to read anything written from a middle-class perspective about the lives of the poor in this period without hearing the shock and horror they contained. The notion of a society divided along very different class lines is evident in numerous letters, pamphlets and sermons. Despite the legions of 'slummers' and missionaries, the lack of understanding of working-class culture is staggering: this truly was another country, a different race or even species – the well-trodden discourse of 'darkest England' reveals as much about middle-class Victorian attitudes as it does about working-class lives.

The readership of *The Times* may well have been shocked to read the report of one London Board school inspector, T. Marchant Williams, in February and March 1884. In the central districts of London including the notoriously overcrowded area of St Giles, Williams calculated that some 24 per cent of families lived in one room only; a further 43 per cent had two rooms while just 33 per cent enjoyed the relative luxury of three rooms.[42] As Anna Davin has shown, Williams' findings echoed those of Charles Booth in East London in 1891 and 1901.[43] Living in one or two or even three rooms meant little privacy for anyone. A family of eight might occupy two beds, or three if a truckle bed could be stowed away during the day under one of the others and if the budget stretched that far.

In some homes multiple beds were unheard of; in others the very poor slept on rags or old clothes on the floor. Rooms had to serve as bedrooms, living rooms and workrooms and if any attempt was going to be made to keep them clean (and despite the concerns of the well-to-do middle classes most working-class wives tried to keep up standards of respectability) then houses had to be vacated during the day. There might be several explanations for the crowded street scenes captured by late century photographers but the need to find space to work was certainly one. When modern readers worry about allowing their children out to play we might reflect that our ancestors had little choice.

Anna Davin cautions us against assuming that the overcrowded conditions within which many London families existed in the 1880s necessarily degraded those that experienced them. Stories of families sleeping two, three or four to a bed; of sisters and brothers sharing limited space; of children running amok in the streets – all these can provoke visions of neglect, incest and hardship. However, this is to accept too readily the fears and warnings of contemporary social investigators, COS visitors and Board school investigators: all of whom reflected middle-class concerns about the poor and their offspring. Both Davin and Jerry White (in his study of the Rothschild Buildings),[44] drawing upon a range of first-hand accounts, describe a world of community support, of neighbours happy to share what meagre food and goods they had with those less fortunate than themselves – hopeful that when it came to their own time of need others would reciprocate. Davin shows us, as Helen Bosanquet discovered, that the backbone of this self-supporting society was its matriarchs: the women of the East End battled poverty, sickness, dirt and their husbands to keep body and soul (and, crucially, family) together.

The evidence suggests that where contemporary middle-class observers saw danger the working class saw companionship, warmth and shared troubles in their overcrowded homes. We might assume that no one could enjoy sharing a bed with siblings or other relatives but clearly this is erroneous: many missed the warmth and security it brought, as this example shows: 'We slept two, three in a bed like nothing. We never had a hot water bottle or extra blankets – we didn't need it. You all warmed another' one resident of the Rothschild remembered.[45] Arthur Harding, who grew up in the notoriously criminal Nichol estate at one end of Brick Lane, also recalled his early life with fondness rather than horror.[46] 'Community' is a word laden with meaning and imbued with a sense of a long-lost past. In our 'broken' twenty-first century society the need to cling to notions of a 'golden age' surfaces frequently, regardless of whether such a 'golden age' ever existed.[47]

Jerry White's wonderful micro-history of an East End tenement in the late

Victorian and Edwardian period shows that, even though many had little them-selves, they were often prepared to share it with their neighbours.[48] This sharing of resources included food and drink, shelter and companionship, and extended beyond family ties and could even result in the suspension of feuds and disputes when times or circumstances were particularly hard.[49] Children were looked after when parents fell sick and could not provide; families clubbed together to find rent for those behind with theirs (and on at least one occasion they prevented an eviction from the Rothschild model dwellings); refugees fleeing persecution in the Russian empire were accommodated until they could find their own digs or were able to move on to America or elsewhere.

The Rothschild was an almost entirely Jewish community, even if it contained a variety of ethnicities: Russian, Lithuanian, German, Polish, 'Dutch' (or English) immigrants all lived there. Did this cultural closeness ensure a sense of commun-ity or was the shared experience of poverty as important in establishing a feeling of unity? The community that White describes (from the oral testimonies he has gathered) suggests that common cause and shared identities were equally important. The residents of the Rothschild Buildings knew what it was like to survive on very little and how to do so while retaining one's self-respect and dignity. Those that fell below this level of respectability would have been unlikely to find a flat in such a block. The tiny minority of tenants who turned to crime or prostitution, or who sought relief in a bottle, or were guilty of excessive violence or abuse, were probably excluded from this community. The drudgery of everyday life in the East End is very apparent, with the burden of domestic chores falling heaviest on the women. In model dwellings such as the Rothschild Buildings, strict rules ensured that landings and stairs were scrubbed and kept tidy; prying neighbours enforced cleanliness in individual flats and rooms. One historian has described them as part of a middle-class attempt to 'civilize and pacify the urban poor'.[50] However, not everyone could either afford, or meet the required standards, to live in one of the many model dwellings that sprang up in the second half of the nineteenth century. For many poorer Eastenders shelter or home meant a room in a lodging (or 'doss') house or, below that, recourse to the detested workhouse casual ward.

From the middle of the nineteenth century some of those influenced by the concerns of proto-social workers, public health reformers and moral crusaders regarding the state of the poor, attempted to improve the conditions in the crowded cities of Britain via building design. Two worthy organizations, the Metropolitan Association for Improving the Dwellings of the Industrious Classes and the Society for Improving the Condition of the Labouring Classes, had been created between 1841 to 1844 and had made some small inroads in re-housing working families before 1875. The former had been founded, as the Rev Henry Taylor, Rector of Spitalfields, declared at its inaugural public meeting in September 1841, 'for the purpose of providing the labouring man with an increase of the comforts and conveniences of life, with full compensation to the capitalist'.[51] Their efforts were well meaning but inadequate; in total fewer than 2,000 families profited from their building programmes.[52] Part of the problem for these early pioneers of social housing was that the rents they needed to charge, even to make the limited profit they desired, were still relatively high in comparison with the costs of living in slum housing. This had the effect of attracting only the better-off, skilled working classes to these new dwellings.[53]

In 1863 the architect Henry Darbishire published a paper on the housing of the poor in which he set out his principles for a new set of buildings initiated by the philanthropy of George Peabody, a wealthy American merchant banker, who had made England his home. Darbishire's approach, which reflected in part the relative failure of previous schemes (by effectively excluding the poor by being too costly to build and maintain), was to build cheaply and with working-class lifestyles in mind.[54] In what appears to be a misunderstanding of working-class culture he declared that: 'if there is anything in the world that a poor man hates or a poor man's children are educated to hate with cordial, sincere, and unquenchable hatred, it is fresh air'.[55] Evidently frustrated that each and every attempt to provide ventilation was covered over or blocked up by tenants, Darbishire presumably did not consider that heating costs represented a large proportion of working families budgets and that drafts – however well intentioned – were not welcome. Darbishire was equally concerned to make his homes easy to clean and keep tidy, thereby helping to instill the moral message of 'improvement' in those that occupied them. Thus, Peabody homes were built of painted brick rather than paper and plaster (which cracked and attracted vermin) and had laundry facilities on site: there could be no excuses for not clean living in a Peabody home. As Martin Gaskell noted, 'this was a severely practical model, and one which involved a very low opinion of working-class interests and expectations'.[56]

The Peabody Trust built a series of large estates across the capital, starting in Spitalfields, all being different but built on the same principles as Darbishire had outlined. The blueprint involved a rectangular block built around a central open space that provided a playground for children and effectively isolated the dwellings from the surrounding area. As John Tarn puts it, the Peabody community 'was in every sense separate, socially as well as physically', so that it could perform its dual role of housing and 'improving' the working classes.[57] The rules that governed tenancy were strict and contrasted starkly with the relative freedom offered by slum landlords: rent was paid in advance; there was to be no toleration of arrears and 'disorderly and intemperate tenants' were to be shown the door immediately.[58] Darbishire's vision, and Peabody's money, reinvigorated the model dwelling movement in the 1860s and the Trust (founded in 1862) was followed by the Improved Industrial Dwellings Company a year later, and the Artizans, Labourers and General Dwellings Company in 1867.

These trusts operated on the principle of a 5 per cent return on investments; a level of profit than many London builders would not consider viable or worthwhile. In this they were helped by the government who, under the terms of the Labouring Classes Dwelling Houses Acts passed in 1866 and 1867, allowed them to take out long-term loans at just 4 per cent. Anthony Wohl argues that these 'unpublicized subsidies' were vital to the model dwelling movement.[59] However, while rents were not pitched at the peak of what the market would stand they were not subsidized either: if the middle classes were seen to be bailing out the working classes they would have fallen foul of the rhetoric of 'self-help' that was espoused by the COS and its supporters like Octavia Hill. Thus, once again attempts of providing homes for the poor were to some extent undermined by a refusal to break the golden rule of Victorian giving: that of not 'demoralizing the recipient'.[60] Wohl has suggested that the Peabody Trust was still able to offer accommodation to those at the lower rungs of the social ladder, albeit not the 'residuum' that so terrified some contemporaries, and this is evident from the occupations of those listed as tenants in 1891.[61] However, the main beneficiaries of the model dwelling movement were still the 'respectable' working man and his family not the poorest inhabitants of the 'abyss'.

The Peabody Trust was not the only benevolent philanthropist housing agency operating in the capital and was in fact one of over 30 such organizations building homes throughout London, many of which are still standing a century or more later.[62] Arguably, the Peabody Trust, by taking advantage of cheap land made available by the Cross Act and loans under the Labouring Classes Dwelling Houses Acts, transcended the line between private and public: Wohl describes it as a 'semi-public body' and we might view it as an important stage in the development of council housing.[63] The model dwelling movement therefore represents the forerunner of state-sponsored social housing but they did not effectively tackle the vast need for new housing in the last quarter of the nineteenth century. Indeed as M. J. Daunton has noted, the 'contribution of philanthropic and local authority activity to the housing stock was, in quantitative terms, negligible before 1914', accounting for a mere 1 per cent.[64] As a result many poorer Londoners were unable to benefit from the charitable entrepreneurship of Peabody and his imitators.

## DOSSERS, CASUALS AND DOWN-AND-OUTS: THE REALITY OF HOUSING CONDITIONS BEYOND THE MODEL DWELLING

For those who could not secure a regular income sufficient to both maintain a patina of respectability and pay the rent necessary to occupy a flat in a model dwelling or a room in a respectable terrace, the lodging or 'doss' house provided a safety net above the final degradation of the workhouse. Doss houses, like those in Thrawl Street, Whitechapel, where Polly Nichols lived, were home to a community of loafers, down-and-outs, and those who had been brought low by a series of circumstances both within and beyond their control. According to the American writer Jack London (who explored the East End in 1902 under the pretence of being a stranded sailor), these low lodging houses were described, with heavy irony, as the 'poor man's hotel'.[65] In 1886 Howard Goldsmid had similarly assumed the guise of a 'dosser' to investigate the reality of life in these 'coffee houses' of East London.[66] Both men were disturbed, as Mearns and Sims had been, by what they saw: the cramped conditions, poor food, drunkenness and bad language, all of which – in their eyes – reflected the degree to which the inhabitants had descended into the 'abyss'.

For many, a bed (or a part of a bed in extreme cases) in a lodging house was as good as it got and the much-derided landlords that provided them were crucial in the 'economy of makeshifts' that maintained London's poor.[67] The builders of model dwellings – ostensibly the architects of social reform through housing – could not afford to let their neat and tidy flats to those at the very foot of the housing ladder. Until the municipal authorities began to take the lead in social housing in the aftermath of the Great War, the provision of cheap accommodation rested with the slum landlord. Jack London made a distinction between the larger lodging houses and those 'little private doss-houses' that were, he declared, 'unmitigated horrors'.[68] The larger houses, such as the one in Middlesex Street that Jack London visited, had subterranean communal areas, which served as communal spaces to sit and chat, drink tea or coffee and make food. Above was a 'smoking room' that was lit until ten – allowing the residents to read the many rules and regulations governing their stay.

Once a guest had braved the smell of the kitchens and had his fill of pipe smoke and conviviality he would retire to his bed for the night. At Cooney's in Thrawl Street, 1866, a bed cost 4 pence a night; by the time Jack London paid for a 'cabin' in Middlesex Street in 1902 the fee was 5 pence.[69] This bought one a bed in a shared room with little space to undress and no privacy whatsoever. This was simply a place to sleep – if sleep was possible among so many strangers – there was no place to store possessions or engender any real sense of 'home' in these larger lodging houses. These were not 'homes' but simply shelters: they offered no hope of improvement (as the model dwellings did) but merely protection from the streets or the horror of the workhouse. As such they were populated by a cross-section of society's 'unfortunates'. Goldsmid acknowledged that not everyone who sought the refuge of the doss house was a 'loafer' – there because of his or her lack of desire to do an honest day's work. The occupants of the Beehive lodging house in Brick Lane came from diverse backgrounds:

> Many have seen better days; respectable artisans whom the waves of trade-depression have overtaken and submerged; clerks elbowed out of a berth by the competition of smart young Germans; small shopkeepers ruined by the poverty of the working-folk among whom their business lay; even professional men – land surveyors, solicitors, surgeons – are now and then to be found among the motley crowd in a 'kip-house' kitchen.[70]

At Middlesex Street the population was exclusively male when Jack London visited it and was made up of those aged between 20 and 40. Older men found it hard to earn even the small amounts needed to pay for a night's lodgings. The experience of the area's prostitutes, including almost all of the Ripper's victims, was similar. Mary Nichols was killed in Buck's Row as she sought the four pennies she needed to pay for her 'doss' and Annie Chapman and Kate Eddowes were also murdered as they went in search of the money to pay for their accommodation, having drunk what they had previously earned on those nights. The lodging houses took in the detritus of the neighbourhood, however drunk or beaten down they were. As long as they could pay they were welcome. Goldsmid described the scene in the nearby vicinity of the Beehive: 'When closing-time comes, and the dram-shops and gin-palaces have sent their contingent to reinforce the representatives of sinning and suffering humanity that crowd the unwholesome street, Thrawl Street is a thing to shudder at, not to see.'[71]

However bad the lodging houses of the East End were they compared favourably, in the eyes of the working-class poor, with the casual wards of the Poor Law Union workhouses. The English Poor Law has a long and well-trodden history which I am not going to engage with at any length here, except to suggest that by the 1880s it was palpably unable to cope with the pressures thrown up by a century of industrialization, population growth and migration.[72] In Whitechapel the workhouse was run with rigid efficiency (in that it deterred all but the really destitute or sickly from its doors). The clerk of the Whitechapel Union, William Vallance, was a subscriber to the COS principles of self-help and resistance to charitable donations. When the Commissioner of the Metropolitan Police Sir Charles Warren wrote to the capital's Poor Law Unions to request their help in distributing tickets for overnight accommodation in lodging houses (in the wake of the homeless' 'occupation' of Trafalgar Square and St James' Park) Vallance answered that while the Board of Guardians for Whitechapel would accommodate any houseless poor that appeared before them seeking shelter, they would not become 'the almoners of private benevolence' by distributing charity tickets. It was the workhouse or no house for Vallance and his union.[73]

The Whitechapel Casual Ward, for the temporary homeless, was situated in Thomas Street and in January 1888 it had beds for 44 men and 25 women who were fed on a very basic diet of bread, gruel and cheese for which they were expected to work at picking oakum, carrying coal and cleaning around the wards. Inmates could enter between 4 p.m. and 6 p.m. depending on the season and were discharged at 6.30 a.m. if they were able. The fear of the 'house' that was shared by many of the working class throughout the nineteenth century is sometimes hard to imagine from the perspective of those used to a state-funded benefit system. We need to remind ourselves that those who took refuge in the workhouse were not merely accepting poor food and hard labour. They were surrendering their freedom and sense of self: once inside the workhouse they wore workhouse clothes, obeyed workhouse rules and lost their rights to vote if they had them. Families entering the workhouse were separated: fathers on one side, mothers on another, children taken away, educated, fostered or apprenticed out if parents remained for any length of time. It is hard, even given the harshness of the mid-Victorian penal system, to imagine a worse fate than turning to a London parish for help in the late nineteenth century. Which in part explains the encampment at the foot of Nelson's Column.

## THE 'WEST END RIOTS' AND THE ROLE OF THE POLICE

The summer of 1887 was notably warm and rough sleeping must have seemed much more attractive than the confines of the workhouse. However, the gathering of so much human flotsam and jetsam in the very heart of the Empire was distressing for its wealthier inhabitants and problematic for the policing authorities, because of previous troubles in the square. In February of 1886 a rally called by the Fair Trade League, a protectionist organization that urged its supporters to resist the attempts of 'the foreigner to rob you', provoked a counter demonstration by the recently formed Social Democratic Foundation (SDF).[74] Led by the well-heeled anti-Semite Henry Mathers Hyndman, the SDF espoused a variation of Marx's revolutionary socialism and gained support from several notable radicals of the age (including William Morris, the future Labour MP William Lansbury and Marx's daughter, Eleanor).

Exactly what happened on 8 February 1886 is still not entirely clear, but a peaceful protest escalated into disorder and rioting.[75] The SDF had been angered by police tactics in the years since their creation in 1881, complaining that while the police had been quick to move on their demonstrations they had allowed organizations such as The Salvation Army and other groups espousing evangelism and abstinence from alcohol to assemble without disruption. That the police were concerned about the activities of The Salvation Army is evident from some of the correspondence held at The National Archives; but it was the awful noise of badly played brass instruments and the reactions of local residents that features most prominently in early reports of the Army's activities. Hyndman's socialists arguably offered a much more serious threat to the peace of the nation than a parade of well-meaning, if cacophonous, evangelists. We can usefully explore the events of February 1886 through the pages of the London press and the report of a parliamentary committee that investigated them.[76]

The police had been informed that there was likely to be some trouble in the square as the socialists and free traders disputed the territory for debating, but it would seem that they feared little more than a bit of 'horseplay' as a number of police witnesses told the committee. The police presence in the square was minimal and the officer in charge, Superintendent Walker, was in plainclothes, as his position only required him to wear uniform on formal occasions. This seems to have led the committee to conclude that there was a lack of visual leadership on the day. The police had placed reserves in various locations close to the square in case of trouble, a tactic still employed by the modern Metropolitan Police in dealing with protest marches and gatherings. The crowd itself contained considerable numbers of what Superintendent Dunlap, himself on duty in the square, described as 'the roughest element'.[77] At about half past three a large body of demonstrators began to move off in a westerly direction, towards Pall Mall. Here is where the confusion about the events of the day is most apparent. Sir Edmund Henderson, then chief commissioner of the Metropolitan Police, was also in the square. He seemingly feared that a 'mob' was likely to cause trouble along Pall Mall and so instructed Dunlap to request the reserves under Superintendent Hume at St George's Barracks, to move off and protect the property in that area. Dunlap then selected a trustworthy constable from A division to deliver the message.

However, something got lost in translation and the police reserves were directed to the Mall, rather than Pall Mall. Just who was to blame for this error concerned the committee who questioned everyone from the commissioner down to the unfortunate constable, William Hulls. PC Hulls told the committee that Dunlap told him to take a message to Hume from Sir Edmund Henderson to 'throw the men along the Mall'. He went as fast as he could, fighting his way through the throng from the foot of Nelson's Column, reaching the barracks in five minutes. Hume received his message and added 'I suppose they are going to make for Buckingham Palace', and then lined up his men and moved them off. Hulls returned to duty and neglected to report the successful completion of his mission to his superiors because he 'saw them all busy on that occasion and did not like to interfere'.[78] Thus, in a faint echo of Balaclava, the men at St George's barracks charged off in the wrong direction leaving Pall Mall and its windows to the mercy of the London mob. The first window was broken at 3.40 p.m. at Messrs Christopher's in Pall Mall East; at the Junior Carlton Club a crowd member mounted the balustrade and addressed his colleagues. A shower of small stones hit the club, breaking more windows. It has been suggested that members of the club had been taunting the protestors from the comfort of their offices but this is not confirmed in the committee report and is hard to clarify for certain.

The press went to town on the riots, condemning the protesters and blaming the SDF for the trouble. *The Times* wanted to know 'whether there is no law that can touch Messrs. Hyndman, Burns and Champion' (the principal SDF leaders), while the *Morning Advertiser* declared that in 'no other capital in the world could fellows like Burns and Hyndman have been permitted to preach the detestable doctrines they did'. Indeed when working-class Parisians had objected to the seizure of the Montmartre arsenal and had declared the Paris Commune in March 1871 the retaliation of the French authorities was absolute, with some 25,000 communards being killed in fighting and a further 10,000 executed or exiled. By contrast the response of the London authorities was therefore more than moderate.

The *Morning Post* dismissed the protesters as being composed of 'a few fanatics, a great amount of loafers and idlers, and a huge contingent of professional thieves' and the *Daily Telegraph* accused the police of being unprepared: 'Practically, London was yesterday afternoon in the hands of the mob, who could have done anything they chose. For the credit of the nation such a miserable scandal must not be allowed to occur again'.[79] Such sentiments were repeated in the pages of the *Birmingham Gazette, Birmingham Post, Leeds Mercury* and *Liverpool Post*.[80] Other papers were careful to point to the very real hardships that some people were experiencing in the capital and the danger of neglecting the poverty and misery of some Londoners. The *Daily News* warned that 'a disposition now

exists to turn empty stomachs and idle hands into materials for social and political agitation' and advised that the authorities act to prevent this happening.[81]
The *Pall Mall Gazette* published an interview with the leadership of the SDF
who denied any responsibility for the rioting in the capital: 'That was entirely
contrary to our wishes' claimed Hyndman, 'We simply [...] set before the people
what we conceived to be the only truth that could bring them permanent and
substantial relief; but we had no idea that they would at once proceed to break
windows, or indulge in any violence whatsoever', before adding the 'time for that
is not yet come, in our opinion. It may come, but this was premature – decidedly
premature'.[82] There is a sense in Hyndman's comments, and in the reportage of
the *Pall Mall Gazette*, that this had very little to do with fermenting revolution. As
the paper noted, the socialist speakers 'accompanied [the rioters] rather than led
them' and the leaders of the SDF were clearly unhappy that political protest had
descended into riot and the looting of shops. As groups of rioters made their way
to Hyde Park they could been seen carrying armfuls of clothing, bottles of alcohol
and other goods, all pillaged from the shops on Piccadilly and its adjacent streets.

This 'final curtain call for the London crowd' recalled the events of June 1780
rather than those of Paris in 1789 or 1870.[83] Historians have mixed views on the
social background of the 'West End' rioters. Gareth Stedman Jones has argued
that they were predominantly drawn from among the East End's casual poor and
he and Eric Hobsbawm have described this group as 'apolitical' in their actions:
these were men that could gather 'to hear Conservative-inspired demands for
protection as a solution to unemployment' and then 'riot the very same afternoon under the banner of socialist revolution'.[84] The underlying apathy of the
unskilled working class is contrasted with the aspirational politicking of London's
artisans – the traditional radicals in the capital's political history. However, Marc
Brodie warns us against too easily accepting such a simple dichotomy: London's
working class had a number of local and personal influences that affected their
political consciousness.[85] Stedman Jones recognizes this, accepting that many
were 'motivated by sectional rather than class interests' in their attendance at
rallies and later union actions.[86] East London's politics was a volatile mix of ideo-
logies and pragmatic demands for change; its poorest classes could be exploited
to swell the ranks of demonstrations for any number of causes.

The verdict of the parliamentary committee was that the police were at fault
for the disturbances. There had been, they concluded, a lack of numbers, a breakdown of communication, and a failure to co-ordinate resources. The committee
was clearly puzzled that the police did not deploy mounted police to marshal
such demonstrations. Sir Edmund Henderson was contrite and admitted that
in future the Met would review its preparations. The committee finished with

these words: 'we conclude our report by a strong expression of opinion that the administration and organization of the Metropolitan Police Force require to be thoroughly investigated; and we hope that this investigation will take place without delay'.[87] Before the end of the following year the police were to be found wanting again, this time because their attempts to police the demonstrations of the unemployed ended in much more than a little 'horseplay'.

Beyond the concerns with the ability of the policing authorities to quell any attempts at socialist revolution and unruly demonstrations was a more deep-seated fear of social unrest caused by the deprivation experienced by thousands of Victoria's subjects. The occupation of Trafalgar Square and St James' Park was an ugly reminder of the plight of London's poorest. The solution was far from clear. That a significant section of British society lived in, or close to, poverty and pauperism was in many ways an indictment of the very system that had made the Empire as successful and powerful as it was at the end of the century. Industrial growth and military might (at least at sea) had made some people very rich; others had grown very comfortable as wages rose and consumption increased. The splendour of the Victorian age is still visible in Britain's modern urban centres. But the very motor of capitalism means that for some to prosper many others have to settle for less. The challenge for the late Victorians and Edwardians was to

THE UNEMPLOYED AND THE POLICE.

Figure 5  'The unemployed and the police', *Moonshine*, October 1887. In this cartoon the suggestion is that the real troublemakers are the political speakers who were using the plight of the urban working classes to call for radical reform.[88]

steer the nation through turbulent waters without suffering a cataclysmic mutiny below decks. The poor had to be helped to become part of the system and to be able to support themselves within it. The alternative was to share the wealth of the Empire more evenly among its vast population; or at least to mitigate some of the worst effects of a market economy on its poorest subjects by using public funds, raised by taxation.

This is where we need to return to the work and ideas of Beatrice Webb and Helen Bosanquet and the ideological battle between collectivism and individualism.

## THE BOSANQUETS AND WEBBS: COMPETING IDEOLOGIES OF REFORM

Helen Dendy was born in Manchester in 1860, the youngest daughter of businessman and former nonconformist minister, John Dendy. After achieving a first at Cambridge, Helen moved to London and joined the COS. She met and married the philosopher Bernard Bosanquet in 1895 and they collaborated on several publications that outlined their vision of 'individualism'.[89] While historians have perhaps neglected Helen Bosanquet her more illustrious counterpart occupies a much larger place in history. Beatrice Potter was born in Gloucestershire in 1858, one of ten children. Her father, Richard, was a businessman and railway director and Beatrice grew up in some comfort and as, her biographer notes, sought 'from an early age, to question her circumstances'.[90] In 1883 she also joined the COS to work with the London poor. The COS was 'professionally pioneering but ideologically reactionary' in that while it adopted the very modern practice of personal visits to those in need, this was accompanied by a very Victorian emphasis on self-reliance.[91] Along with other reforming bodies in the capital (such as the 'observation post' at Toynbee Hall, where young men from good families were urged to settle after completing their degrees at Oxbridge to help instill the benefits of education and self-improvement among the local working poor [92])the COS stressed the importance of personal contact with the poor and working classes.

However, Beatrice clearly wanted to do more than the 'ladies work' undertaken by Octavia Hill and her COS visitors and she ventured to Manchester to look at social conditions there and to broaden her political outlook. In 1886, after working as a rent collector at Katherine Buildings, Whitechapel (one of the capital's new model dwellings), she published her first article in the *Pall Mall Gazette* on the subject of unemployment in the East End.[93] In this Beatrice firmly rejected attempts to create work for the unemployed by means of artificial schemes of public works and demonstrated a philosophy that was very close (in its attitude towards pauperism at least) to that of Helen Bosanquet. The two women had, therefore, similar beginnings and shared experiences in social investigation. By 1890, however, Beatrice had rejected individualism and had declared herself a socialist, if not a revolutionary one.[94] After a chastening experience with Joseph ('Radical Joe') Chamberlain, Beatrice met, and then married, Sidney Webb whose cockney charm and avowed intellect must have helped overcome his unprepossessing looks. They forged a strong intellectual partnership and, as Fabian socialists, made a major contribution to the history of Labour politics in Britain.

The story of the intellectual 'war' between the Bosanquets and the Webbs has been told elsewhere in more detail and with much greater depth than this volume has space to allow and so what follows is a relatively brief summary of their different positions with regard to poverty and the role of the state.[95] Although they adopted different approaches to the problems of society, and, in particular, poverty, the Bosanquets and Webbs, according to A. M. McBriar, 'certainly shared a feeling characteristic of many intellectuals in the later Victorian age: a sense that the traditional values of earlier Victorianism no longer provided a satisfactory way of reconciling man to society and the universe'. McBriar goes on to add: 'Not being either revolutionaries or deniers, they were in search of a new creed to live by, a new "collectivism" that would restore a sense of true community to a society become divided and disharmonious.'[96] Helen Bosanquet had refined the rhetoric of 'deserving' and 'undeserving' recipients of charity and poor relief. Instead she recognized that some people could be helped while others were beyond redemption. In a collection of essays published in 1895 Helen failed to see any real future for the 'residuum', who did no useful work as far as she could see:

> they pick up 'bits and pieces' of work and are paid so little that they have to rely on supplements and charity. [The residuum] is economically dead. It may be possible to galvanize it into a temporary appearance of life, to raise up a social monster that will be the terror of the community; but the best that can be really hoped for is that it should gradually wear itself away, or in the coming generations be reabsorbed into the industrial life on which it is at present a mere parasite.[97]

C. S. Loch shared Helen's opinion that the 'residuum' was beyond redemption while believing that the rest of the working class could be improved by raising individual standards.[98]

Beatrice Webb believed that co-operation, trade unionism and state supplements might be used to help workers lift themselves out of poverty, while accepting that there were distinctions to be drawn between those who were out of work as a result of economic circumstances and those who were deemed idle and shiftless. Beatrice was aware that 'the industrial organization, which had yielded rent, interest, and profits on a stupendous scale, had failed to provide decent livelihood and tolerable conditions for the majority of the inhabitants of Great Britain'.[99] Fabians argued that it was society, through the infrastructure of the State, which had the power to redress the problems caused by market economics. Ultimately socialists had little time for philanthropy, seeing it as 'an aspect of wealth and privilege that should abolished'.[100] Home visits could be seen as intrusive and as a continuation of middle-class attempts to control the behaviour of the working classes for their own ends rather than simply an act of selfless giving.

As a result, Helen Bosanquet has suffered from being characterized as representing old-Victorian values of self-help but it is more appropriate to see her as someone struggling with the huge social problems she saw everyday in her COS work. Reconciling the need to support those in need without reducing them to a life of dependency was uppermost in her mind. She was a realist and her views bear closer inspection because she asks difficult questions that resonate today. In writing that 'many of our attempts to "elevate the masses" are only attempts to train them to our own standard, not because it is intrinsically better, but because it is what we are used to and can understand' she challenged the prevailing wisdom that the middle classes necessarily knew best.[101] She went on to warn her readers that: 'We need to be quite sure that we really *want* to cure poverty, to do away with it root and branch. Unless we are working with a whole-hearted and genuine desire towards this end we shall get little satisfaction from our efforts'. In what might be regarded as a critique of middle-class philanthropy she added that 'in the absence of poverty the rich would have no one upon whom to exercise their faculty of benevolence'.[102]

For all this Bosanquet was optimistic that the solutions for society's social problems lay in the institution of the family; at a time when some socialists were convinced that the family could not possibly survive the ravages of capitalism. Bosanquet had faith in the East End matriarch, even if she had little in their menfolk. 'Among a certain low type of men the prevailing expression is one of vacuity, of absence of purpose or character; among the women corresponding to them the prevailing expression is that of patient endurance', she opined.[103] She rejected Fabian socialism and opposed the provision of school meals as undermining the family and as a 'subsidy to lazy parents', not as a benefit to poor incomes.[104]

In 1909 the two camps came crashing together in the Poor Law Commission Report where they differed in their findings. Bosanquet, who authored the major report, defended the role of private charities while in the minor report

THE REAL STARVER OF THE POOR.—JOHN BULL VAINLY ENDEAVOURS TO RELIEVE THE DISTRESS

"The great difficulty of relieving the distress among the unemployed is that the principal part of the assistance supplied is certain to get into the hands of [the professional loafer, cadger, and thief, who are always on the look-out to intercept such bounty, to the detriment of the deserving."—*See Newspapers.*

THE ONLY APPARENT REMEDY.—"HARMLESS TO THE POOR, BUT FATAL TO VERMIN."

**Figure 6** 'The real starver of the poor. – John Bull vainly endeavors to relieve the distress', *Fun*, November, 1887. In this cartoon *Fun* illustrates the problems of providing benefits to poorer families, suggesting that the criminal 'residuum' as well as those deserving of help would exploit this.[105]

Webb championed the cause of bureaucratic socialism as the way forward for welfare policy.[106] McBriar sets out the distinction neatly: 'The COS believed that economic independence for all was desirable, and that this could achieved by a "wise administration" of charity and the Poor Law; Socialists, on the contrary, aimed at an economic dependence on the State which would [in the view of the Bosanquets] be degrading to the working class and to the whole community.'[107] In a recent volume Kathleen Martin has warned against seeing such a clear distinction between the two camps, suggesting that the Webbs had strong reservations about the value of social insurance.[108] Writing in 1896, C. S. Loch, secretary of the COS, set out the default position of the organization: 'To shift the responsibility of maintenance from the individual to the State is to sterilize the productive power of the community as a whole and also to impose on the

State ... so heavy a liability ... as may greatly hamper, if not also ruin it. It is also to demoralize the individual'.[109]

Clearly we are still struggling to address this conundrum in our modern society. The provision of state benefits is sometimes accused of creating a 'dependency culture' and tabloid newspapers delight in printing occasional stories of 'greedy benefit scroungers' who abuse the welfare system at the expense of the 'honest' majority. Neither of these women were revolutionaries although both would have described themselves as feminists; both believed that women had a more important role to play in society than Victorian society was prepared to allow them. Neither of them saw the birth of the welfare state in 1945 although both lived long enough to see the creation of old age pensions in 1908: this must have been viewed with satisfaction in both camps. Indeed the move towards state interference or intervention, whichever way it is characterized politically, was well underway as the new century dawned. In 1900 Britain spent approximately £8.4 million on poor relief, the only form of 'social security' funded from taxation. On the eve of the First World War this had leapt to £43.3 million and now included unemployment and health insurance, pensions and social housing schemes.[110]

## 'BLOODY SUNDAY' AND THE EVENTS OF NOVEMBER 1887

Having considered the contrasting attitudes towards solving the social problems of the day, as expressed by two leading female philanthropists, we can now return to the more serious expressions of discontent that so unnerved contemporaries. The spring of 1886 had brought protestors to the centre of London, with riotous consequences as we have seen: the following hot summer had led to scenes of hardly less horror from a middle-class perspective as large numbers of unkempt Londoners lounged about and undertook their ablutions in the fountains of Trafalgar Square. Later in 1887 the situation became markedly worse and the venue was, once again, Trafalgar Square.

The year 1887 marked Queen Victoria's fiftieth year on the throne but not everyone was content to join in the festivities. As the homeless gathered in Trafalgar Square the socialist agitation that had led to the previous year's riots resurfaced, as a large banner was unfurled with the legend 'We will have work or bread'.[111] Local residents complained: 'It is impossible for any large meeting to be held without its being attended by a considerable number of roughs and thieves whose only object is to promote disorder for their own purpose'.[112] As autumn approached, the police, now under the stewardship of Sir Charles Warren, who favoured a militaristic no-nonsense approach to policing, decided to clear the square of its temporary occupants. Meetings were broken up with force and, faced with regular demonstrations of the unemployed and Irish Home Rule agitators, Warren took the decision to ban all meetings in the square. Warren's action provoked a storm of protest at the restriction of freedom of speech and assembly.[113] *Reynolds's Newspaper* asked 'Are we in London or St. Petersburg?' in a direct comparison between tsarist Russia and Liberal England.[114] The Metropolitan Radical Federation called a meeting in the square to protest the imprisonment of an Irish MP. On 13 November marchers converged on the square from all over the capital and this time the police had taken note of the committee of 1886's report and had stationed mounted officers 'at every angle of the square' with ranks of policemen positioned on all sides.[115] Warren had no intention of allowing the marchers to hold their rally and a police baton charge surged into the ranks of the protestors. A desperate battle ensued and while the supporting cavalry from the Life Guards were not required the police caused some 200 casualties among the protesters and two or three men were killed. The debacle even became the subject of a popular song as the story of 'Bloody Sunday' unfolded.

> It is within our memory's range
> How, in Trafalgar Square,
> Warren and all his myrmidons
> Forbade assembly there;
> How p'licemen with their truncheons,
> And soldiers with drawn swords,
> Attacked unarmed defenceless crowds,
> As though 'twere savage hordes.
> So, Remember Trafalgar Square,
> Oh! We'll soon have a meeting there;
> Our leaders are few, but they're staunch and they're true,
> And ready to suffer and dare
> Remember Trafalgar Square,
> Its trials and triumphs to share;
> When outrage and murder are called 'law and order',
> Remember Trafalgar Square![116]

In reality the soldiers, with or without drawn swords, were not involved in the fracas. The press reacted with a mixture of admiration for the police efforts and condemnation of their rough-hand tactics. In this they reflected the character of the newspapers and their editors. The *Pall Mall Gazette* led with the headline,

'At the point of a bayonet' before describing the police as 'ruffians in uniform'. Although the military were not called upon, the *Pall Mall Gazette* reported that they had been issued with live rounds and were ready to ride the protesters down 'beneath the hoofs of the chargers of the Life Guards'. The writer reminded the reader of the carnage that had occurred at a Reform rally in Manchester in 1819 and suggested that, save for the 'marvelous forbearance and good temper of the crowd' the 'Peterloo massacre' could have been repeated in Trafalgar Square.[117] The *Daily Chronicle*, by contrast, praised the self-control of the police but blamed the authorities for letting the demonstration happen in the first place. *The Times* were quick to support the police and Warren in particular for 'his complete and effectual vindication of that law which is the sole bulwark of public liberty'. The *Standard* attacked the 'selfish and cruel demagogues who bring together these ignorant crowds to serve their own ambitious purposes', and the *Daily Telegraph* was similarly quick to point the finger at rabble rousers 'carrying red flags and thick sticks'.[118]

Most seemed to accept that things could have been a lot worse; two policemen were stabbed and several heads broken but initially it was not thought that fatalities had occurred. In fact one person, Alfred Linnell, did collapse after the disturbances and died in hospital 12 days later. His funeral was occasioned by some protest at the actions of the police: 'Remember Linnell's martydom!' urged the closing line of Halliwell and Lewis' popular song. Linnell was a law writer, a minor member of the bourgeoisie, not a creature from the abyss. In an incident reminiscent of recent public demonstrations, Linnell was supposedly injured when a mounted police officer attempted to move a small crowd.[119] The coroner found for the police – there were no visible hoof marks on the deceased 'only small bruises by the left knee [that] should not have caused his death'.[120] The truth was hardly as important as the symbolism of Linnell's death. William Stead at the *Pall Mall Gazette* would use 'Bloody Sunday' as a stick to beat the chief commissioner with: Warren's militarization of the police would come back to haunt him, and eventually lose him his job. His final denouement would be in South Africa, at Spion Kop, the scene of one of the British army's heaviest defeats in the nineteenth century.

'Bloody Sunday' and the 'West End riots' of 1886 spread unease throughout Victorian society but they did not really threaten the hegemony of the ruling elites. Socialists such as Hyndman and Burns could posture all they liked, but England was not ready for revolution. This was not France, which had seen popular uprisings in 1830, 1848 and 1871 and had a much more politicized population in its capital and a more developed revolutionary spirit. After 'Bloody Sunday' radicals adopted different, less physical, tactics, perhaps aware that the capital had grown less tolerant of violent demonstrations which, as we have seen, were viewed as the manipulation of 'rough elements' by power seeking mountebanks. When the authorities attempted to suppress freedoms the press would howl. But revolution? That was quite another thing. Instead efforts to deal with the social problems of inadequate and insufficient housing, unemployment (a word that was first included in the *Oxford English Dictionary* in 1888) and poverty were continued.[121] The threat of 'outcast London' was less a cry for revolution and more a plea for help. Socialists now began to develop the trade union movement as a platform for social and economic reform.[122] Other politicians recognized the need for 'something to be done' and Winston Churchill was to repeat these concerns 22 years later when he alleged that the 'greatest danger to the British people is not to be found among the enormous fleets and armies of the European continent' but at home in the 'unnatural gap between rich and poor' and the 'constant insecurity in the means of subsistence and employment. Here are the enemies of Britain. Beware lest they shatter the foundations of her power'.[123] We might observe that politicians are quite adept at highlighting the problems that face society, but are much less able to effect lasting change.

These then were the conditions under which the Ripper's victims all lived and worked. Whitechapel was a desperate place to inhabit in the nineteenth century and despite the attempts of reformers to improve the area it remained a district stained by poverty, neglected and overcrowded well into the twentieth century. In this part of the capital many of its inhabitants were simply driven by the need to survive. In doing so one section of this society turned to prostitution and this became another 'great social evil' for middle-class reformers to concern themselves with. This is the focus of the following chapter.

# 6

# City of Dreadful Delights:
## Vice, Prostitution and Victorian Society

One of the first things that anyone reads about the Ripper murders is that all of the victims were prostitutes, or 'unfortunates' as contemporaries preferred to describe them. However, it is probably more accurate to say that all of the women killed by the Whitechapel murderer had been selling themselves for sex on the streets shortly before they met their death, and their individual paths to this desperate measure will be considered later. The Victorians' relationship with prostitution – indeed with sex and sexuality – has been the subject of intense historical enquiry since Steven Marcus published his 'startling and revolutionary perspective on the underside of Victorian life' in 1964.[1] Since then there has been a growing body of work that has debunked the prevailing belief that the Victorian age was entirely suffused with prudery, including the notion that they covered up their table legs to protect the innocent.[2] However, it is certainly true that the Victorians were very concerned with the problem of prostitution and throughout the nineteenth century attitudes towards sex and sexually transmitted diseases informed debates about the sex trade and those who worked in it.[3] In this chapter we will meet some of the key speakers in this ongoing discussion and consider some of the ways in which Victorian society sought to deal with the social problems occasioned by prostitution. We will also look at the ways in which reformers sought to deal with prostitution and, in particular, with child prostitution and so-called 'white slavery' (which we term 'people trafficking' in the twenty-first century).

As Sigsworth and Wyke have written, [it] 'is difficult to resist the impression that prostitution resolved itself into a physical expression of the class structure of Victorian society'. So while the clients were drawn from the ranks of working-, middle- and upper-class men, the suppliers were exclusively working class women and girls.[4] It was suggested that upper-class gentlemen from the West End were preying on the daughters of the working classes in the East. The *Pall Mall Gazette*, under the zealous direction of its now familiar campaigning editor, William Stead, actively promoted the 'decadent aristocrat' thesis to explain the murders in 1888.[5] That he was able to do so can be explained by the phenomenon of 'slumming' that saw middle- and upper-class Londoners regularly travelling to the rougher parts of the capital to experience the excitement of working-class nightlife and to observe the poor in their natural habitats. They went because such areas were, as Seth Kovan notes, 'anarchic, distant outposts of empire peopled by violent and primitive races'. They were, he continues, both 'prosaically dull and dangerously carnivalesque'.[6] Slumming fed a vicarious interest in the world of the 'other' in the same way that reading about the adventures of explorers and missionaries, or viewing the exhibitions at the British Museum or in innumerable travelling sideshows fired the imaginations of nineteenth-century Britons. While 'Darkest Africa' might have been far beyond the horizons (and pockets) of most Victorians, the East End was, as Kovan points out, merely a short and relatively inexpensive journey by hansom cab, omnibus or the new underground railway. Thus, Whitechapel and its environs attracted all sorts of visitors in the second half of the nineteenth century, many of whom came – as we have seen in the previous chapter– with the higher purpose of trying to help improve the living conditions of the people that dwelt there. Others, like Henry Mayhew and Frederick Greenwood, came to investigate and comment upon what they saw. Still others came to play and gawp and satisfy their lusts.

## CONTEMPORARY DESCRIPTIONS OF PROSTITUTION IN LONDON

Henry Mayhew dedicated the first 100 pages of his study of London's labouring poor to the problem of prostitution in London, which was penned by his colleague, Bracebridge Hemyng.[7] Prostitution was rife in Victorian London. Hemyng conceded that the real numbers of women engaged in the trade was almost impossible to determine but that there could be anywhere between 8,000 to 80,000 or more operating in the late 1850s. Many of these were to be found in the East End but areas such as Haymarket, Charing Cross, Regent Street and the West End more generally were frequently referred to as locations for prostitution. The French writer Guy de Maupassant wrote a short story in the late nineteenth century entitled *A Night in Whitechapel* in which two friends are shocked by an encounter with a young woman outside a local pub:

> Under the softening influence of alcohol we looked at the vague smile on those lips hiding the teeth of a child, without considering the youthful beauty of the latter. We saw nothing but her fixed and almost idiotic smile, which no longer contrasted

with the dull expression of her face, but, on the contrary, strengthened it. For in spite of her teeth, to us it was the smile of an old woman, and as for myself, I was really pleased at my acuteness when I inferred that this grandmother with such pale lips had the teeth of a young girl. Still, thanks to the softening influence of alcohol, I was not angry with her for this artifice. I even thought it particularly praiseworthy, since, after all, the poor creature thus conscientiously pursued her calling, which was to seduce men. For there was no possible doubt that this grandmother was nothing more nor less than a prostitute.

This passage reflects the debilitating effects of alcohol and poverty that characterized the lives of many street prostitutes in the capital. Hemyng had divided prostitutes into three classes: 'those women who are kept by men of independent means; secondly, those women who live in apartments, and maintain themselves by the produce of their vagrant armours; and thirdly, those who dwell in brothels'.[8] His neat division must have blurred the reality: some women would have fallen between these positions and many women turned to prostitution as a desperate attempt to feed themselves or their family when other forms of employment had dried up or alcoholism had rendered them unfit to pursue any other calling. Hemyng found that brothels even contained married women, such as the French woman he met in Haymarket, who 'loved her husband, but he was unable to find any respectable employment, and were she not to supply him with the necessary funds for their household expenditure they would sink into a state of destitution, and anything, she added, was better than that'.[9]

Prostitutes in Whitechapel worked the streets for paltry returns. They feature in Hemyng's survey as 'Those who live in low lodging houses'. Typically they would earn a few pennies for servicing their clients, often exactly the sum they needed to pay for that night's rent or 'doss'. That they drank to relieve the tedium and grim reality of their lives is hardly surprising. Like modern-day sex workers (many of whom are addicted to hard drugs such as heroin or crack cocaine) nineteenth-century prostitutes were commonly dependent upon alcohol. This allowed many observers to dismiss them as part of the 'residuum', that broad unwashed mass of humanity that blighted the streets of the capital. The ability to categorize prostitutes as somehow the antithesis of respectable womanhood further coloured attitudes towards them. As we shall see these attitudes changed across the century but arguably continue to resurface in modern strategies to deal with the problem. According to Hemyng since most of the lodging houses were owned and run by immigrant Jews many women had few qualms about avoiding the rent whenever possible. Known as 'bunters' some managed to live a fly-by-night existence flitting from room to room without paying their debts.

One (with the delightful sobriquet of 'Chousing Bett') told Hemyng that she 'never paid any rent, hadn't done it for years, and never meant to' and then she continued, revealing the latent anti-Semitism in nineteenth-century Britain, 'They was mostly Christkillers, and chousing a Jew was no sin; leastways, none as she cared about committing'.[10]

Reading Hemyng's account of his visits to prostitutes and his conversation with them one is struck by the way in which he is seemingly intent on describing these women as coming from a world quite apart from his own and presumably that of his readership. There is also the possibility that his subjects are aware of his desire for danger, authenticity and difference. Sitting in a public house with 'Chousing Bett', 'Swindling Sal' and discussing the talents of 'Lushing Loo' we are bound to wonder if these women are having a joke at the po-faced journalist's expense. We learn that these street prostitutes can earn £8 or £10 a week but that £4 or £5 was more likely; how much of this was true or involved an element of property crime as well is much harder to establish. Clearly whatever these women earned, much of it went in rent (unless they were successful at 'bunting') or on drink. Lushing Loo, when she did appear, promptly spent the half crown Hemyng gave her on a 'drain of plane' (gin) until she was 'perfectly drunk' and started to sing. When asked her history she again revealed that she was quite aware of this form of reformist enquiry: 'Oh, I'm a seduced milliner ... anything you like', before going on to tell her interrogator a fairly typical tale of a descent from a respectable upbringing from which she ran away for a soldier, a broken heart, desperation, prostitution, drink and now merely a wish to die. The story may be melodramatic, it may be either true, false or a compilation of half-truths: whatever it is, it probably serves as a blueprint for many of London's 'unfortunates' in the second half of the century.[11]

## A BRIEF HISTORY OF PROSTITUTION AND ITS TOLERATION IN BRITAIN

Prostitution has had a long history of toleration in Britain and while there were several attempts to control and suppress the trade throughout the eighteenth and nineteenth centuries it has never actually been made illegal. It was tolerated because it supposedly protected the innocent young women of the middle and upper classes from the rapacious desires of young and older males. 'Sexual desire in men was considered to be overpowering whereas in women it was passive and controllable' writes Paula Bartley.[12] By the middle of the nineteenth century prostitutes were being 'catalogued with the detritus of society; they were "dissolute", "fallen", "wretched", the "Great Social Evil" of a society that was eager to stress its morality and progress'.[13] In many respects prostitution was tolerated so long as it was not too overt, too brash, too sexually threatening. In eighteenth-century London streetwalkers who harassed passersby on the Strand or in St Paul's churchyard would find themselves rounded up by the watch or City constables and dragged before the magistracy to be reprimanded, fined or sent to the Bridewell House of Correction. Those who kept a lower profile or worked in one of the capital's more exclusive high-class brothels escaped such unwanted attention.[14]

The Victorian middle classes feared that prostitution would pollute respectable society, wrecking marriages, breaking-up the family home and destroying the very fabric of the nation. While at one level it was conceded that young men needed an outlet for their 'natural' lusts it was also recognized that prostitution carried the twin threat of moral and physical disease. The early Victorian period was no less blighted by venereal disease than had been the supposedly more libertine Hanoverian age that preceded it. Medical science still offered very little by way of a cure for syphilis and at least one member of the Royal Family was believed to have contracted the often-fatal condition. By the second half of the nineteenth century there had been some decline in incidents of syphilis but the emergent medical profession still pressed for measures to control its spread.[15] As we have seen in relation to housing policy the Victorian period cannot be seen as one of creeping and inevitable state intervention. Early attempts at public health policy floundered as the Board of Health was wound up in 1858, some four years after its key proponent, Edwin Chadwick, had himself been ousted from office.[16] The newly created, and much less prominent, Medical Office was headed by John Simon who adopted a much less interventionist approach to public health while at the same time being fully committed, as Chadwick was, to the importance of raising standards of health in Britain and its Empire. The other important development of 1858 was the Medical Act of that year which went a long way to legitimizing the position of scientific medicine in the public consciousness. The 1858 act enshrined in law the 'statutory definition of a medical practitioner' along with a register and a general medical council to police it.[17] The medical profession had arrived and this newfound legitimacy was to manifest itself in a determined assault on prostitution and the curse of venereal diseases.

The Crimean War had exposed the problem of sexually transmitted diseases within Britain's armed forces. Politicians and military leaders along with moral crusaders and medical practitioners bemoaned the state of the 'thin red line' that protected the wealth and power of the Empire. The dual theme of public health and public morality was in evidence here, as indeed it was to remain throughout the second half of the nineteenth century. That soldiers and sailors consorted with prostitutes was considered to be inevitable. After all few servicemen were married or were allowed to have their wives with them on campaign or in barracks. 'Lushing Loo' herself had been with a number of soldiers and regaled Bracebridge Hemyng with this charming ditty that neatly sums up the problem of venereal disease and, in this case at least, petty crime:

> The first I met a cornet was
> In a regiment of dragoons,
> I gave him something he didn't like,
> And stole his silver spoons.[18]

The response to these problems was to create legislation that would target the perceived polluters of the military machine: the street prostitutes operating in the barrack towns and naval ports of Britain. The Contagious Diseases Act (CDA) of 1864 (along with amendments and extensions to the acts in 1866 and 1869) affected 18 protected districts that contained major garrison stations and threw a 10-mile cordon around them. The acts enabled the arrest and compulsory medical examination, by a military surgeon, of any woman suspected by plainclothed police of being a 'common prostitute'.[19] If the woman was found to be diseased she could face detainment and treatment in a 'lock hospital' for up to a year. The act enshrined the 'double standard' of Victorian gender politics and concentrated all its attack on disease upon the body of the working-class prostitute rather than on the actions of her clients. The examination was particularly invasive and this, along with the acceptance of prostitution that the acts implied, led to a strong response from Victorian feminists and social moralists against what they saw as an attack on women and the state regulation of vice.[20]

From the 1870s onwards Josephine Butler organized an active campaign for the repeal of the CDA, welcoming on board interested parties from across the political and social spectrum. Butler met with fierce opposition but by 1883 had managed to persuade a significant number of MPs to back her cause.[21] Butler had formed the Ladies National Association for the Repeal of the Contagious Diseases Acts, which was able to recruit prominent female voices, such as Florence Nightingale, to argue that the CDA not only represented an attack on female civil liberties but also 'implicated the state in sanctioning male vice'.[22] This latter imputation was a crucial one; prostitution was not illegal as we have already established but the idea that in some way the state should accept it as a *legitimate* activity was anathema to many Victorians. The CDA were repealed in 1886 and must be considered to be a failure of state intervention in public health. The acts, in targeting garrison towns, completely ignored the fact that most prostitutes operated in London. Any attempt to extend the acts to the capital would have failed as medical experts estimated that in order to treat all the infected street-walkers in London the authorities would have to double the number of hospital beds then available. The cost of administering the CDA in London was thus pro-hibitive. Any soldier or sailor wishing to use a prostitute was more than capable of taking one of the many trains to London or other towns and cities not covered by the legislation. The *cordon sanitaire*, as it was, was therefore largely ineffectual.

Historians have debated the underlying reasons behind the introduction of the CDA as well as considering the repeal campaign within the context of evolving feminism in the nineteenth century. Clearly the authorities were concerned with the health and effectiveness of the armed forces – a concern that continued to inform debates about morality and sexual health throughout the century. These debates were also closely linked to concerns about the state of the working classes more generally. Naturally these areas are hard to separate: it was working-class men that filled the ranks of the armed forces, and working-class men that worked the mines, manufactories and other industries that fuelled industrial growth and underpinned the power and wealth of Empire. In 1885 the Rev J. M. Wilson addressed a public meeting in London calling for a campaign of social purity 'for the good of your nation and your country'. He was speaking in the aftermath of national concerns about the Empire, the defeat of General Gordon, the threat of nationalism in Ireland and socialism at home as well as rising feminism that chal-lenged the status quo of Victorian patriarchy.[23] These concerns resurfaced at the turn of the century as proponents of eugenics looked at the degraded specimens that were called upon to defend the Empire in southern Africa. Thus we can view the CDA as part of a series of measures aimed at controlling the behaviour and health of the working classes. In particular the CDA were an attempt to impose middle-class values and respectability on working-class women and to remove from them one of their opportunities to earn an income that was not controlled by male society. As Jeffrey Weeks has written: 'Repressive public sanctions [such as the CDA] would make the move into prostitution a different kind of choice than when it could constitute a temporary and relatively anonymous stage in a woman's life'.[24] Hemyng was aware of this when he surveyed the returns of prostitutes arrested by the Metropolitan Police between 1850 and 1860. Of the nearly 42,000 women (all 'disorderly' it should be noted – as was stated earlier it was rowdy drunken behaviour that got one arrested not prostitution *per se*) many gave respectable occupations before the magistracy. Now it may be that they did so in the hope of more lenient treatment or to help fulfil a contemporary discourse of 'fallen womanhood', but it is also indicative of the vulnerability of working-class women to the fluctuations of the lifecycle and the job market. So while it is possible that working-class women enjoyed a life of prostitution, at least as far as it allowed them some degree of freedom, however degraded, it was but one option available to them, and perhaps one that was viewed differently within working-class communities than it was by middle-class commentators who never needed to descend to that level of personal sacrifice.

The testimonies of individual East End women who turned to prostitution are sadly lost to us (if they ever existed at all) and we are reliant on sifting through the words of those who, like Henry Mayhew, Bracebridge Hemyng and Josephine Butler, wrote about the women they met or 'rescued' from the streets. The Women's Library on Old Castle Street, Whitechapel, houses the collected letters of Butler and the archive of the Ladies National Association for the Repeal of the CDA, as well as records of the National Vigilance Association and the Association for Moral and Social Hygiene; but within these there is little that brings us to a closer understanding of the working girls of East London. These women do appear in the registers of the Thames Police Court where magistrates such as Lushington regularly fined, imprisoned or reprimanded them for being drunk and using 'obscene language'.[25] Women rarely appear charged as prostitutes or for prostitution for this was not a crime in itself. We can but presume that many of the women brought in for drunkenness were streetwalkers, arrested for causing a nuisance and for being disrespectful to police officers who tried to move them on. Julia Lefair (a French immigrant perhaps or maybe 'Lefair' was simply an elegant *nom de plume*?) appears on more than one occasion for drunk and disorderly behaviour. Lefair gave her age as 28 or 29 and is one of the very few women between June and December 1888 who is referred to as a 'prostitute'. Ellen Mansfield (27) was sentenced to 14 days hard labour for 'soliciting prostitution' in August of that year while Lefair herself was discharged without further sanction.[26]

We know that Catherine Eddowes had been arrested for being drunk and incapable on the night she was murdered but had been let out of police custody when she had sobered up. This must have been, as it had been in the eighteenth century, a fairly regular way of dealing with inebriated streetwalkers (and others). The police must have known that many of these women would simply have been reprimanded and released by the magistrates and so a short spell in the cells was sufficient punishment for the majority of them. Those who were obstreperous might well expect more severe treatment, especially if they resisted attempts to move them on and assaulted the constable (verbally or physically) in the process. Elizabeth Stride, who met her death on the same night as Eddowes, had been prosecuted at Thames Police Court on 8 August 1888 (the night after Martha Tabram was brutally murdered in Gunthorpe Street) for being drunk and using obscene language; she was fined 5s or offered five days' imprisonment – she paid the fine. There are occasional examples of offenders being prosecuted for their direct involvement in the sex trade. Elizabeth Parker and Isabel Smith, both women in their early twenties, were charged with keeping brothels. Parker was fined £10 and Smith (alias Hayes) received a slightly higher sanction of £15: the 'madams' both paid up.

As Jeffrey Weeks has noted, the CDA allowed the Victorian police 'an easy opportunity for general surveillance of poor neighbourhoods' outside of the capital and the enforcement of legislation to penalize vagrancy and drunkenness effectively meant that the police did not need specific laws to combat prostitution within London itself. The prosecutions of Elizabeth Parker and Isabel Smith in 1888 may also reflect the implementation of legislation passed in 1885 to suppress brothels.[27] The clampdown on indoor prostitution had the unwanted (but surely not unforeseen) effect of pushing women onto the streets and into the arms, not only of 'bullies' (or in modern terms, 'pimps') but also in the path of the Ripper. The year 1885 had also seen the Rev Wilson demand a return to 'social purity' as we saw earlier. That year had been dominated by the exposé of child prostitution in the capital by the editor of the *Pall Mall Gazette*, and this story, like that of the CDA, is worth repeating because it tells us something about attitudes towards sex and sexuality in the late Victorian period.

## THE 'MAIDEN TRIBUTE' AND THE TRAFFICKING OF WOMEN IN THE NINETEENTH CENTURY

On 4 July 1888 the *Pall Mall Gazette* issued a warning to its readership:

> We say quite frankly to-day that all those who are squeamish, and all those who are prudish, and all those who prefer to live in a fool's paradise of imaginary innocence and purity, selfishly oblivious to the horrible realities which torment those whose lives are passed in the London Inferno, will do well not to read the Pall Mall Gazette of Monday and the three following days. The story of an actual pilgrimage into a real hell is not pleasant reading, and is not meant to be. It is, however, an authentic record of unimpeachable facts, 'abominable, unutterable, and worse than fables yet have feigned or fear conceived.' But it is true, and its publication is necessary.[28]

This wonderful journalistic device helped ensure that over the next few days the paper enjoyed unprecedented sales and its editor, the renewed attention that he and his cause desired. Stead wanted to hurry along legislation that had stalled

in parliament to raise the age of consent for girls from 13 to 16. The Criminal
Law Amendment Act of 1885 had been opposed in the House of Lords by those
peers who felt it was an unnecessary and unwelcome interference into the private sphere. Stead believed otherwise and was determined to bring the matter
before the court of public opinion. At the heart of the debate lay the thorny
subject of child prostitution, which Stead saw as a terrible indictment of late
Victorian society. In brief he alleged that in London young virgins were being
bought and sold and placed in brothels for the sexual gratification of those with
the money to pay for them. He used the language of Greek mythology to invoke
the 'Maiden Tribute' that saw annual sacrifices made of young Athenian girls
and boys to appease the Minotaur of Crete. With colourful language and a clear
understanding of the dramatic, Stead declared that in modern London many
more young girls were being sacrificed to 'minister to the passions of the rich'.
He attacked the 'dissolute rich' that both preyed on these 'maidens' and refused
to enact the legislation that would stop it. He called upon the democratic process
to right this wrong, even declaring that 'unless the levying of the maiden-tribute
in London is shorn of its worst abuses – at present, as I shall show, flourishing
unchecked – resentment, which might be appeased by reform, may hereafter be
the virus of a social revolution. It is the one explosive which is strong enough to
wreck the Throne'.[29] The inference here was that since certain members of the
Royal Family were known to enjoy the seedier side of London entertainments
they might well have indulged in this particular activity.

William Stead was not the first person to raise the subject of child prostitution; the Criminal Law Amendment Act of 1885 had arisen from a campaign
begun some five years previously. Alfred Dyer had published a pamphlet in 1880
decrying *The European Slave Trade in English Girls* in which he showed how girls
as young as 13 were taken to the Continent, often under false pretences, to work
as prostitutes. Once there they were virtual or actual prisoners of the brothel
keepers and hired 'bullies, frequently ex-convicts, are at hand to frustrate any
attempt at their rescue'.[30] Dyer agitated for reform of the law that allowed this
situation to exist. The Home Office despatched its own barrister, Thomas Snagge,
to investigate Dyer's allegations. Snagge found that the problem was quite as bad
as Dyer claimed with the discovery that 33 British girls and women had been
taken to Continental brothels between the years 1879 to 1880.[31] Dyer's campaign,
which drew strong vocal support from Josephine Butler and others, eventually
forced the establishment of a House of Lords select committee. Snagge was able
to show that traffickers were able to exploit the relative ease in obtaining false
birth certificates that claimed girls as young as 15 were actually 21 (and so not
subject to Continental restrictions on the age of prostitutes) but also that under

English law it was not a crime to push a 13-year-old girl into the trade. The committee framed the legislation that was eventually to become law in 1885, in part because of the efforts of Stead and his supporters. Gladstone's administration had other issues (trouble in the Sudan and agitation for the extension of the franchise at home for example) and dragged its feet over passing the Criminal Law Amendment Act. Thus, while not the instigator of the campaign, Stead's intervention in July 1885 was crucial to its eventual success.

Stead set about the process of exposing the trade by finding his very own maiden to sacrifice. He drew on the help of a former procuress and brothel madam, Rebecca Jarrett, who was willing to help Stead find a young girl fit for his purposes. In June 1885 Jarrett went to Charles Street in the poorer part of Marylebone and told the occupant, Nancy Broughton, that she 'wanted a girl for a place'. This in itself was not suspicious; many young girls went into domestic service in London. However, four or five girls were rejected for being 'too big or too old' before 13-year-old Eliza Armstrong applied.[32] On Derby Day, 3 June, Armstrong left Charles Street in the company of Jarrett – distinctive for her limp and the cane she used as support – and seemingly disappeared. *Lloyd's Weekly Newspaper* reported that Eliza had been taken to a 'French accoucheuse' (a midwife), presumably to determine whether she was a virgin or not.[33] Eliza had been taken to a house in Poland Street where she was undressed and given chloroform (which she said had no affect) before Stead came into her room as if he was a client. Eliza was not otherwise harmed by Stead or anyone else but he showed a rather callous attitude towards the girl. After she had been examined and drugged she was taken off to Paris to be cared for by the Salvation Army while Stead wrote up the experiment for the pages of the *Pall Mall Gazette*.

Stead's intention was to demonstrate that he could easily buy a child for the purposes of sexual exploitation. However, when the story broke the girl's mother, Mrs Armstrong, claimed that she knew nothing of the actual destination of her daughter, instead believing that was going off to be a domestic servant. This was crucial because if Jarrett and Stead had taken Eliza (or 'Lily' as she was to be known in Stead's articles) *against* her mother's wishes then they had broken the law. Mrs Armstrong was understandably keen to refute neighbourhood gossip and brickbats that she had sold her daughter into sexual slavery. The result was a very public trial of Jarrett and Stead for 'unlawfully taking Eliza Armstrong aged 13, out of the possession and against the will of her father'.[34] In fact it took two trials to finally determine guilt or innocence and in November 1885 Stead himself made the closing statement in his defence:

I believe everyone in court knows perfectly well that the reason I did all these things was in order, by private enterprise and private adventure, to achieve a great public good. Last May, when we began this work, the battle appeared to be going against us all round – the battle for womanhood, the battle for purity, the battle for the protection of young girls. The Criminal Law Amendment Act, which had been introduced as urgent in 1883, was hung up, having been watered down before it was hung up. Everything appeared to be lost, but there is great virtue in individual resolve, and at that time I and my few helpers descended into the thick of the fray. We succeeded in one month in driving back the host of the enemy and in planting the standard of purity, virtue and chastity within the lines that had been held by our insulting foe.

Jarrett and Stead were found guilty while others involved were acquitted. Stead was awarded first-class prisoner status and saw out his three months in Holloway Prison, retaining his uniform after his release and forever wearing it on the anniversary of his conviction. Jarrett suffered much more and was effectively abandoned by Stead who felt she had let him down both in court and in the less than particular way she had arranged for Eliza Armstrong to be 'bought'. *The Times* regarded the sentences as appropriate 'warnings to fanatics of all kinds' adding that 'the zealot bows to the law, but is not the less a zealot'.[35] It clearly had little time for Stead's campaigning style of journalism. The *Standard* was even more scathing:

> The mere recital of the abominations prompted and carried through by the principal defendant almost suggests a doubt whether anything short of monomania can have led to the idea that such a sacrifice of all that was right and true and virtuous in the lives of so many people was really demanded as the price to be paid for a victory over vice.[36]

This was a view not shared by the *Daily Chronicle*. While it accepted that Stead was a fanatic, and that he had certainly broken the law through his actions, it at least credited Stead with acting from the best of intentions in noting that he 'sought to accomplish a great good in the interest of society'.[37]

So what are we to make of the scandal of the 'Maiden Tribute' and the exposé of child prostitution in Victorian Britain and elsewhere? Arguably the most significant effect of Stead's newspaper campaign was in the passing of the Criminal Law Amendment Act in 1885. This piece of legislation raised the age of consent for girls to 16 but also set in place measures to protect young women and girls from exploitation in the sex industry. Persons procuring women under the age of 21 for prostitution within Britain or the Empire were liable for a prison sentence of up to two years and if the girl was under 13 the sentence could be extended to 'penal servitude for life'.[38] It also highlighted the issue of the exploitation of working-class girls by members of the aristocracy and elite. This echoed the treatment of working women by the CDA and resurfaced in the attacks on gentlemen in the wake of the Ripper murders. Middle-class moralizers such as Stead were quick to point to the poor example that many pleasure seeking 'toffs' were setting to the working classes they ruled. The 'Maiden Tribute' therefore offers us another glimpse into the ongoing class war between the middle and upper echelons of late Victorian society.

It also illustrates once more the gulf in understanding of working-class lives and culture by the more comfortable middling sorts. Stead's campaign built upon Dyer's less sensational one but both operate from the principle that young women were the 'sexually innocent, passive victims of individual evil men' rather than a consequence of a deeply unequal capitalist society.[39] This followed from the traditional view that saw prostitution as individual failings of character rather than an effect of society itself. Therefore philanthropy directed at prostitutes in the nineteenth century grew out of the prison reform movement, which spent time inside gaols talking to inmates about their path to crime. Prisons were seen as corrupting institutions and 'fallen' women were viewed as redeemable but this was made more difficult if they were exposed to other criminals. Thus reformers argued that separate institutions should be created to help such women escape from prostitution. In Magdalene asylums prostitutes were subjected to a disciplined regime of moral education and industrious training to instil middle-class standards of femininity. Josephine Butler rescued working girls from the streets of Liverpool and attempted to re-educate them as 'respectable' members of society. Similarly Ellice Hopkins helped establish a number of Ladies' Associations for the Care and Protection of Young Girls across the country. These had the aim of preventing young women from falling into prostitution.

Stead's campaign, building as it had on Dyer's original exposé of the traffic in British girls, should not obscure the fact that earlier in the century the trade had also operated in the opposite direction. Bracebridge Hemyng's survey of London prostitutes had revealed that along with the export of poor unfortunate English girls, unscrupulous Europeans (one assumes that the English were not involved . . .) regularly brought young women from the Continent to work as prostitutes in London. Again it would appear that women from Belgium (this was the subject of a complaint to the magistracy at Marylebone Police Court but other nations may well, in Hemyng's opinion, have been involved) were 'imported' into Britain under false pretences and then effectively imprisoned in brothels. In Hemyng's rather colourful language these Continental mesdames were 'made to fetter themselves to the trepanner, and they, in their simple-mindedness, consider their deed binding, and look upon themselves, until the delusion is dispelled [by whom one is bound to ask], as thoroughly in the power of their keepers'.[40]

Mary Kelly, often considered to be the Ripper's final victim, had herself been trafficked to the Continent but had made her escape and return to Britain. Whether her experience was typical or, in managing to remove herself from an overseas brothel, she showed an exceptional presence of mind, we will never know. Mary did avoid sex slavery abroad but the fate that she exchanged it for she could never have imagined. Hemyng recounts the story of a London whore whom he does not name who he met in a refuge but who had shared Mary's experience. At 16, and with her parents in financial difficulty, she had advertised herself for a position in service. Her advertisement attracted the attention of a French woman who preferred English servant girls and was offering a high wage. However, when she reached France it soon became clear that her mistress had other, much less respectable intentions towards her. Luckily she was saved by one of the clients of the brothel, a young Englishman who effected her escape with the assistance of the English consul and the deployment of the young man's personal wealth. Unfortunately when she arrived back in England no one was prepared to believe her story and as a result she 'found it difficult to do anything respectable, and at last had recourse to prostitution; – so difficult is it to come back to the right path when we have once strayed from it'.[41] Do we believe this tale of exploitation or should we view it as another attempt by the subject of Hemyng's investigation to tell him exactly what he wanted to hear? People trafficking was a reality in the nineteenth century just as it remains a reality today. Many of its victims are deluded, seduced, greedy or simply desperate to escape the situation they find themselves in. As with much of the related history of the Whitechapel murders it is sobering to think that so little has really changed in 120 years.

## REVISING THE HISTORIOGRAPHY OF PROSTITUTION

There are different ways to view prostitution in the late Victorian period. Judith Walkowitz's seminal study of prostitution effectively challenges the view of prostitutes as mere passive victims of male lust. Instead she sees them as independent and assertive. They also seem, when interviewed by reformers in prisons such as Millbank (where Rebecca Jarrett was left to rue her involvement with journalism), to have had higher expectations of life than other working-class women. 'Living in a society where status was demonstrated by material possessions' Walkowitz contends, 'women sold themselves in order to gain the accoutrements that would afford them "self-respect"'.[42] In this analysis we see the prostitute as a member of the urban working class, and this is particularly appropriate to the prostitutes of the East End. Walkowitz argues that the 'stereotyped sequence of girls seduced, pregnant, and abandoned to the streets fitted only a small minority of women who ultimately moved into prostitution'. The women working the streets of Whitechapel and its environs were often local girls, former domestic servants and had 'lived outside the family – indeed, they would most likely have been half or full orphan. Before going onto the streets, they had already had sexual relations of a non-commercial sort with a man of their social class'.[43] Prostitutes had much more control over their own trade, at least until the late 1860s and 1870s, than many do today. Bullies certainly operated in the East End along the Ratcliffe Highway but many British prostitutes were able to work without being exploited by a pimp or gang master. There was also a form of unity among the 'fallen sisterhood' that bound prostitutes together in times of hardship. They sat outside of 'respectable' society but it is much less clear that they were outcast: again this seems to be a rather middle-class view of respectability. Working people realized that prostitution was often a necessity and not a choice for some women.

In 1857 William Acton asked who are these 'somebodies that nobody knows'?[44] Hemyng had defined them by the class of men that used them (as 'kept mistresses, demimondaines, low lodging house women, sailors and soldiers' women, park women and thieves' women'). But this was an oversimplification. Prostitutes were drawn, at least according to the contemporary reform organizations, from the vulnerable trades. About half were former servants, others were dressmakers, barmaids, flower girls – those working-class women that were exposed to poverty when times were hard. East End prostitutes like 'Swindling Sal', who was interviewed by Hemyng, were perhaps exceptional in that they were very outgoing in their answers; most prostitutes were more 'ambivalent and defensive about their occupation.'[45] Their decision to prostitute themselves was probably more circumstantial than deliberate. As Walkowitz has noted, the lifestyle of prostitution offered some advantages and 'some women may have found the shorter hours and better pay of prostitution a temporary solution to their immediate difficulty'.[46]

The lack of male partner was often cited as the reason for women turning to the streets and this may well have been an important consideration. Observers also cited the very nature of Victorian cities as centres of vice because they offered too much freedom and anonymity. The overcrowding that typified cities such as London compounded the problem, forcing thousands to live in parlous conditions with the inevitable add-on problems of disease and pollution. This physical state of the poor figured prominently in the works of social observers and reformers.

In a middle class inspired tautology, immorality was associated with poverty, which simultaneously was associated with the working class. Prostitution, it was supposed, resulted from the generalised indecency of the working class as large families lived, ate, drank and slept together in one room, which made the cultivation of chastity impracticable.[47]

Thus we return once again to the recurrent theme of middle-class morality and a desire to control the behaviour of their social inferiors. The Victorian period saw a shift in attitudes towards sex and sexuality but also towards children and childhood. The 'Maiden Tribute' in some ways exemplifies this shift. As the notion of adolescence gradually began to establish itself in the Victorian consciousness the middle classes developed clear ideas about what was (and what was not) appropriate behaviour and pastimes for their own offspring. They then began to apply this viewpoint to the children of the working classes. However, the children of the working classes (as we saw in Chapter 5) inhabited an entirely different world to their rich compatriots. Working-class children aged 12 and above routinely worked and spent considerable amounts of time unsupervised. The independence that Walkowitz noted in East End prostitutes was a product of the freedom many young people enjoyed in the capital. This scared the middle classes who sought to control and restrict the work and leisure activities of working people, or at least to try and mould them into acting in ways which they themselves felt comfortable with. Throughout the nineteenth century, Victorian society saw wave upon wave of reforms designed to limit the ability of the 'ordinary' man or woman to enjoy themselves: drinking, gambling, bare-knuckle boxing, dog fights, bullock hunting – all were curtailed or banned during this period.

## IMAGINING THE LIVES OF EAST END PROSTITUTES: THE VICTIMS OF THE RIPPER

Finally we might spend some time looking at the sort of women that walked the streets of Whitechapel. Hundreds if not thousands of women chose this desperate option in the last decades of the nineteenth century and, as we noted earlier, few if any have left behind them any indication of why they did so. In recent years one of the more heartening developments in 'ripperology' has been a movement to reveal the lives of the Ripper's five canonical victims. This has not been an easy exercise since working-class lives typically produce little in the way of documentary evidence. These women have achieved fame or have, rather, drawn the attention of the world because they were brutally murdered by an unknown assassin who has resisted investigators' best efforts to unmask him for over a century. One might ask who cares about the victims? Perhaps because we now live in an age where the victim is increasingly prominent in discussions about crime or, more cynically, because there is precious else new to write about the Whitechapel case, the histories of Polly Nichols, Annie Chapman, Elizabeth Stride, Kate Eddowes and Mary Kelly are now of increased interest. This was particularly evident at the Jack the Ripper exhibition in 2008 at the Museum of London Docklands which stated its intention of contacting the relatives of the deceased in advance of its opening. To date there has only been one volume dedicated to the victims, by Neal Stubbings Shelden, which is useful if a little uninspiring in its presentation.[48] It does, however, along with what little we might glean from the police reports and press cuttings, help us imagine the lives of these five East End prostitutes and thereby project a composite image of the low lodging house 'unfortunate' that Hemyng was at pains to describe.

We have already noted some of the circumstances of the Ripper's victims in Chapter 2. All but Mary Kelly were well into their thirties or forties, all had experienced broken relationships at least in part because of their personal strug-gles with alcoholism. Each one of them had friends and family who would have missed them but were drawn from the very bottom rung of society and as a result, had these women not been murdered in such a brutal and sadistic manner, the murders might have failed to register in the wider public consciousness. Even now their deaths have not been marked by any official memorial in the area in which they lived and worked. Some enterprising individual has stencilled their names on the streets in which they died but apart from their graves there is little or nothing to remember them by. The same fate is likely to befall the 13 victims of Peter Sutcliffe or the five women murdered by Stephen Wright in Ipswich.

So what can we add to the memory of the five canonical victims of Jack the Ripper? Well, in the case of Mary Kelly very little at all. As Sheldon notes she has left us almost nothing apart from the unreliable evidence provided by her boyfriend Joseph Barnett. Kelly hailed from Limerick in Ireland, one of a family of eight children. Her family crossed the Irish Sea to Carmarthenshire where her father worked 'as a gaffer at an ironworks'.[49] Kelly married a local man and after he died in a mining accident she decamped to Cardiff (where, according to Thomas Williams, she met and became Dr John Williams' lover). It was at this point that Kelly, aged about 18 or 19, fell into prostitution. By 1884 Kelly had been up to London and had travelled to France and back, escaping the clutches of a Continental madam who would have imprisoned her in a brothel as we have seen. She avoided that fate but met a worse one. All of this is largely conjecture since the real Mary Kelly is as elusive as her killer. Again this provides the conspiracy theorists with more ammunition. Walter Dew says he remembered Kelly as a frightened woman and had often seen her 'parading along Commercial Street, between Flower-and-Dean Street and Aldgate, or along Whitechapel Road'.[50] But then by November 1888 surely most East End prostitutes were living with the fear that they might be the next victim of the Ripper. That this did not stop them going out to look for customers should not surprise us; they prostituted themselves because they had little other way of existing.

Mary Ann Nichols had married in 1864 to William Nichols, a printer from Oxford, and by 1876 the couple were living in the newly built Peabody Estate in Duchy Street in Stamford Hill. They must have been earning enough money and living a respectable working-class life to have been able to afford the rent and meet the strict criteria that Peabody buildings required. However, there it seems that Mary and William had a temporary separation in 1876, perhaps on account of Mary's drinking or because William was having an affair with another resident in the block. Whatever the truth the pair finally parted in at Easter 1880 and Mary moved away. She turned up in the records of the Lambeth workhouse in 1882 and 1883 before moving in with Thomas Drew, a blacksmith, for about a year. This relationship also failed and by 1887 Mary was back in the workhouse. The final twist in Mary's life was in May 1888 when she wrote to her father to tell him that because of her good attitude in the workhouse the guardians there had found her a position in service in Wandsworth with Mr and Mrs Cowdry. Mary told her father, with a touch of irony perhaps, 'they are teetotalers and very religious so I ought to get on. They are very nice people and I have not much to do'. In July the workhouse received a letter in which Mrs Cowdry suggested that Mary had run away from service with property amounting to £3 10s. Mary went north and moved into a lodging house in Spitalfields and prostituted herself to pay the rent and feed her drink habit. A good-tempered and very small woman, Mary clearly struggled with life and failed to take advantage of the last opportunity that was given her.

Annie Chapman married her husband, John, in Knightsbridge in 1869. John was a coachman and by 1873 when Annie had produced two children, he was working in the employ of a member of the nobility in Bond Street. Shelden is unsure why Chapman left this position but speculates that it might have been because of Annie's dishonesty or poor behaviour. He did, however, eventually manage to obtain work out of town in Berkshire in the household of Sir Francis Tress Barry who was to serve as MP for Windsor from 1890 to the memorable election of 1906 (which saw the beginning of the end of 'Country House' government). By the end of the 1870s Annie had already succumbed to alcoholism and this may well have caused her to lose as many as five babies in her lifetime. She had returned to London in 1880 with her crippled son, John Alfred, to seek medical help at a London hospital. She may also have remained in London because her husband had little time for her when she was drinking. She returned to Berkshire in 1882 but, having supposedly weaned herself off the drink in London, soon found herself reaching for a bottle when she was with John. On 26 November her eldest child died of meningitis. Emily Chapman was only 12 years old and the grief the family felt only exacerbated Annie's alcoholism. Within two years her drinking habit had reached such a state that she was effectively expelled from her home by her husband's employers. Annie self-destructed at this point and went on the tramp, eventually ending up in Spitalfields living in a common lodging house and relying on prostitution. Annie received an allowance from John but this abruptly stopped in the summer of 1886 when he fell ill and was forced to give up his job in Berkshire. When Annie Chapman died in a backyard on Hanbury Street she was about 47 and had a terminal illness affecting her lungs and brain. She seems to have been a well-mannered woman, literate, industrious and quiet who only turned to prostitution when she had no other options.[51]

Elizabeth Stride's story has already been told in part in Chapter 2 with the supposed loss of her family in a maritime disaster. Stride had arrived in London in 1866 from Sweden where her family name was Gustafdotter. Aged 26 she married John Stride, a man considerably older than herself, and 'opened a coffee hall' in Poplar, East London two years later in 1871. Her life seems to have been one of fantasy fuelled by alcohol, which may explain her claim that her husband was killed when the *Mary Alice* sank on the Thames in September 1877. Despite this the census records that Neal Shelden has consulted suggest that in 1881 the couple were still living in Poplar but separated that year. Stride was admitted to the Whitechapel workhouse infirmary just after Christmas 1881 and was discharged on 4 January 1882 and placed in the workhouse proper. Thereafter she appears to have lived in Flower and Dean Street in a common lodging house, as her fellow victims Polly Nichols and Annie Chapman had. John Stride died in 1884 and soon after Liz Stride made one of her frequent appearances before a police magistrate for being drunk and disorderly. She found the company of another East End resident, Michael Kidney, but this was another difficult relationship that probably ended when she accused him of assaulting her in 1887. Her story matches that of the other women killed by 'Jack'. 'Long Liz' (so called because she was unusually tall at 5 ft. 5 in.) was an alcoholic whose relationship collapsed and, losing the financial support of her husband, fell into casual prostitution and a desperate life in and out of the workhouse.

Catherine Eddowes was born in Wolverhampton and only settled in London, with her common law husband Thomas Conway, in 1868 when she was 26.

By then she was already an alcoholic. In 1871 she and Thomas were living in Southwark where Catherine was working as a laundress and they had two children aged 7 and 3. She had a third child in 1873 at the nearby workhouse, though the couple were not inmates. In 1881 the family were living in Chelsea and their children were attending school. All was not well, however, and in a familiar scenario the couple split up, with Thomas citing his common-law wife's drinking as the main reason. Catherine went to live in Spitalfields were her sister had gone some years previously and she alternated between prostitution and piecework in and around Brick Lane. Here she met a local market labourer called John Kelly and moved into his digs on Flower and Dean Street. The couple stayed together but both seem to have enjoyed a drink and Catherine was, like Liz Stride, to make at least one appearance at the Thames Police Court. Her drinking almost saved her life. When PC Robinson found her outside a shop on Aldgate High Street at 8.30 p.m. one night he tried to get her to stand up but she was far too drunk. She was taken to Bishopgate Police Station and allowed to sober up. At 1 a.m. she was sent on her way after giving a false name and address as Mary Anne Kelly and wishing the constable a cheery 'Good night, old cock'. Three quarters of an hour later another policeman found her mutilated body in Mitre Square. According to Neal Stubbings Shelden hundreds lined the route of her funeral as testament to her popularity.[52]

Catherine Eddowes does seem to have been a less desperate woman than Nichols, Chapman or Stride. Perhaps her popularity explains the crowds but then again perhaps this was merely a reflection of the publicity that surrounded the case and the fact that she was, at that point, the most brutally murdered of the four victims. That was to be surpassed in the slaying of Mary Kelly, and the evisceration of her corpse is almost made manifest in the lack of any real biographical detail about her.

Overall Neal Stubbings Shelden is to be commended for his painstaking research into the five canonical victims of the Whitechapel murderer even if his book would have greater merit if he had been much more circumspect in listing his sources. As a result much of this information is open to challenge and as with so much of the case we are not necessarily that much closer to the truth. However, a pattern has clearly emerged from these mini biographies of the murdered women. They were all prostitutes but they did not start out that way. These women largely fell into prostitution as their lives collapsed. They shared an experience of failed marriages, lost children, poverty and petty crime. Much of this was due to alcoholism but this in itself probably reflected the desperate nature of their lives. They must also have shared this experience with thousands of other women in the East End and elsewhere. If we can create a composite of the common prostitute in the East End then she probably resembles someone like Polly Nichols, Annie Chapman or Kate Eddowes: a woman down on her luck, without a solid working male partner, unable to find regular 'respectable' employment and forced to sell herself in order to find a bed for the night and enjoy the pennyworth of gin that helped her forget how miserable her life was.

## CONCLUSION

In late Victorian London prostitution occupied the minds of many social commentators, journalists, feminists and reformers as well as magistrates and the policing authorities. Prostitution was a problem: a social problem and an individual problem for the women involved. Indeed we might add that it has ever been thus and remains the case today. The Ripper's victims were prostitutes of the lowest class and as a result in this chapter we have not looked at the more affluent end of the sex trade – at the expensive brothels of the West End and at the lives of courtesans and escorts that catered to a wealthy clientele. These establishments rarely suffered from interference from the police since the men that frequented them had important connections to protect. But 'Jack's victims would not have been able to find work in the bright lights of the West End – their ravaged lives determined that the dark streets, alleys and court of the East End was where they would work. They may have shared their West End sisters' need for money but they also exchanged their favours for little gain. Theirs was a desperate existence and one that in at least five cases ended in tragedy.

Prostitution was not a crime *per se*, in that few women were prosecuted for selling their bodies. However, prostitutes were viewed as a part of the 'criminal class' that was closely associated with the East End of London. The existence of this class is far from clear but Whitechapel and its environs was certainly a breeding ground for crime and criminality, as Chapter 7 will outline.

# 7

# Crime and the Criminal Class
# in Late Victorian London

The Whitechapel murders represent an extraordinary crime for any period of history but contemporaries believed that the area in which they occurred was a breeding ground for criminality of the basest sort. We have already considered Victorian attitudes towards murder and prostitution and touched upon other forms of violent crime when looking at the Irish community in the East End and at the garrotting panics in the mid-century. This chapter will look at crime more generally and in particular at property crime in the late nineteenth century. In doing so we will explore attitudes towards all forms of theft including highway robbery, burglary and housebreaking. The role of the police courts, where magistrates such as the much despised Mr Lushington presided, will be examined to see how they operated both as disciplinary institutions and as arenas for the resolution of disputes between neighbours living in the packed slums of the East End. We will then turn our attention to the more formal courtroom at the Old Bailey where more serious property crimes were tried. Using the trial records and the reports of cases in the London press this section will analyse the nature of crimes committed, look at what was stolen and how, and try to understand victims' responses. The role of the police will be left to Chapter 8 so this chapter will close by studying the way in which the criminal justice system dealt with those found guilty of all forms of theft in the nineteenth century and show that by the 1880s the main weapon in the state's armory was the prison. How did we reach this situation when at the beginning of the century some thieves were being executed for very similar acts of crime?

There is a rich secondary historiography of crime and criminality for the nineteenth century that has examined the ways in which society attempted to explain criminal behaviour. In the early part of the century criminal actions were considered to be personal failings – in much the same way that we saw reformers characterize poverty as an individual malaise rather than a societal problem. By the last quarter of the century, however, contemporaries were beginning to view criminal behaviour as resulting from the collective activities of a distinct group within society. In particular the notion prevailed that a criminal class existed in the period – a subclass below the respectable working classes that lived entirely by criminal activity and had rejected the Victorian work ethic in favour of the easy pickings available from those better off than them. This was largely a fiction, created by the writings of Henry Mayhew and others, that has to some extent been perpetuated by historians who have relied too heavily on contemporary texts. This chapter will use more recent work to undermine the concept of the criminal class and discuss the reasons why it may have been a useful tool for the Victorian authorities to enforce harsher disciplinary practices.

## HISTORIOGRAPHY AND THE IDEA OF A CRIMINAL CLASS

The second half of the nineteenth century saw the emergence of the science of criminology and the attempt to understand criminal behaviour. Earlier in the century the idea that personality and behaviours could be understood by analysing cranial shape (phrenology) and that patterns emerging from data analysis (statistics) could throw light on all manner of criminal activity had gained a foothold in contemporary consciousness. Both enabled a new discourse of criminality to take root as offenders began to be regularly described 'in terms of the external factors acting upon their will – their social environment, their physical and psychic constitution, or a mixture of the two'. As Martin Wiener has suggested this scientific approach 'led gradually to a subtle weakening of moral judgment of the individual'.[1] This contrasted with the views of earlier in the century, which had tended to see criminality as the manifestation of personal failings in the individual.

This new scientific approach allowed for new ways of dealing with the problem of crime and criminals. In short, if the problem was in society or the environment in which the offender had grown up or inhabited then these could be changed; if the problem was within the individual's head or body then perhaps that too could be altered. Failing that, the logic of this new science was that criminality had to be eradicated: bred out over time or driven out by reformatory punishment. The identification of what we might characterize as 'genetic' blueprints of criminality had another important consequence for contemporary attitudes towards crime. As criminal deviance was increasingly constructed as occupying a distinct place in Victorian society – a parallel society at odds with the honest hard-working one as espoused by Samuel Smiles – it appeared that a criminal class had been created to live parasitically upon the fruits of Victorian industrial success. In

1861 Henry Mayhew published his study of the poor and criminal of London in which John Binny declared:

> Thousands of our felons are trained from their infancy in the bosom of crime; a large proportion of them are born in the homes of habitual thieves and other persons of bad character, and are familiarised with vice from their earliest years; frequently the first words they lisp are oaths and curses. Many of them are often carried to the beershop or gin palace on the breast of worthless drunken mothers, while others, clothed in rags, run at their heels or hang by the skirts of their petticoats. In their wretched abodes they soon learn to be deceitful and artful, and are in many cases very precocious. The greater number are never sent to school; some run idle about the streets in low neighbourhoods: others are sent out to beg throughout the city.[2]

Later in the century the eminent Victorian psychologist Henry Maudsley described the criminal class as the 'step-children of nature', morally hamstrung by the environment in which they had been born and with little prospect of dragging themselves out of it without outside assistance. Charles Booth drew a similar conclusion from his extensive statistical study of the working classes, viewing much criminality as hereditary.[3] The Rev W. D. Morrison, a prison chaplain and long-time critic of the prison regimes of the nineteenth century, wrote in 1891:

> There is a population of habitual criminals which forms a class itself. Habitual criminals are not to be confounded with the working or any other class; they are a set of persons who make crime the object and business of their lives; to commit crime is their trade; they deliberately scoff at honest ways of earning a living, and must accordingly be looked upon as a class of a separate and distinct character from the rest of the community.[4]

That the patterns of behaviour displayed in later life were learned in infancy was very much a feature of Victorian discourse. Thus, children and youth were corrupted by exposure to poverty, immorality, idleness and crime, and themselves drawn in to the whole sorry business of delinquent behaviour. Older criminals taught younger ones, gangs of pickpockets infested the city streets, hiding away from the arms of the law in the tenements and rookeries that so worried polite society. Binny described how:

> Many of these ragged urchins are taught to steal by their companions, others are taught by trainers of thieves, young men and women, and some middle-aged convicted thieves. They are learned to be expert in this way. A coat is suspended on

the wall with a bell attached to it, and the boy attempts to take the handkerchief from the pocket without the bell ringing. Until he is able to do this with proficiency he is not considered well trained.

This lively description, which could be Fagin's den, has sometimes been swallowed whole by subsequent authors without considering the extent to which this discourse was a useful one for those pressing reformist agendas in the second half of the century. For the Victorians the concept of a criminal class was intrinsically linked with growing urbanization. The cities and towns of mid-nineteenth century England were seen, with their desperate poverty and squalid slums, as a breeding ground for crime and we cannot separate the notion of criminal classes from the fears about the Victorian town and city that were discussed in Chapter 3. The chaplain of Preston Gaol wrote in 1849 that:

> It is the large town to which both idle profligates and practised villains resort as a likely field for the indulgence of sensuality or the prosecution of schemes of plunder. It is the large town in which disorder and crime are generated.

Mayhew and his contemporaries saw a hierarchy of criminals that formed the so-called 'criminal class'. At the top was the 'swell mob', the more successful pickpockets and thieves that appeared to ape the behaviour of the middle classes, dressing in fine clothes and promenading at church on Sundays. These individuals feature in many of the contemporary reports and accounts such as that of James Greenwood. As a youngster Greenwood had been introduced to the world of Victorian journalism while working as a compositor in a printing works. In 1869 Greenwood published his main work, *The Seven Curses of London*, in which he explored the themes of neglected children, professional begging, prostitution, gambling, drunkenness and crime. He did so with a sense of curiosity and offered solutions that reveal a strong link to contemporary middle-class values and beliefs. Greenwood was particularly concerned with the effect that cheap literature, the 'penny dreadfuls' as they were called, had on impressionable youth. He equated this 'poison-literature' with the spread of disease. 'A tainted scrap of rag' he stated, 'has been known to spread plague through an entire village, just as a stray leaf of "Panther Bill", of "Tyburn Tree" may sow the seeds of immorality among as many boys as a town can produce'.[5] Greenwood told his readers of an 'army of male and female thieves, twenty thousand strong' and of the poor 'hard-worked policeman who must have such a terrible time of it in keeping such an enormous predatory crew in anything like order'.[6] He described their language – the thieves cant – with terms such as *sinker* (forged coin), *bug hunters* (thieves who robbed drunks at night), *fine wirers* (long-fingered thieves adapt at emptying ladies purses) or the charming practice of *going snowing* (stealing linen that was hung out to dry). Greenwood was able to distinguish between the hardened criminals who he believed were beyond the reach of reform, and those that could be set on the right path. The message of reform was being clearly and firmly put. Greenwood, in common with many of his contemporaries, believed that education, work and religion could help many other offenders return to the straight and narrow.

Henry Maudsley had made links between those suffering from mental illness and the criminal elements in society. He had argued that deviance was not a personal choice but a product of heredity and environment. His work built upon the investigations that had been ongoing since the 1860s by medical professionals working within the prison system. After 1865 all prisoners were subject to medical examination under the terms of the Prison Act and phrenology was a particular feature of their work. Dr George Wilson studied the heads of 464 prisoners and claimed that 'moral imbecility' could be discerned in a large proportion of convicts. In 1870 James Bruce Thomson declared that the 'physical organization of the criminal is marked by . . . a singular and stupid look'.[7] Thomson found both mental and physical defects in the prisoners he studied, along with a lack of intelligence and a propensity for violence.

On the Continent the idea that a person's physicality could provide insights into their mental and moral health were at the heart of Cesare Lombroso's 1876 work, *The Criminal Man*. Lombroso, an Italian physician and psychiatrist, outlined the theory of the 'born criminal' with which he developed a new branch of criminology that he termed 'criminal anthropology'.[8] History has not been kind to Lombroso: he has been labelled racist and his ideas ridiculed, especially after the Second World War when the evidence of Nazi atrocities, perpetrated on the grounds of heredity and biological race, were exposed. However, while Lombroso, himself a Jew, may have been simplistic in his interpretation of his data it was not out of place during this period. As Mary Gibson and Nicole Hahn Rafter have suggested, 'many of Lombroso's views were standard for the time and rooted in humanitarian impulses'. They seem crude and in some ways silly to a twentieth-century audience but they echo the work of Wilson and Thomson and others who believed that a criminal class existed in the nineteenth century and wanted to find ways to reform and combat it. Lombroso's interest lay in studying the criminal rather than the crime they had committed. Like Maudsley he saw crime as a 'natural' activity rather than an individual choice, and therefore some-thing that 'would always remain part of the human experience'.[9] As he developed his research over the last quarter of the century Lombroso classified criminals using physical features such as head shape, eyes, facial hair and tattoos. Some of his findings are frankly bizarre: arsonists, he declared, were generally effeminate and possessed luxurious hair while he stated that nearly 'all criminals have jug ears, thick hair, thin beards, pronounced sinuses, protruding chins, and broad cheekbones', characteristics that must have been common to many members of the Italian working and peasant classes.[10] Lombroso was not alone in his findings; in London a sketch writer at *The Graphic* was keen to point out the physicality of the criminal class, as he watched the comings and goings in the London police courts. He observed that the 'out-standing ear is one of the signs of the criminal class, precisely as the ear close to the head is the sign of civilization and peaceful tendencies'.[11] Ears that protruded were clear examples of criminality as were bullet heads and jutting jaws.

Lombroso's work on tattoos attracted the amused attention of the *Pall Mall Gazette* who commented that it 'is rather curious that people who are often "wanted" by the police should voluntarily identify themselves by almost indelible marks' before going on to conclude that this form of personal adornment demonstrated that 'savagery is always very close to our civilization, and that the criminal and the indolent easily glide back into the manners of Australians and Red Indians', while accepting that there were notable differences between the tattoos of felons and those of native peoples.[12] The *Glasgow Herald* was also clear that there was a world of difference between the use of tattoos by criminals which might be to 'conceal a brand of shame' such as the 'D' for deserter from the armed forces) and the 'heraldry of the savage' which marked the body of the Maori king.[13] The *Gazette* undertook a more detailed analysis of Lombroso's work in an article in 1887 entitled 'The science of crime' summing up his conclusions as follows:

> M. Lombroso states that no less than 40 per cent of prisoners are born, or habitual criminals, whom no house of detention, no penal servitude will change, and to whose existence the public had better accustom themselves, adjusting their minds to the existence of this latest of natural phenomena, a phenomena which, to use the philosopher's reasoning, is as necessary as birth and death.[14]

Lombroso's theories, however wild or generalized they might appear to us, were therefore in circulation in the period of the Ripper murders. The public's appetite for crime news, as demonstrated in earlier chapters, clearly ran to devouring the latest theories for explaining the workings of the criminal mind. Just under a year after the 'double event' the *Gazette* commented that when 'Jack the Ripper is finally caught it will be very interesting to see whether his physiognomy corresponds with that thus graphically described by Professor Lombroso'.[15] In 1890 Havelock Ellis, more noted for his work on sexuality, contributed to the debate with his volume in The Contemporary Science Series called *The Criminal* which took a very similar line to Lombroso in examining the physicality of offenders.[16]

Lombroso, in accepting that criminality was inevitable, was in effect arguing for a new attitude towards crime and its prevention. The new science of criminology could be used, he believed, to assist in the fight against crime just as much as new methods of detection. While there is much that is innovative in the approach of Lombroso and others towards understanding and defining criminals and criminal behaviour, they were treading a well-worn path that stretched back at least as far as the last decades of the eighteenth century. Jeremy Bentham's 1791

WHITECHAPEL, 1888.

First Member of "Criminal Class." "FINE BODY O' MEN, THE PER-LEECE!"
Second Ditto, "UNCOMMON FINE!—IT'S LUCKY FOR HUS AS THERE'S SECH A BLOOMIN' FEW ON 'EM!!!"
"I have to observe that the Metropolitan Police have not large reserves doing nothing and ready to meet emergencies; but every man has his duty assigned to him, and I can only strengthen the Whitechapel district by drawing men from duty in other parts of the Metropolis."—*Sir Charles Warren's Statement.* "There is one Policeman to every seven hundred persons."—*Vide Recent Statistics.*

**Figure 7** 'Whitechapel, 1888', *Punch* (October 1888) pokes fun at the police and at the same time provides its readership with a stereotypical characterization of the 'criminal class'.[17]

design for the panopticon or 'Inspection-House' envisaged a prison system in which offenders could be observed, controlled and analysed. We will return to the use of the prison and punishment policies at the end of this chapter because they are crucial to understanding nineteenth-century attitudes towards crime and the so-called 'criminal class'.[18] Before that it is necessary to explore the ways in which criminals were prosecuted in the period and to look at the problem of crime as it was reported in the newspapers. Thus, we will first look at the work of the Thames Police Court that covered the Whitechapel area before moving up the criminal justice system to see the sorts of crimes that came before the Old Bailey, London's premier criminal trial court.

## LONDON POLICE COURTS: THE NATURE OF SUMMARY JUSTICE IN THE LATE NINETEENTH-CENTURY CAPITAL

In response to widespread concern about crime and a perceived lack of law and order towards the end of the eighteenth century, seven police courts were established in London in 1792. These followed the pattern of the investigative office created by the Fielding brothers at Bow Street with a justice of the peace and a team of thief-takers. By the late nineteenth century these 'police courts' were dealing with a wide range of petty crime, vagrancy and interpersonal violence and were to some degree an arena for the resolution of all manner of disputes that arose from everyday life.[19] Unfortunately only partial records survive from these early magistrate courts but those of the Thames Police Court do exist for the period. In addition the London newspapers regularly reported on the proceedings of these courts, although it is likely that they selected only those cases that were particularly interesting or chimed with contemporary fears or preoccupations with certain forms of offending behaviour. We also have a late nineteenth-century sketch of the police courts, and a detailed, if very descriptive, tract on a selection of offenders that were brought before them that offers anecdotal observations without specifying which court is being examined.

The Thames Police Court had been created as part of the general reform of policing in 1792. In 1821 the Lambeth office was merged with Thames and in 1845 a purpose-built court was established in East Arbour Street in Stepney. Throughout the last quarter of the nineteenth century the court served the population of the East End and was presided over by the notoriously harsh magistrate Mr Lushington and his colleagues Thomas Saunders and Montague Williams. Lushington, as we shall see, was not prepared to tolerate drunkenness, bad language, gambling or attacks on the police and handed out fines and short prison sentences to thousands of petty offenders each year. Mr Saunders, by contrast, was said to be 'an acute, discriminating, and merciful magistrate', according to *The Graphic* at least.[20]

The records of the Thames Police Court are not complete but we do have a series of registers of proceedings that cover the 1880s.[21] There are two sets of registers; one covers all offences arising from arrests (and so, usually, features brief details of the police officer involved) while the other consists of cases brought by summons. There is some overlap between the two registers but, as we shall see, the first set is most predominantly concerned with criminal activity. For the purposes of this study I have surveyed the first court register for January to December 1887. The decision to pick the year before the Whitechapel murders was deliberate: incidents in the court between August and December 1888 have been referred to in other chapters and there is some sense in picking a period not coloured by extraordinary events that might affect the workings of the court.

The police office at Thames was a summary court: the cases were heard before the magistrate and a clerk, no jury sat and all judgements were made by the sitting justice. He therefore wielded tremendous power in his courtroom. By the middle of the nineteenth century common assaults and petty thefts had been made summary offences rather than crimes for which a judge and jury were required. The late nineteenth-century magistracy had a range of options open to them when offenders were brought before them. They could send offenders on for a full jury trial if the crime was suitably serious. Alternatively they could punish minor offenders with fines and short spells of imprisonment (or order a beating if they were small boys). They could acquit them if no prosecutor appeared or the case was unlikely to stand up to close examination, or simply admonish them and send them on their way. The court dealt with a tremendous variety of offences. Offenders were charged with thefts and burglaries, assaults and rapes, drunkenness and foul language, criminal damage, failing to maintain their families and not sending their children to school. Those prosecuting were individuals who had fallen victim to crime – violent or property – and the officers of the Metropolitan Police who were playing an increasingly proactive role in the prosecution process. However, this was a local court serving the local community and we should not simply view it as an arm of state authority in the East End. Throughout the century the number of criminal prosecutions increased and there are some clear reasons for this. As Jennifer Davis has observed, the estab-lishment of the Police and the police courts made it much easier for offenders to be caught and prosecuted 'quickly and decisively'.[22]

Table 7.1 shows that most of those brought before the courts were men, a factor that is consistent with all studies of crime and criminality throughout the eighteenth and nineteenth centuries. Men dominated statistics for property crime as well as those for interpersonal violence and so it is no surprise to see that 77 per cent of hearings featured a male defendant. Indeed if we were to remove the category of disorderly behaviour (which covers cases of drunkenness, drunk and incapable, foul language, refusing to move along or to quit premises when asked – which meant the pub in many cases) then the proportion of male offenders would rise to around 85 per cent overall. The large numbers of women arrested and then prosecuted for their bad behaviour when drunk has thus distorted the figures to some degree.

**Table 7.1** Hearings at Thames Police Court, January 1887–December 1887 (Court Register 1)

| Type of offence | Male | Female | Total | Males | Females |
|---|---|---|---|---|---|
| Property | 381 (84%) | 74 (16%) | 455 (27%) | 22% | 4% |
| Violence | 352 (84%) | 65 (16%) | 417 (24%) | 20% | 3% |
| Disorderly | 337 (62%) | 208 (38%) | 545 (32%) | 19% | 12% |
| Regulatory | 244 (85%) | 44 (15%) | 288 (17%) | 14% | 2% |
| Total | 1314 (77%) | 391 (23%) | 1705 | | |

While it is necessary to say something about the nature of all the offences prosecuted here I do not intend to spend too much time on the regulatory business of this court. The offences covered under this category include dangerous (or 'furious') driving, desertion (of the armed forces or one's family), refractory paupers (who have refused work or absconded from the workhouse), damage to property or throwing stones (usually the antics of small boys) and cruelty to animals. There are some very serious offences here of course; a Mrs Donovan was prosecuted in August 1887 for kidnapping children and using them to help her beg on the streets, but this was a rare crime.[23] The numbers are generally small and, if taken together with the administration of the Education Act and the prosecution of individuals under the various property acts that controlled lettings and house building, can be seen as part of the general regulation of everyday life in the capital rather than as strictly *criminal* behaviour. Instead we will look in more detail at the prosecution of disorderly persons, at petty theft and interpersonal violence, for it was these that occupied most of the business of the Thames office in 1887.

On almost every page of the Thames court's registers offenders appear charged with some form of disorderly behaviour. *The Graphic* noted that a considerable number of these types of offenders were presented before the court on Monday and Tuesday mornings, 'when the offenders have had their week's wages to pitch away over the pewter-covered counters of the publicans'.[24] If we take 1 June 1887 there are 17 hearings listed of which all but one mention drunkenness in the nature of the offence. Elizabeth Shand and Hannah Morebly were discharged after being arrested for being drunk and disorderly the previous evening. John Edmonds and Mary Botely were not so fortunate: both had compounded their crimes by using foul language to the police and Edmonds received a 40s fine (which he paid) while Mary was sent to gaol for 14 days. John Doyle and Maria Mitchell were picked up for being drunk and fighting and were bound over to keep the peace for six months on pain of losing their £10 recognizance. Bella Blue-Eyes, a young woman of only 18 ('at first sight she looks thirty' stated Redding Ware, the author of a small pamphlet describing offenders appearing at the police courts of the capital) was in the police court because she had 'been found drunk, hysterical and blasphemous, in a gutter, whence she has been removed by a severe-faced policeman, and "run-in"'.[25] Redding Ware had some sympathy for this costermonger's wife who had had her eye gouged out by her husband in a jealous rage. In his view this was the sorry tale of a 'mere child' who was 'mercilessly converted into a woman' who tried to live up to 'the high living and drinking bouts of her athlete of a husband, and in a couple of years she is a complete wreck'.[26] Helen Bosanquet had noted that East End women were worn out by 25 and almost all of 'Jack's victims were broken women in their late thirties and forties. Bella received 14 days' imprisonment for her drunken behaviour as she had no funds to pay the 10/- fine offered as an alternative. How many of those women found dead drunk on the streets were trying to wipe out the misery of their desperate lives, as Bella surely was, we can only wonder at.[27]

Nicholas Buckley drunkenly refused to go home when PC Elliot asked him and gave him a mouthful of abuse instead: the magistrate fined him 10/- with the threat of seven days incarceration if he failed to pay. In a similar incident a 19-year-old youth with a record of violent behaviour was charged with disorderly conduct and using obscene language. John Downey had already served six months for assaulting a policeman but this does not seem to have improved his temperament. One evening two gentlemen had complained about his boorish drunken behaviour to which Downey responded by pushing them off the pavement. The men then took their complaint to the nearest police officer. When a police constable told Downey to go home and sleep off his drunkenness, he received a mouthful of invective and a refusal. Downey was fined 5s and discharged.[28] John and Agnes Kemp (possibly a married couple or perhaps siblings) were jointly accused of being drunk and refusing to return home: Agnes caused some damage as she was arrested and they were fined 60s between them. In neither case is the motive for the drunken actions of the defendants at all clear. Indeed the only explanation necessary might be the consumption of too much booze, but in some instances the underlying tensions of life are revealed by the prosecutions in the police court. Edward Robinson had worked at the Rose and Crown pub in Bromley before he was dismissed for what the paper called his 'drunken habits'. In the ensuing three months Robinson had continually returned to the pub to vent his anger at his former employer. On this occasion he had overstepped the mark, challenged the entire pub to a fight while inebriated and assaulted one of the customers; Mr Lushington fined him 10s.[29]

On Valentine's Day, 1887, the register reveals that Elizabeth Stride (the Ripper's third canonical victim) was fined 2s 6d for being drunk and disorderly and using foul language. Many of the women who appeared thus charged were prostitutes as the East End's unfortunates who infested the streets frequently fell foul of the Metropolitan Police's attempt to clean up the area. Many were like 'Long Liz' Stride and would have made regular appearances at the police courts. However, those who were prosecuted here represent just a small proportion of those displaying drunken behaviour on the streets. The police could hardly hope to arrest everyone they found in an inebriated state, especially as that then meant escorting them back to the nearest police station to be formally charged. Even those that did find themselves propped up in front of the desk sergeant must have had a good chance of escaping a court appearance. Many would simply have been shut in a cell until they had sobered up, as Catherine Eddowes was on the night of her murder. Drunkenness also extended to the arrest of persons for being drunk in charge of vehicles. In January 1887, Richard Riches was remanded in custody after being charged with running over a man in the street while under the influence of alcohol. The newspaper reported that Riches was found by PC Thomas Baker at 9.50 p.m. surrounded by a crowd and quite incapable of controlling his horse and van.[30]

Historians of crime have now established that in the eighteenth century the summary courts were being used by large numbers of persons to prosecute assaults.[31] The same is clearly true in the 1880s. Interpersonal violence accounted for around a quarter of all offences heard at Thames and slightly more if those cases brought by summons are included. A summons cost 2s which was not an insubstantial sum for a working-class person to find and so it is worth noting that considerable numbers of people felt that the seriousness of the attack upon them was worth the outlay. However, much of this assault was probably fairly trivial and assault itself was open to wide interpretation throughout the nineteenth century. According to the Police Code Book for 1870:

A common assault is the beating, or it may only be the striking, or touching of a person or putting him or her in fear.[32]

Under this definition a gentle shove could constitute an assault and one can easily imagine how inebriation might have led to numerous assault prosecutions using this criteria. The Offences Against the Person Act 1861 contained a number of offences such as grevious bodily harm (GBH) and wounding that allowed action to be taken by the police but common assault was still extremely vague. Assaults were not indictable (and therefore had to involve a more serious use of violence to be heard before a jury) and were subject to classification by the police themselves and ultimately were dealt with at the discretion of the magistrate. 'Assault' was usually deemed to mean reckless, but not necessarily intentional, violence, while 'battery' implied the intent to cause harm. Under the 1861 act any assault that caused harm – and this could mean merely bruising or minor breaks – was termed 'actual bodily harm'.

The more serious offence of GBH was actually two separate offences. Wounding carried a maximum sentence of five years' imprisonment whereas GBH could be punished by life. In January John Haley came before the magistrate at Thames accused of wounding and cutting John Day. The victim alleged that he had been rudely awakened at 1 a.m. by Haley knocking at his door and accusing him of stealing his hat. When Day denied this Haley struck him in the face with a stone and as the pair grappled Day felt a stabbing pain in his side. He could not tell the magistrate what weapon his assailant had used but he was sure it was Haley who had wounded him as there was a light on in the room. The police were called to the house in Devonshire Street and PC Hawell of H division (which covered Whitechapel) found Day with blood on his face and side. Day's wife told the court that three men had come to her house and threatened her husband, demanding he return the missing hat and a local surgeon confirmed that he had treated John's wounds. Mr Lushington was evidently convinced there was a case to answer as he committed Haley for trial.[33]

If a court believed that there was an intention to kill the victim then a charge of attempted murder could be levelled. These broad definitions of interpersonal violence have to some extent survived into current legislation, the most recent reclassification being in 1998. The number of offenders charged with more serious incidents of violence are small: just 26 men in 1887 compared to 311 for common assault. It is notable that while women were accused of violence they appear in much smaller numbers (just 64). There was a large degree of discretion involved in the prosecution of assault. An assault without a weapon or without an associated attempt to steal was not indictable, but if one was to add one of these things it became much more serious. We should note the comment of the criminal registrar in 1909.

> There is no ... clear rule, and (it may be said) no uniform practice as to the degree of violence which makes it proper to prosecute an assault as an indictable offence ... Many of the common assaults and still more of the assaults on police constables, now disposed of summarily, amount in reality to malicious wounding, causing grievous bodily harm, or even felonious wounding, and if they were sent for trial, would swell the number of indictable offences against the person.
>
> *Criminal Registrar* (1909)[34]

Once again the numbers of persons appearing before Lushington and his fellow magistrates is not a clear and certain picture of violence in London in this period. Only a relatively small number of assaults would have resulted in prosecutions: again the involvement of the police would have been partial given the number of beat officers available and many people would have chosen to ignore assaults or respond in kind rather than go to the law. This is particularly true for domestic violence as historians have shown that only a small proportion of women were prepared to take their husbands and partners to court, preferring to suffer in silence or find other ways to try and curb their behaviour. The wife that went to law risked a lot: she could find the family breadwinner locked up, fined or indeed freed to meet his vengeance at a later date. Thus the so-called 'dark figure' of unrecorded crime is very evident in cases of assault and domestic assault in particular. Because all of the cases recorded in the first register are brought in by police constables it is difficult to be clear who the victims are in many of these assaults. However, by looking at the second register (of cases brought by summons) the prosecutor is more obvious. The following table gives a brief indication of the nature of assaults prosecuted in this way at Thames.

**Table 7.2** The nature of assault prosecutions at the Thames Police Court by summons, January to December 1887

|                             | *Number*   | *Percentage* |
|-----------------------------|------------|--------------|
| Male on male                | 110        | 22%          |
| Male on female (domestic)   | 221 (112)  | 45% (23%)    |
| Female on male              | 21         | 4%           |
| Female on female            | 138        | 28%          |
| Totals                      | 490        | 100%         |

The unsurprising result is that most violence was perpetrated by men and more often than not it was women who were the victims. It is also worth noting the large numbers of persons that appear here. If we include the assault cases brought in directly (those listed in the first register) then we can estimate that around 20–24 cases of assault were being dealt with by this court each week in 1887. This is a not inconsiderable amount of petty violence if we remember that many or indeed most assaults did not result in a hearing of any kind. The table also shows that women were not averse to attacking each other even if they seem to have refrained from assaulting their menfolk. This last statistic is slightly problematic: men were much less likely to report an assault on their person by a woman for reasons of pride and notions of masculinity. The 21 cases that do appear are unusual and may well include complaints from elderly males or young boys, possibly servants or employees. One was written up by the court reporter from *The Illustrated Police News* in September 1887 and serves to remind us that tales of parental cruelty towards children are not new. Jane Sibley of Mile End had married her husband and taken on the responsibility for his 6-year-old son, Alfred, and his two siblings. The family lived on Turner Street in a shared lodging house owned by Henry Eade. Eade had often heard little Alfred cry out or scream and feared that he was being abused by his father and stepmother. One Friday night when Sibley's husband was out, Eade heard Alfred's cries and decided to intervene. He warned Jane that 'You had better be careful . . . I think you will go too far with the boy. I do not think you fairly treat the boy'. Mrs Sibley protested that she was simply 'holloaing more to the boy to frighten him than beating him'. When Henry Eade encountered Mr Sibley he told him to sort his wife out saying that, 'If this goes on I shall have to stop it'. Sibley told him to mind his own business. At this point Eade decided to involve the authorities and alerted a constable. Alfred was examined by a local doctor after the policeman noticed marks on the child's legs, some of which seemed to be burns. Mrs Sibley claimed she had pushed the child and he had fallen against the stove but the policeman was unconvinced. On a more thorough examination Alfred was found to have burns on his legs, thighs and buttocks, as well as bruising to his forehead. Some of these showed signs of systematic abuse over a long period. The court decided that the injuries were not consistent with the child accidently falling against the stove and the boy's 8-year-old brother testified that after Alfred had been caught stealing sweets his stepmother had forced him to sit on the stove as punishment. He struggled and she beat him with a stick – which is how he had sustained the injuries that so alarmed Mr Eade and the constable. Justice Lushington committed Jane Sibley for a jury trial for her cruelty. Violence towards children was endemic in the period and beatings common so it is interesting that in this case the close-knit nature of East End dwellings resulted in a prosecution for cruelty and hopefully saved young Alfred from a more serious fate at the hands of his stepmother.[35]

The high proportion of attacks on women by men includes 112 instances that can quite clearly be described as domestic violence or wife beating. In all these cases the parties share the same surname and while this could be coincidental or represent other familial relationships it is more likely that these are wives bringing their husbands to court (or at least obtaining a summons against them). As we noted earlier this was a risky strategy to pursue and it is not surprising that in many of these hearings the case was dismissed because the complainant failed to appear. Several women may have threatened their abusive spouses with a court appearance but have not actually needed to attend to see their spouses punished. By obtaining the summons they achieved a sort of moral victory rather than the pyrrhic one that might have followed had their husbands been fined or even imprisoned by the magistrate. What is clear is that many East End women were prepared to go to law to try and arrest abusive behaviour in the home; sometimes this could have particularly severe and unexpected consequences for the convicted wife beater. In March 1887 a man appeared at the Thames court to ask the magistrate's advice. In January he had been prosecuted by his wife for assaulting her and had been fined £6. Unable to raise the funds he was sent to prison. Meanwhile his wife had sold his home and moved away. The unfortunate husband had also failed to find work on his release from gaol and was not able to comply with a court order to support his estranged wife with 10s a week. What, he asked the court, could they do to help? The answer was stark: what his wife had done was perfectly legal and there was nothing the justice could do to help him. The newspaper reported this case perhaps as a salutary warning to others who might be inclined to use violence to resolve domestic issues.[36] The figure for domestic violence could indeed be even higher given that many cohabiting couples lived without seeing the need for a formal marriage ceremony, therefore, many of the 109 other cases of male on female violence could be described as domestic.

Much of this violence received relatively little sanction from the magistracy. On many occasions no prosecutor appeared to back up their complaint (the summons or perhaps the knowledge that their assailant had spent a night or two behind bars was often satisfaction enough) and in others the magistrate dismissed cases for lack of evidence. Offenders could be fined or sentenced to short periods in prison of up to a month, and this was invariably the outcome for individuals who assaulted policemen. More serious cases could be sent for trial if actual or grievous bodily harm could be proven and the court routinely bound parties by recognizance (which required them to enter into a financial bond to ensure their future good behaviour) where it could not resolve the matter by agreement or fines. All of this again reflects what we already know about 'common assault': it covered a tremendous range of violent action, much of which was relatively petty. The amount of assault prosecuted at the Thames court does, however, reflect the fact that this was a rough and violent area of the capital and that much of this violence was fuelled by drink. Indeed the correspondent at *The Graphic* believed that Thames Police Court heard more cases of assault, actual violence, attempted murder and murder than 'probably any other court in the Metropolis'.[37]

This was also an area associated with crime and criminality as we have seen throughout this book. The figures in Table 7.1 show that prosecutions for theft and other forms of property crime accounted for just over a quarter of all hearings. As with assault, the number appearing in the police court charged with some form of theft is in no way an accurate record of the extent of pilfering that went on in the period. In her study of the London police courts Jennifer Davis argued that many employers (whether large or small businessmen) would have been reluctant to go to the law in many cases: 'Sentiment might prevent some small employers from prosecuting those with whom they worked closely' and we should not discount the fact that those with larger workforces may well have shared similar emotions. Others may simply have not wanted to take the time out of their busy lives to attend court, especially if this meant closing business in order for other employees to testify. After all, employers had the ultimate sanction: they could simply dismiss the thief and refuse to provide them with a reference for future employment. This may well have served as a more severe punishment than anything the court could administer.[38]

Individuals were accused of stealing all sorts of property that reflect both their needs and opportunities for theft in this part of London. In many instances the magistrates remanded suspects brought in for a few days while evidence could be gathered or the owner of the property found. The examination and re-examination of suspects had been a feature of the summary courts of the eighteenth century and can in itself be viewed as a disciplinary function operated by the magistracy. Suspected thieves could be arrested and imprisoned for a few days or a week before being released with a caution.[39] Minor criminals could be sent to prison for short periods as William Dover was in August 1887: having stolen £1 4s and 6d the 18 year old was sentenced to a month of hard labour. Robert Richards was offered a choice after he was found to have stolen a pewter pint pot from a local pub, either pay a £2 fine or go to gaol for 14 days: he paid the fine. John Farrington's offence was more serious as he had broken into a shop in Spitalfields and had stolen a camera lens valued at 15s; the magistrate ordered that he be fully committed for trial. This case made the pages of *Lloyd's*

*Weekly Newspaper* which gave the victim's name as Henry Schwero, a music seller, of 1 Fieldgate Street.[40] The London press routinely sent reporters to the police courts but given the number of cases heard it had to be something either exceptional or topical for the papers to report it. In March, George Carlton and Henry Cranfield, described as 'rough-looking fellows', were convicted of assaulting and robbing a Chinese seaman on the West India Dock Road. The magistrate said it was 'an abominable thing that poor inoffensive Chinese could not walk the streets without being assaulted and robbed'. He sentenced the pair to two months' imprisonment with hard labour.[41] Not all property crime was as direct as some of those noted above, nor were all the culprits easily identified as members of a criminal class. Charles Lawrence was a veterinary surgeon who was well known in the East End. He pleaded guilty to embezzling money from a firm of iron merchants and, despite them intervening on his behalf, he was sentenced to six months in prison – the maximum sentence the court could award.[42]

As we noted earlier the reporting of crime at the police courts can only offer a glimpse into the workings of the summary courts. Reporters would have been necessarily selective about the cases they chose to bring to the attention of their readers. The salacious, the topical and the unusual would have been the staple fare of the court reporter. In the *Pall Mall Gazette* the police and magistracy had, after the Trafalgar Square and Hyde Park debacles, an implacable critic, and at Thames it would seem that Mr Saunders JP was under scrutiny by the editors and reporters that observed goings on in his courtroom. The inconsistency of justice was highlighted in this report from late 1887: 'Mr Saunders of Thames Police Court does not seem to improve in his notion of justice' it declared, before going on to note that the magistrate had fined one offender just 5s for running over a man's leg while 'careering round a corner' in charge of a milk van but then sentenced Edward Buckley to 14 days' imprisonment for simply stealing a pane of glass 'from a stall outside a shop', despite him making no attempt to escape. Finally the exasperation of the *Gazette* was complete when 'a lad named Costin was charged with the theft of a German sausage. This dreadful offence was too much for Mr. Saunders who committed Costin for trial'.[43] Many of those brought before the court were offered the alternative punishment of a fine or a short period of imprisonment. In some of the capital's other police courts, Marlborough Street for example, most defendants chose to pay the few shillings fine. At Thames, according to Robinson of *The Graphic*, most of those convicted preferred to take their chances inside and 'work it off' to use a contemporary expression. 'Money is always "tightish" Stepney way', he explained, and 'every unfortunate cannot expect a little private benefit – a "friendly lead", as it is called, a whip round of friends, relations, and acquaintances – to meet the expenses of the very unlucky day which has brought matters to so sorry a pass'.

Robinson's detailed overview of the workings of the London police courts were published over three editions in 1887 and include some wonderful illustrations of the court. We see policemen giving evidence, defendants receiving advice from their solicitors (when they could afford them) and women weeping in the dock, as well as the interior of a Black Maria – the police vehicle that carried offenders to and from the courtroom in East Arbour Street. After offering some delightful vignettes from Bow Street in his second report *The Graphic's* correspondent concluded by noting that:

> Police cases are not always amusing, however – there are dreary desert wastes, over which the whole staff has to plod, and it is 'hard lines' on the student of human nature if he has dropped in when School-Board cases and Gas summons are being stolidly listened to by a sorely-affected stipendiary. Now and then in a School-Board case there is a glimmer of interest, but in a Gas dispute – despite the subject of discussion – there is not the spark of light and life. The reporters slip down from their seats, the clerk of the court yawns ominously, the policemen show signs of utter weariness, visitors, interested in coming cases, drop into fitful slumber. The magistrate sits patient and resigned, the gas collector produces a whole army of defaulters, who file in, one after the other, with the invariable plea that they have not burnt one-half of the quantity of gas charged for. These gentlemen [the Gas collectors] summoned to appear are the only beings in Court who betray the slightest amount of excitement over the details – the collector turns over his dropsical note-book and calls therefrom the number of thousands of feet of gas consumed, and the amount due to the company in consequence and the magistrate invariably agrees with him: 'judgement with costs' and calls the next case. At length the collector's last dreary statement is heard and his soporific presence is removed.[44]

Fortunately for the cub reporter sent to cover proceedings in the police court the opportunity to attend the sittings at the higher court at the Old Bailey presumably followed from a successful initiation at the lower end of the criminal justice system. While the summary courts represent the arena in which most Londoners would have encountered the law and have made their complaints, the Old Bailey was where the most serious (and therefore more newsworthy) crimes were prosecuted and judged.

# THE OLD BAILEY: LONDON'S CENTRAL CRIMINAL COURT

Between January 1850 and December 1899 London's Old Bailey courtroom heard over 52,000 trials for a wide variety of offences as Table 7.3 shows.

**Table 7.3** Trials at the Old Bailey, 1850–1899

|  | Theft | Killing | Sexual offences | Royal offences | Deception | Damage to property | Breaking peace | Misc | Totals |
|---|---|---|---|---|---|---|---|---|---|
| 1850s | 7,871 | 322 | 408 | 2,029 | 1,467 | 71 | 762 | 184 | 13,114 |
| 1860s | 5,562 | 408 | 482 | 1,631 | 1,340 | 126 | 863 | 243 | 10,655 |
| 1870s | 3,932 | 425 | 494 | 929 | 1,587 | 130 | 811 | 212 | 8,520 |
| 1880s | 4,502 | 455 | 954 | 1,295 | 2,059 | 194 | 996 | 258 | 10,713 |
| 1890s | 3,858 | 448 | 1,222 | 510 | 1,983 | 151 | 923 | 251 | 9,346 |
| Totals | 25,725 | 2,058 | 3,560 | 6,394 | 8,436 | 672 | 4,355 | 1,148 | 52,438 |

What is immediately apparent is the dominance of crimes against property in the statistics. Theft (which includes the sub category of 'violent theft') accounts for 49 per cent of all crime tried at this level of the criminal justice system. If we included forgery and fraud (which come under 'deception') and coining (dealt with under 'Royal offences' as an attack on the currency was considered to be an attack on the monarch) then we can push this figure to 77 per cent. Interpersonal violence accounted for just 12 per cent and as we have seen a large amount of violence came before the summary courts. Trials for sexual offences, (rape, assault with intent to rape and bigamy) constituted around 7 per cent of the business of the court and a variety of miscellaneous offences (conspiracy, returning from transportation, performing an abortion, concealing a birth – to name but a few) made up the remaining 2 per cent.[45] We have already looked at murder in an earlier chapter and other forms of violence and sexual crime cannot be covered in any depth here. Therefore this chapter will concentrate on the key property crimes that concerned the late Victorians. If we take another look at the Old Bailey records it is possible to construct a more detailed table for analysing property crime over the second half of the nineteenth century.

**Table 7.4** Property offences at the Old Bailey, 1850–1899[46]

| Offence | 1850s | 1860s | 1870s | 1880s | 1890s | Totals |
|---|---|---|---|---|---|---|
| Simple larceny | 2,220 | 1,187 | 846 | 960 | 779 | 5,992 |
| Theft from master | 1,483 | 678 | 466 | 267 | 212 | 3,106 |

(*continued*)

| Offence | 1850s | 1860s | 1870s | 1880s | 1890s | Totals |
|---|---|---|---|---|---|---|
| Robbery (includes highway robbery) | 382 | 674 | 521 | 713 | 583 | 2,872 |
| Pocket picking | 858 | 619 | 339 | 251 | 211 | 2,278 |
| Embezzlement | 673 | 529 | 268 | 211 | 156 | 1,837 |
| Theft from a specified place | 628 | 350 | 267 | 277 | 264 | 1,786 |
| Mail theft | 141 | 155 | 167 | 303 | 357 | 1,123 |
| Housebreaking | 270 | 149 | 98 | 209 | 145 | 871 |
| Receiving | 231 | 162 | 111 | 78 | 93 | 675 |
| Animal theft | 172 | 142 | 80 | 142 | 83 | 619 |
| Extortion | 28 | 24 | 21 | 43 | 66 | 182 |
| Game law offences (poaching) | 1 | 0 | 2 | 2 | 5 | 10 |
| Other[47] | 8 | 3 | 0 | 0 | 2 | 13 |
| Totals | 7,871 | 5,562 | 3,932 | 4,502 | 3,858 | 25,725 |

Table 7.4 shows that there was quite a lot of variation in the prosecution of certain offences across the 50 years covered by this survey. How do we explain the peaks and troughs in crime statistics? This might reflect changes in legislation or in patterns of prosecution or indeed in perceptions of the seriousness of certain forms of lawbreaking. In general property crime was much higher in the 1850s than it was at the end of the period. This perceived fall in crime has in part been attributed to the gradual establishment and development of the Metropolitan Police from 1829 onwards. However, it also reflects moves towards using the magistrate courts to deal with a wider range of minor property crime. It was in the 1830s and 1840s that, as Clive Emsley has noted, a 'flowering of the statistical movement' occurred in England and Wales, largely due to the work of Criminal Registrar Samuel Redgrave, who organized the way in which the statistics of crime were presented.[48] This data was made available to the public and may to some extent have fuelled concerns about the amount of crime in society and the concomitant threat to private property and persons. Fluctuations may also have been the result of economic factors such as unemployment or agricultural depression. The 1880s, which saw an economic downturn after several decades of growth, has notably higher numbers of prosecutions at the Old Bailey than the decades either side.

As Table 7.4 demonstrates it was the offence of simple larceny for which most defendants were brought to trial in this period. After 1827, the distinction between 'grand larceny' (the theft of goods to the value of one shilling – or 12 pence) and 'petty larceny', was abolished. Simple larceny now covered all forms of theft that had no other aggravating factors that were prosecuted under more specific legislation (such as burglary, theft with violence or theft from a master for example). Burglary is the next highest subcategory which, if we include housebreaking, accounted for just under 20 per cent of offences prosecuted here. Stealing from one's master was clearly dealt with more severely in the earlier part of our period, the offence having been formally created in 1823 as a result of widespread concerns arising from the rapid industrialization of Britain in the late eighteenth and early nineteenth centuries. Masters had long been concerned with the depredatory habits of their domestic staff but this new law appears to have been aimed more at workers in the new industrial centres. Robbery generally meant theft from the person on the street either by single individuals or by groups of thieves. As we saw earlier the 1860s witnessed a 'moral panic' about street robberies by gangs of garrotters who attacked their victims from behind.

Pickpockets were less feared because they eschewed violence but were no less criminal. Picking pockets was also an offence that was more likely to feature younger defendants and women. Embezzlement often involved stealing from one's master or employer but usually meant the embezzlement of money rather than the theft of property or goods. Much of this form of theft was prosecuted through the summary process (as we saw in the case of the well-respected but light-fingered vet prosecuted at Thames) and it is also quite likely that servants and clerks found to be stealing from their employers would simply have been dismissed without references or the prospect of finding work elsewhere. Therefore, though the Old Bailey merely represents the numbers of cases that reached trial, it is by no means a true reflection of the amount of crime in society. Goods stolen needed to be sold on or exchanged and so thieves needed receivers to 'fence' their ill-gotten booty. Thus receivers account for fewer than 3 per cent of those accused of property crimes at Old Bailey. The Victorians had a ready made image of the receiver in Dickens' Fagin (himself based upon the real-life character of Ikey Solomon) but the reality was probably much more prosaic: second-hand clothes dealers and pawnbrokers were sometimes complicit in facilitating the market in stolen property in London.

Before looking in detail at robbery, burglary, shoplifting and a number of other specific offences, let us finish this brief introduction to the range of offences heard at the central criminal court. The theft of mail is interesting as the postal service (created in 1841) was still a relatively new organization. It would seem that the majority of those prosecuted for taking letters and parcels (and the money, postal orders and goods they contained) were employees of the Post Office. The elaborately named Weston Montacute was among 30 Post Office employees prosecuted in 1888 for stealing the mail out of a total of 38 prosecutions for this particular offence. Montacute was sent to prison for five years.[49] In the same year there were 22 prosecutions at the Old Bailey for animal theft.

Peter Wallace stole a horse and harness from a carman's cart in December 1888 while he was delivering goods at the Albert Docks, while Alfred Stewart made off with six chickens and five pigeons. Stewart was caught by a policeman after a long chase through the back alleys of Mile End and received a sentence of 15 months' imprisonment.[50] Poaching, an offence that was featured heavily in the caseloads of magistrates in the countryside around London in the eighteenth and nineteenth centuries, was understandably less of a problem in the capital proper.

Finally, there were two trials for extortion in 1888. Margaretta Becker was accused of demanding money with menaces from a Leornhart Krott in May but acquitted. Krott had run a restaurant in Amsterdam where he had employed Becker as a waitress. She followed him to London claiming he was the father of her child, which he vigorously denied. Despite the fact that Krott seems to have been a very shady character – accused of living in a brothel, being expelled from Antwerp by the authorities there and arrested on suspicion of being an anarchist and possessing dynamite by the Hamburg police – the Old Bailey jury found insufficient evidence to convict him on this occasion. In the other case William Milne was convicted of threatening William Harris, a pork butcher, to obtain money from him. Milne told Harris that he had receipts that proved that Harris had bought bad meat from Smithfield market – meat that Milne had sent there – and promised that unless the butcher paid up he would expose him and ruin his business. However, Harris was presumably wise to this scam and confident that he was careful in selecting what he bought from market: he called for a constable and had Milne arrested. In his defence Milne argued that he was simply trying to expose the trade in so called 'croaker' or diseased meat and that to shut him up Harris accused him of extortion when he had not asked for any money at all. As he stated in court, 'My only object has been to get inquiries to stop the traffic in diseased and bad meat'.Unfortunately for him the jury did not believe his story and he was sent down for three months' hard labour.[51]

It is perhaps more useful to look at the percentages of individual crimes as prosecuted at the Old Bailey rather than at absolute numbers. If we do so then for the key offences we get the following table:

**Table 7.5** Property offences at the Old Bailey, 1850–1899 by percentage occurrence[52]

| Offence | 1850s | 1860s | 1870s | 1880s | 1890s |
|---|---|---|---|---|---|
| Simple larceny | 28 | 21 | 21 | 21 | 20 |
| Burglary | 9 | 16 | 18 | 23 | 23 |
| Theft from master | 19 | 12 | 12 | 6 | 5 |
| Robbery (includes highway robbery) | 5 | 12 | 13 | 16 | 15 |
| Pocket picking | 11 | 11 | 9 | 6 | 5 |

(*continued*)

| Offence | 1850s | 1860s | 1870s | 1880s | 1890s |
|---|---|---|---|---|---|
| Embezzlement | 9 | 10 | 7 | 5 | 4 |
| Theft from a specified place | 8 | 6 | 7 | 6 | 7 |
| Mail theft | 2 | 3 | 4 | 7 | 9 |
| Housebreaking | 3 | 3 | 2 | 5 | 4 |
| Receiving | 3 | 3 | 3 | 2 | 2 |

Table 7.5 reveals that prosecutions for robbery increased significantly at the end of the 1850s (probably reflecting fears about garrotters) while larceny fell slightly and then remained fairly constant to the end of the century. We can see that pocket picking and thefts from masters fell away (presumably because these are more often dealt with by the police courts) and the same is possibly true for embezzlement. Receiving, as we might imagine given its close relationship with all forms of theft, is stable throughout the nineteenth century while mail theft increases – perhaps with an increased quantity of letters and parcels in circulation. The first offence that I would like to look at in detail, however, is burglary (with the related crime of housebreaking) because trials of unwanted intruders clearly grew in proportion to other offences over this period.

The crimes were broadly the same: burglary was the illegal entering of premises at night to commit a felony (which was usually theft) while housebreaking took place during daylight. Burglary was considered to be more serious because the inhabitants were likely to be asleep in their beds and so the level of fear was increased. We should note that in both offences the term 'house' could also include 'attached buildings, shops and warehouses'.[53] Housebreaking could be quite opportunistic, especially as many premises were largely unprotected and open for most of the day – only being secured at night. Burglary could equally be a matter of trial and error – the trying of door handles or looking for open windows or breaks in the fence – but it was suggestive of premeditation.

Between 1 January 1880 and 31 December 1889, 1,034 defendants stood trial for burglary at the Old Bailey. The overwhelming majority of defendants (96.1 per cent) were male and over 80 per cent of trials resulted in a guilty verdict (and around 40 per cent of defendants chose to plead guilty in the hope of a more lenient sentence). We can now look in detail at some of the cases that touched, in some way, on the East End of London.

In June 1888 Frederick Frewer, an assistant at Telford's pawnbroker's shop on Whitechapel High Street, took in a silver hunter watch brought in by a James Smith who gave his home address as somewhere in Bethnal Green. Several days later Joseph Jones, who worked in his father's pawnbroker's on Church Street,

Spitalfields, received a signet ring pawned by Richard Wood. Several other pawnbrokers were also the recipients of watches and jewellery over the last two weeks of June and early July that year, ranging across North and East London. The goods – 84 watches, 30 rings, 18 or 20 chains and 6 or 8 brooches – had been stolen from the premises of Selloff Seligmann in Lower Clapton. Mr Seligmann had retired for bed at 11.30 p.m., having closed his shop up at 10 p.m. leaving his stock of jewellry and watches in the window. At 8 a.m. the next day, he came down to find that he had been burgled: the thieves had entered through the rear of his property and had made a great deal of mess, lighting the gas and scattering the floor with matches and jewellry that they either did not want or could not carry. The watchmaker called the police who sent an officer round at 9 a.m. that day. He reported that the intruders had slipped the catch of a rear window and had climbed in over the top of the shutters before ransacking the jeweller's stock and making their escape without disturbing the sleeping owner. While most of the pawnbrokers who gave evidence at the Old Bailey had simply taken in the goods they had been offered, one clearly suspected something was not quite right and decided to ask a few questions when James Keightley appeared in his establishment on Kingsland High Street. Edward Brooks had received a list of stolen goods (goods were often advertised as stolen and details posted in the *Hue and Cry* or the *Police Gazette* as well as in the more general newspapers of the day) and this watch attracted his attention. 'Does this belong to you?', he enquired of Keightley. 'Yes', he replied 'I bought it in the "Lane" [Petticoat Lane, or more properly Middlesex Street, Spitalfields] on Sunday morning'. Keightley went on to add that he wanted to pawn the item so as to have some money to attend the Alexandra Park race meeting. As soon as he realized the pawnbroker was suspicious Keightley took off, with Brooks in pursuit. Brooks soon caught the thief and, after a struggle, and with the help of a nearby jeweller, handed him over to a police constable to be charged. When he was searched at Hackney Police Station he was found to be in possession of five silver watches and one gold one, a gold ring and a gold key. When they went round to Keightley's home address they caught his wife, Hannah, attempting to hide other items before rounding up Martha Wood who had also been pawning stolen watches and jewellery as a result of the raid on Mr Seligmann's shop. Another suspect, Richard Wood, was picked up after he ran away from a police detective who was searching Keightley's home. Wood denied being involved declaring 'the Lord strike me blind, I never committed the burglary', but it was later found that he had also pawned some of the items taken from the jeweller's premises and so he too faced trial. Keightley claimed that he was just pawning the goods for a man he refused to name while his wife denied any knowledge of the affair; Wood too pleaded his innocence and told the court that he was asked to pawn a few things by a passerby who had noticed in what a poor state his boots were and offered to get him a better pair.[54] Wood stated he was out of work through sickness and had been duped by the supposed good Samaritan: 'I was too ill to work or I should not have met him'. The court did not believe him but there was not enough evidence to convict anyone of the burglary: Wood and Keightley were sent to prison for receiving stolen goods (the former for nine months the latter for five years) while Hannah and Martha escaped punishment this time.[55] This was a straightforward, if daring, robbery: the value of the goods stolen was in excess of £300, a large sum of money for the 1880s. Perhaps Keightley was innocent of the theft as he claimed. The case reveals a great deal about the trickle-down effect of property crimes such as this: the thieves were unlucky that one of the pawnbrokers was both vigilant and prepared to risk his own life in pursuing a criminal. Most of them simply pocketed the watches and other items and turned a blind eye to wherever they had come from.

David Silverberg and his sweetheart, Esther Harris, returned home to the jeweller's shop that Silverberg owned on Great Alice Street, Whitechapel, to find the street door open and a man in the parlour with a roll of cloth under his arm. The thief tried to escape but Silverberg secured him and called the police. The burglar, a young man of 19 years, was convicted and sent down for nine months.[56] Another Jewish business was the target of a burglary, this time in White's Row close to where Mary Kelly's body was found five years later. Henry Morris was convicted of stealing two watches, chains, £2 in cash and thirty pairs of boots from Hirsch Moses and his wife. Morris had surprised Johannah Moses in the bedroom where she slept with her sick husband (he was too ill to attend court) but fortunately for her an alert policeman had seen Morris use a nearby ladder to force his way in through the Moses' window. PC Thick, who was a sergeant by the time of the Whitechapel murders, recognized Morris from the Middlesex sessions of the previous year: this probably helped to earn Morris a five-year sentence for this particular robbery.[57]

A burglary in Mile End three years later resulted in a vicious assault on the policeman who captured one of the thieves. PC Weir of H division stopped three men at 1.30 a.m. as they wheeled a costermonger's barrow down the street. Dennis Bryan told PC Weir that he was behind with his rent and 'was going to do a shift' [i.e. move house at night to avoid his debts] but the policeman insisted on searching the barrow. As he opened a bundle the other two men ran off and Weir seized Bryan – a struggle ensued. Bryan bit the policeman's nose and then his hand, breaking the skin and drawing blood before kicking him and running off. Weir and another officer took the barrow to the station and issued a description of the thief before Weir's wounds were dressed. PC Weir was off work for two weeks and perhaps the seriousness of the attack explains the lengths to which the Metropolitan Police went to catch the perpetrator. Six weeks later Weir accompanied Inspector Abberline to Birmingham in plainclothes where a man fitting Bryan's description had been sighted. Bryan was arrested and at his trial a jemmy was produced that the police deposed had been found close to the spot where Weir had stopped the three men in Pelham Street. A detective with the Criminal Investigation Department (CID) told the Old Bailey that the jemmy that had been found corresponded with marks on the shutters of Mrs Woodland's pawnbroker's: her premises had been robbed earlier that evening of two quilts, four shawls and several other items. The jury found Bryan guilty of the burglary (but innocent of wounding PC Weir), and guilty of causing grievous bodily harm to Thomas Ockwell, another policeman who had tried to arrest Bryan in the wake of a robbery in Whitechapel High Street that year. Ockwell, a police constable with 18 years service under his belt, was on duty when he heard the smashing of glass 300 yards away. Hurrying to the scene he stopped Bryan who was coming towards him and demanded to know what he had in his bundle. The two men struggled on the ground before Bryan aimed seven or eight blows at the policeman with his own truncheon before making off with it and goods stolen from Barnet Goldschmidt's shop. The constable came to his senses shortly afterwards and his whistle summoned help. He was treated by Dr Bagster Phillips who told the court that 'his scalp was all pulp and jellied'. The extent of the constable's injuries left him permanently deaf and unfit for service; 'he will probably never be able to resume duty', Phillips told the jury. Ockwell was able to go with Weir and Abberline to Birmingham to identify his attacker. This time the jury and ignored the defendant's claim that his identity had not been proven and that the witnesses that appeared against him were 'influenced entirely by the circumstance of his being known as belonging to the criminal class'. The judge sentenced him to 12 years behind bars.[58]

Housebreaking was sometimes opportunistic but also relied on sound intelligence as to the whereabouts of the inhabitants. Breaking into a house during the day certainly carried many risks but was perhaps less dangerous than doing so at night when the occupants were more likely to be at home. One solution, of course, was to watch a property and note the comings and goings of the household. On Christmas morning 1887, Charles Statham, his wife and their servant visited his father-in-law to enjoy the season's festivities. They returned to find their had been home broken into, seemingly with a jemmy, and the house ransacked. The housebreakers had taken a 'marble clock, a silver cruet stand, 13 silver spoons, and other articles', valued at about £15. Statham, a small businessman running a delivery service, told his wife and servant to go and stay at her father's for the night and in the morning he went to the Thames office to give evidence about the goods taken from his home. When he got back he found that thieves had broken in again. This time they had been seen coming out of John Tattersfield's house (Statham's neighbour). When he challenged them they shoved him aside and ran off, with Tattersfield in hot pursuit. It being Boxing Day there was no one about, even on the usually busy Mile End Road. The criminals split up but as one ran into Grove Road Tattersfield called to a nearby policeman who caught and arrested the thief. One of the thieves had escaped this time but Henry Burrows – who confessed to another housebreaking in the previous year – was sentenced to ten months' hard labour. Mr Statham's property was recovered.[59] Statham's property had been found in Bow in a room occupied by Jane Ward who was convicted of harbouring the person who had committed the first robbery on the Statham household and of attempting to pawn the stolen items. The judge sent her to prison for a year.[60]

The ability of John Tattersfield to keep up with Burrows having seen him exit Statham's house was crucial in persuading the jury of Burrows' guilt. Even when the evidence seemed stacked against the defendant any doubt that could be sown in the minds of the jurors might help secure an acquittal. Emanuel Krost kept a provisions store on Brick Lane and one June evening he locked up his premises to go out for an hour. As he opened his gate on returning he noticed his barrow had been moved; puzzled, he went over to examine it. As he did a man jumped out of the passageway and tried to get past him. 'What do you want here?', Krost demanded, but the intruder mumbled something incoherently and fled, slamming the gate in Krost's face and making for Flower and Dean Street. Krost was aware of the poor reputation of the area and was afraid to go after the man. Instead he returned to his shop to find he had been robbed. He described the scene to the court:

> the door leading to the shop parlour was broken open, and another door was open – I missed from a chest of drawers a few dozen briar pipes, three of which were in cases – one was silver mounted, and had an amber tip, and another was mounted with silver and amber, also some cigar-cutters; two suits of clothes were on the ground ready to be taken away, and two linen shirts, half-a-dozen towels, value altogether 7l. or 8l.

Krost reported the crime to the police who arranged an identity parade of 10 or 12 local men. He picked out George Cullen as the man he had seen based on his height and the fact that he had noticed he was not wearing a collar. Cullen's lawyer caused the jury to question Krost's identification on the grounds that after 9 p.m. it would have been dark. Krost was sure it was Cullen as the lights from the local pub flooded his yard. Cullen had been arrested on the following day by Walter Dew – then a young policeman but later to become famous as the detective that caught Dr Crippen – as he patrolled on Brick Lane with a detective investigating the break-in. Both were in plainclothes and their studying of Cullen and several others brought a fair amount of abuse in their direction. Cullen threatened Dew saying 'G – blind me, if ever you attempt to take me I will chevy you – that means stab you', as the officer told the court. However, despite Dew's suspicions and Krost's identification, Cullen, perhaps because his lawyer was able to mount an effective challenge or on account of his relative youth (he was just 18), was found not guilty.[61]

Both Statham and Krost were quick to tell the court that they had secured their property prior to going out. Home insurance was a relatively new concept, being offered by Lloyd's of London from 1887 onwards, but throughout the period the police and papers reminded the public that they had to take responsibility for making their homes hard to steal from. As *Reynolds's Newspaper* warned, 'Every unoccupied dwelling and every unfastened door or window is a standing invitation to the burglar and housebreaker to enter, and one of which they are not slow to avail themselves'. The police had discovered 28,915 windows and doors open as they patrolled and the paper further condemned 'the reprehensible practice of certain shopkeepers who are in the habit of exposing goods for sale without keeping any effectual watch over them'.[62]

By 1881 the failure of the police to effectively thwart so-called 'professional' burglars and housebreakers revealed itself in the satirical periodicals of the day before emerging in direct attacks on police competence more generally in newspapers such as the *Pall Mall Gazette* and *Reynolds's*. In February 1881, *Punch* reported the fictional meeting of the 'Association of Burglars' (presided over by Mr Matthew Arnold Sikes, with interjections from the floor by Mr Smashem among others). Here the scientific nature of 'modern' burglary was praised and it was remarked (by a retired felon) that it was a lot safer and less risky now than it had been in his day. The meeting, after the obligatory vote of thanks to the chair, broke up with 'each member going to somebody else's house in the fashionable quarter now known as Burglaria'.[63] At the same time *Funny Folks* gently mocked the *Daily Telegraph* for advising its readers to take precautions against burglars, such as fitting electric door handles or keeping geese, by itself recommending the buttering of doorsteps and the distribution of orange peel – both presumably designed to cause intruders to slip and fall, to then be swept up by the maid servants in the morning.[64] By 1887 the situation was apparently unchanged with

*Moonshine* again suggesting that Mrs Muggins would not have her plate and Dresdenware if her husband had invested in a 'Patent Electric Burglar Detector'. While the article is clearly satirical it is also indicative of the necessity of individuals protecting their homes (and the goods therein) by all means possible and not to rely upon the police to do so.[65]

While both burglary and housebreaking were serious offences that reminded late Victorian society that their homes and property were vulnerable to the most skilled members of the criminal class, it was highway robbery that carried the greatest threat to contemporary sensibilities. Around 16 per cent of property prosecutions in Table 7.3 were for some form of robbery, which was slightly up on previous decades. Despite this the *Daily News*, in reporting an article penned by the surveyor-general of prisons, Edward Du Cane, in 1887, noted that highway robbery had 'all but disappeared' and suggested this was as a result of the improvements in banking facilities and transport links which had removed the necessity for individuals to carry large amounts of money around with them. Unfortunately people were not solely robbed of money and street robberies – muggings, as we would understand them in the modern context – were a regular feature of life in the late nineteenth-century capital.

Highway robbery has been highly romanticized in popular culture and the Victorians were familiar with the tale of Dick Turpin's ride to York from Harrison Ainsworth's epic novel *Rookwood* and the many versions reprinted in the penny dreadfuls of the day. The reality of Turpin's life and crimes was very different as recent work has shown: he and the Gregory Gang terrorized the Essex countryside before Turpin moved on to murder and horse theft in Lincolnshire. He never owned a horse called Black Bess, let alone rode her to within sight of York Minster.[66] The echo of Turpin and the masked cavaliers of the highways can be heard in the reporting of street robberies as 'daring' by the London press: burglars and some pickpockets were 'experts', muggers were 'daring'.

This was how James Flewett was described by the press when he was involved in stealing from John Dudley on Tower Hill in August 1887. As the retired engineer was crossing the road he dropped his cigar. As he bent down to retrieve it three or four men surrounded him and knocked him to the ground. Dudley struggled to get hold of Flewett who kicked him in the hip while he was on the pavement and pulled his watch and chain from his pocket. All the robbers escaped but the victim – who walked with a stick that was also stolen from him – was able to identify Flewett in a parade from suspects gathered by the police.[67] James Flewett, a resident of Whitechapel, was aged 25 and claimed he was at home at the time of the robbery having failed to get work at Billingsgate market that morning. Despite a number of witnesses that confirmed this he was convicted and sentenced to 5 years and 25 strokes of the lash. Some 12 years later a James Flewett stood trial at the Old Bailey and was gaoled for 18 months for highway robbery. He was 38 and had 13 other offences proved against him; it seems likely that this was the same man who had robbed the engineer.[68]

Plenty of other robbers were tried at the central criminal court in this period and the circumstances of their crimes are similar to Flewett's. At 7.30 on a cold January evening, George Hammersley, a caretaker, was at the junction of Commercial Street and High Street, Whitechapel, when several men emerged out of the thick fog and pushed him about. They took his watch and chain and ran off. Despite his inability to positively identify the men due to the conditions, another witness corroborated his story and the men were convicted and imprisoned for a year. The other culprits were later rounded up and prosecuted for the theft in February and April at the same court.[69] John Wade was visiting London on business in March 1888 and had arrived outside the Snider's factory on Buck's Row, close to where Polly Nichols was to become the Ripper's first canonical victim less than six months later. As he entered the building three young men approached him, one of whom grabbed him around the waist and removed his watch and chain with force. James Elliot was eventually convicted of the attack and sent down for a year after confessing to a further robbery in 1886.[70] It took the police four months to track Elliot down but this does demonstrate that they actively pursued actions against this type of offender and were not simply reliant on criminals being caught red handed or arrested in the immediate aftermath of their crime.

Clearly then the lack of cash was no disincentive to street crime: watches were easily pawned or sold on and made tempting targets for small gangs of robbers. Others became victims when they left one of the area's many drinking establishments a little the worse for wear. John Ford was drinking with William Warner in a pub on the Whitechapel Road and the pair left just before 11 p.m. and went their separate ways. The next thing Ford remembered was Warner's hands in his pocket as he attempted to steal his money. As Ford tried to stop him, Warner, who was very drunk, cut Ford's finger with a knife before he got away. The victim made his way to the London Hospital to get his wound dressed before pressing charges against his acquaintance for robbing him of over 17s in change. The jury found Warner guilty of the attack and he received a nine-month prison sentence after Ford spoke up for him in court.[71]

This section has looked at the prosecutions of property offenders at the Old Bailey and has hopefully shown that while a range of criminal activity was dealt with, much of it could be described as relatively petty and opportunistic. This was the nature of much of the crime that troubled Victorian society. With few exceptions the perpetrators were working-class men, many of whom appeared and reappeared before the judges at the Old Bailey and the magistracy at the police courts with depressing regularity. It has been suggested that the nineteenth century saw the development of a disciplinary assault on the depredations of the working-class criminal that was out of proportion to the actual level of crime and its consequences. The identification of a section of society as representing a real threat to order was echoed in a drive to identify a 'criminal class' that could be held responsible for committing the lion's share of robberies and thefts. Once it had been established that crime was not simply the product of individual failings but was in fact a by-product of industrialization and urban living then a scientific approach might be usefully employed to counter it.

Here the Victorian state, itself a much greater and more all-encompassing entity than its Hanoverian predecessor, was able to take centre stage. The idea that crime was something that could be measured, studied and that criminals could likewise be analysed, understood and reformed, was abroad in the late eighteenth century. However, it was the state bureaucracy, wealth and determination of the Victorians that allowed the emergence of social agencies intent on controlling and rehabilitating offenders. The emergence of what professor Gatrell calls the 'policeman-state' is one of the most interesting meta-narratives of the nineteenth century. In this period crime became 'the repository of fears which had little to do with its relatively trivial cost to the society and economy at large. It came to be invested with large significance because it provided a convenient vehicle for the expression of fears about social change itself'.[72] In the final section of this chapter we will look at the ways in which these ideas about crime and criminals determined the ways in which society punished those found guilty at the Old Bailey and elsewhere and how these methods may have differed from the generations that preceded them. The eighteenth century has been characterized as the age of the gallows, the 'bloody code' of Hanoverian justice cowing an awed populace into submission. By the early decades of the nineteenth century the gallows had largely been abandoned in favour of transportation and the prison. By the time the Ripper stalked the streets of London the prison had reached its apogee and we can now explore this change in detail.


## PUNISHING FELONS: THE TRIUMPH OF INCARCERATION

Most capital statutes for property crimes had been repealed by the end of the 1830s and hanging remained a residual punishment rather than a primary one. The death penalty had been under attack from the late eighteenth century; hardly used after 1840 it was abolished for all crimes except murder and treason in 1861. Reformers had argued that hanging was an inappropriate punishment for property criminals in that it effectively treated the petty offender and more heinous criminal in a like manner. Many of those sentenced to die at the end of a rope avoided such an end by having their sentences commuted to transportation or imprisonment. To many observers there seemed little logic behind the decisions that were made; execution had become little more than a lottery. In reality there was some pattern to deciding who would die and who would get a second chance. The nature of the crime was important – violent offenders were more likely to hang – as was the age and character of the defendant. Women rarely faced the hangman but primarily because they did not commit the crimes (such as highway robbery and horse theft) that brought most people to the scaffold and were consequently not deemed to be a threat to society. That dubious honour was reserved for young and unmarried males between the ages of 18 and 25 – the subgroup of society that has consistently held the most fears for those in authority and with property to protect.

Reformers had argued that the death penalty was ineffective as a deterrent given that many offenders realized that they stood a good chance of avoiding the ultimate punishment. Indeed, given the lack of professional police forces until the 1830s, most might well have believed that they would have to be particularly unfortunate to be caught at all and this, as we shall see in the next chapter, was one of the driving forces behind the creation of the Metropolitan Police in 1829. Along with concerns about executing petty thieves for their crimes were worries about the nature of public hangings. Contemporaries, Charles Dickens for example, feared that the spectacle of public execution, which drew tens of thousands to witness multiple hangings outside the debtors' door at Newgate Prison, was in danger of conveying the wrong message to the watching crowds. Hanging crowds were infested with pickpockets; spectators paid homeowners for the privilege of watching the show from upstairs windows; apprentices took time off work to come and see the early morning entertainment. Executions were not seen as manifestations of state power but as a crude form of titillation for the London mob. Dickens witnessed the executions of Frederick and Maria Manning at Horsemonger Lane Gaol in November 1849 and wrote: 'When the two miserable creatures who attracted all this ghastly sight about them were turned quivering into the air there was no more emotion, no more pity, no more thought that the two immortal souls had gone to judgment, than if the name of Christ had never been heard in this world.' In 1868 executions moved inside with Michael Barrett being the last person to suffer the ignominy of being hanged in front of an expectant crowd of some 2,000 people – many of whom had gathered overnight so as to have a good view of the Fenian's last moments.

Australia had been receiving criminals from the mother country since 1787 and thousands of convict workers had arrived to help carve out a new country from the continent's unforgiving climate and terrain. After a period of forced labour convicts could hope to be given a ticket-of-leave and perhaps establish their own farmstead or business in this new world. Some did very well, others made their way back home, but not a few failed to reach the colony at all or died soon after their arrival. As the new nation emerged in the nineteenth century it increasingly objected to its use as a dumping ground for those the English authorities wished to expel from society. In 1853, penal servitude was introduced and transportation was effectively abolished in 1857 although a few offenders were sent to Australia over the next decade. The new punishment that came to dominate penal policy was imprisonment. Experiments in the 1770s had led to the passing of the Penitentiary Act in 1779, which allowed local magistrates to build new prisons. In 1816 the first purpose-built national prison, Millbank Penitentiary, had opened for business on the banks of the Thames in London (although disease and an overly harsh regime closed it before the century was out). Once hanging and transportation had gone imprisonment dominated the penal agenda until the introduction of probation and non-custodial sentences in the early twentieth century.

As has been noted earlier, the Victorian period saw a change of emphasis in viewing the offender. While the final decades of the long eighteenth century had been dominated by ideas about the reformability of criminals, by the second half of the nineteenth century opinions were hardening – a process that was reflected in the development of the prison. Increasingly a perception gained ground that there 'was little point in attempting the reformation and education of those who the social Darwinian and positivist thinkers were describing as innately criminal and inferior'.[73] The growing bureaucratic state of the Victorian period allowed much better record keeping and the techniques of social investigation led to more analysis of statistics and the increased classification of criminals. Prisoners were photographed, measured and interviewed to determine what made them criminal. Their physiognomy was the subject of debate in the same way that other outsiders' – immigrant foreigners and native peoples – were.

Crucially the keeping of records meant that criminal convictions carried more weight than they had previously. A criminal record could now dog an individual's life as never before. Being 'known to the police' and being discovered in suspicious circumstances could lead to short-term imprisonment by a magistrate. Those offenders released early from prison on a 'ticket-of-leave' (the term was used for prisoners in English gaols as well as transportees to Australia) were at risk of being picked up by the police as suspicious persons if they stepped out of line in any way at all. Indeed there was concern expressed by some that the word of a policeman carried too much weight and could constitute an abuse of power. It is little wonder that an antipathy festered between the boys in blue and those recently released from Pentonville and other prisons. The sentence of penal servitude gave judges and magistrates the power to hand down severe sentences to relatively minor, if annoying, offenders. Persistent offending could be rewarded with long periods of incarceration. Thus we see offenders being sentenced to long terms of incarceration for petty thieving if they regularly appeared in court. Until the later decades of the century prisoners might hope to avoid this fate by offering a range of pseudonyms when they appeared in court or arrived at prison. The police and prison authorities in London used certain police detectives as 'recognizing officers' to identify recidivists in staged parades in the exercise yards of Victorian gaols. This had an unexpected consequence in that it acquainted many of the criminal fraternity with Scotland Yard's finest.[74]

Legislation that had followed in the wake of the 'garroting panic' of the 1860s had introduced the concept of the habitual offender and had allowed the police to track those leaving prison and keep tabs on them thereafter. In 1871 the 1869 Habitual Offenders Act was superseded by the Prevention of Crimes Act. This piece of legislation subjected a person under supervision 'to a penalty of twelve months' imprisonment with hard labour for various specified offences, and persons who have been twice convicted of "crime", the second time on indictment', to be 'placed under a term of active supervision, not exceeding seven years, by the Court, in addition to any other punishment which may be inflicted upon them. During this period, supervisees are required to report themselves to the police in the same manner as license holders'. However, this was not always easy for the police to administer, as Assistant Commissioner of Police James Monro was to complain in his 1886 report on the workings of the Convict Supervision Office. He noted that criminals bent on returning to crime simply did not report to the police as the act required, so the 'criminals that most require to be continually watched often evade supervision altogether'.[75] By the 1880s Monro claimed that his office always strived to help former prisoners rehabilitate themselves within society. The Convict Supervision Office actively liaised with charities to find men work 'so that no convict, or person under police supervision just discharged from prison, can complain that he or she cannot obtain work, or by being thrown on the world friendless and destitute is being forced again into crime'.[76] Whatever the reality the principle of the habitual offender informed attitudes within prison walls and prison reformers engaged in heated debates throughout the century on how best to treat those convicted by the courts.

English prisons operated for much of the nineteenth century in a two-tier system. There were a small number of newly built state prisons and a large number of local gaols that dated back to the eighteenth century and were administered by county quarter sessions and justices of the peace. The local institutions came under central inspection in 1835 before being finally amalgamated into a national prison network under the Prisons Act of 1877. The transformation of the prison was a lengthy process; reform came in waves and was often the product of compromise between different groups. The local magistracy were reluctant to surrender their long-established control over the imprisonment and punishment of offenders but the increased costs of the criminal justice system necessitated the relinquishing of power in return for central funding, albeit small funding at first. In some respects the Victorian period demonstrated the problems the authorities had in trying to standardize the treatment of offenders. In 1865 the Prison Act had amalgamated the old houses of correction (which had existed since Elizabethan times to punish vagrants and minor offenders), and the county gaols that had been originally created to house those awaiting trial or execution. The 1865 act created state-run convict prisons. In 1867 there were 126 local prisons, controlled by county and borough magistrates, paid for by rates and used to house petty criminals serving sentences of no more than two years alongside debtors, convicts awaiting execution and those awaiting trial. In addition there were just nine state-financed convict prisons, plus an asylum for criminal lunatics. These were the institutions used to finally replace transportation to Australia as a penal option.

Between 1839 and 1895 the careers of two men, Joshua Jebb and Edmund Du Cane – both former soldiers – helped shape the English prison system. Joshua Jebb had designed a model penitentiary that allowed for the separation of criminals from each other throughout their confinement. The 'separate' system was a controversial regime that advocated solitary confinement in the belief that it would force prisoners to undergo a crisis of conscience that would lead to a reformation of their characters.[77] This policy was made manifest at Pentonville, which opened in 1842. As Michael Ignatieff's seminal study describes, the prisoners at the London gaol were held in isolation, masked when in contact with other prisoners, controlled by a series of bells and forced to undertake menial tasks with religious instruction as their only diversion.[78] It drove some prisoners mad and probably failed to reform many others. The alternate system presented by opponent of solitary confinement was silence: prisoners could associate with each other during working hours but were not allowed to speak. Both systems were supposed to instill the principal of reform through internal contemplation.

However, Edmund Du Cane was less interested in improving the morals of his charges. In this respect he represented the late century attitude towards criminal justice in that he saw criminals and criminality as an inevitable problem of the age. For Du Cane reform was definitely secondary to control. Thus the prison system gradually merged the separate and silent systems into a universal process for breaking the spirit of new arrivals so that they could quickly become acclimatized to a regimented existence. Before penal servitude replaced it, prisoners under sentence of transportation had been 'softened up' for a period of nine to eighteen months before they boarded ships bound for Australia. From 1853 onwards convicts might typically expect to receive a sentence of eight to ten years in prison. For the first nine months a prisoner would be held in solitary confinement then transferred to a public works prison – where he would be set to work improving the fortifications of the naval dockyards or on some other similar project. At Chatham convicts were, as Du Cane proudly reported, 'employed in excavating, pile-driving . . . brick-laying, concreting, stone-dressing and setting' as well as removing the excavated soil and operating steam locomotives and other machines. For working-class men this was not particularly onerous work but for those felons from the middle classes this sort of hard labour must have come as a rude shock to the system.[79] At least this was productive work; prisoners on short sentences in local gaols or serving out their first nine months of solitary confinement had much less worthy employment.

The debate about whether prisoners should be kept in a separate or silent system was complemented by a parallel debate about the nature of work they should be required to perform. Some believed that prisoners should be used to defray the costs of their confinement and instigated schemes that used convict labour to make products, such as mailbags or shirts that could be sold at a profit. Naturally this did not please either those that felt a more punitive form of work was called for or local labour (represented by the trade unions) that resented the competition. Lord Carnarvon, who headed up a House of Lords committee in 1863, argued that the 1865 Prisons Act had called for the use of the 'treadwheel, shot drill, [and] crank' and felt that allowing felons to undertake productive labour, however menial and backbreaking, was 'less penal, irksome, and fatiguing' and therefore less of a punishment. Du Cane himself, despite the success of the public works scheme, tended to side with Carnarvon. Therefore Victorian prisoners were familiar with the treadwheel, hand crank and the numbing tasks of breaking rocks and picking oakum.

The treadwheel had originally been conceived as a functional device that could pump water or grind grain but was seen by Du Cane as a perfect tool to focus criminal minds on their reformation. The amount of distance prisoners travelled on the treadwheel and indeed the height they climbed, varied from institution to institution. At York they climbed 6,000 ft. a day, while at Stafford they were required to ascend half the distance of Mount Everest (16,630 ft.), Salford pushed their inmates even harder. It was, as one contemporary termed it, 'a dreadful punishment' and the old, infirm and very young were supposedly excused from it. Accidents happened and fatalities were not unheard of. The hand crank was situated in cells and was a more solitary punishment. Once again it had a practical application but was generally used for pointless labour. At Coldbath Fields Prison the inventive prison authorities had connected the crank to the treadwheel so that prisoners turning one were in opposition to those operating the other. The number of turns a prisoner made on the crank was carefully recorded and an inmate who failed to complete his allocation faced a loss of privileges or food. Those not compelled to climb the treadwheel or turn the crank could be forced to pick up, carry and then put down a 24-pound cannonball for several hours. This last exercise had no practical application whatsoever.[80]

The progress of every inmate was carefully recorded and they were kept informed of how they were progressing. Three stages and four classes of progress were involved. For the first nine months, as was noted earlier, each prisoner was held in solitary confinement only being allowed out of his cell for exercise and to go to chapel. At stage two he was kept in at night but was able to associate with other prisoners at work. In the final stage he obtained a conditional release from gaol but remained under police supervision until he completed the 'portion of his sentence which remained unexpired at the time of his release'.[81] Each prisoner wore a badge denoting which stage he had reached. As he progressed each inmate could earn points for good behaviour and 'industry', which could lead to early release, increased visiting rights or to a pot of money which was allocated on release. Points or marks were recorded on a card that the prisoner could see, ensuring, in Du Cane's view, that 'day by day, week by week, and year by year, he can count and record the progress he is making towards an advance in class, an accumulation of money, and towards conditional release; and he is made perfectly to see and feel that his fate is in his own hands'.[82] Bad behaviour resulted in a loss of points and incurred additional punishments such as floggings and the application of manacles and chains. Each prisoner was supplied with a set of prison rules many of which would not, in the opinion of at least one contemporary, be given a 'moment's regard outside prison walls'. So a prisoner who blew his nose at the wrong time or was caught short on the treadwheel would suffer additional punishment and the potential loss of good conduct marks. Therefore one had to be totally committed to earning one's freedom from the Victorian prison system. Parole, or more properly the 'ticket-of-leave', was conditional, and as we have seen convicts were watched and could be recalled if they re-offended even in a minor way.

Du Cane determined diets, work and living conditions, all based on scientific principles, to meet this overarching theory of punishment and confinement. The notion of progression even extended to prisoners' diets. In the early weeks or months, the food allowed was barely sufficient to keep felons alive, it was what Sean McConville has termed 'scientific starvation'. Du Cane argued that abstinence from food was not only beneficial to the health of offenders but also declared that if prisoners were too well fed others might be encouraged to commit crime in order to get a good meal. This echoed the principle of less eligibility that had characterized the treatment of paupers after 1834. Thus, prisoners could expect to lose weight inside, and feel 'eternally hungry'. The Howard Association, which reported on the defects of the prison system in 1872, noted that each inmate 'goes to bed hungry and gets up hungry, in fact he is always hungry; and this lasts for not weeks, not months, but for years'.[83] A lack of meat and with little or no attempt made to introduce vegetables (excepting the ubiquitous, but often mouldy, potato) to the diet led to outbreaks of scurvy and virtual malnutrition. Bread was hard, suet pudding inedible and gruel (or 'stirabout') sometimes the only sustenance on offer. The only food item that seems to have met with prisoners' approval was the hot chocolate and even this came with a patina of grease.

Thus, with a considerable number of habitual offenders coming in and out of prison and existing on poor diets the effect on them was devastating. As was the denial of sleep, not as a form of torture but simply from the practice of sleeping on a hard board. Mrs Maybrick, gaoled for the murder of her husband (himself a recent Ripper suspect), complained that 'insomnia was my constant companion' and this must have been true for many inmates.[84] After 1877, when local prisons came under central administration, new arrivals were routinely denied mattresses as part of the softening-up process. For those on short sentences this could mean that they spent their entire time in gaol sleeping on the cold flags. Depriving convicts of company and of reading material – excepting the Bible of course – was also supposed to help focus the mind of the individual on reformation. As the prisoner progressed through the system they could improve their conditions and achieve a better diet, work allocation, improved bedding, greater opportunities for association with other prisoners and leisure activities, but it was a slow and gruelling process that destroyed men's spirits and crippled them physically.

Austin Bidwell, who was incarcerated at Chatham Prison, wrote in his 1888 autobiography a poignant verdict on the prison system:

> The English system is a vast machine in which a man counts for just nothing at all ... The prison does not look on him as a man at all. He is merely an object which must move in a certain rut and occupy a certain niche provided for it. There is no room for the smallest sentiment.

His advice to those caught within this machine was simple:

> Move with it and all is well. Resist, and you will be crushed as inevitably as the
> man who plants himself on the railroad track when the express is coming. Without
> passion, without prejudice, but also without pity and without remorse, this machine
> crushes and passes on.[85]

Thus the picture that emerges from the nineteenth century is of an unbending
punitive system of imprisonment that illustrates Michel Foucault's concept of
deepening discipline in the period.[86] Bidwell's analogy of the machine is apt;
the application of a rational systematic punishment was appropriate in such a
scientific epoch.[87] The prison allowed for the exact measurement of sentencing
that fitted the crime in a way that transportation and execution did not. Once
in prison convicts had to keep to a narrow path in order not to fall foul of the
disciplinary system. In doing so they were observed at every turn, and continually
measured and examined to make sure they abided by the process of reformation.
Unfortunately, this did little to rehabilitate individual convicts and prepare them
for a normal existence outside of prison. Recidivism was high, as was mental
illness and physical degradation. Du Cane's reforms largely failed to provide
an effective punishment policy. Conflicting ideas about how prisoners should
be treated; arguments over local or national control; spiraling costs; a lack of
uniformity and of a body to oversee the reforms, all contributed to this failure.[88]
As will become clear with the police, the prison system was beset with a number
of problems that compromised its role and purpose.

## CONCLUSION

There was no criminal class in the late nineteenth century nor is it a very useful
way in which to understand criminal activity or motivations. Naturally in any
society there are those who choose the easy route over the more industrious
one but we should not be seduced by Binny and Mayhew or by the writings
of those with an investment in justifying their increased role in crime fighting
and prevention. Hopefully this chapter has shown that crime was a very varied
activity in the period. The courts were largely but not exclusively concerned with
property offenders but this varied depending upon the level of the court system.
The summary courts, as they had in the previous century, largely regulated daily
life and dealt with tremendous numbers of East Londoners who came in after a
night of drunken excess or for committing some fairly minor theft. Many of those

appearing there and at the Old Bailey were recidivists – repeat offenders unable or unwilling to keep to the straight and narrow path. By the 1880s the majority of those that received custodial sentences were processed through Sir Edmund Du Cane's mechanistic prison system, which had effectively abandoned any pretence at reformation or rehabilitation almost by mid-century. English prisons may have once held vaunted ambitions to reintegrate convicts into society as changed men but for Du Cane and his contemporaries the prime consideration was in controlling those sent to gaol at the least cost to the public. What happened to them when they were released was of little concern. The result was that men emerged from penal servitude broken, resentful, malnourished and, in many cases, mentally disturbed by the experience. None of this equipped them for the world of work, instead it inured them to hardship and propelled them back into their former, criminal, pursuits. Sadly, we seem to have failed to draw any useful lessons from the history of prison administration and continue to fill our cells with short-term offenders who have little hope of reclamation.

In the final chapter of this study we turn to the forces that were supposed to deal – in the first instance at least – with the problems of crime and disorder on the streets of the capital. The Metropolitan Police famously failed to catch the Ripper and there are many reasons for this, not all of them straightforward or obvious.

# 8

# Watching the Detectives: The Police and the Hunt for Jack the Ripper

On 8 October 1888, one week after the 'double event', the *Pall Mall Gazette* published the first of a series of articles entitled 'The police and criminals of London'. The first of these was an attack on the appointment, if not the person, of Sir Charles Warren as chief commissioner of the Metropolitan Police. The article began by claiming it had no axe to grind with Warren over the events in Trafalgar Square, before going on to do exactly that.

> The collapse of the mainspring of the Metropolitan Police Force as a thief catching organization is due to Sir Charles Warren, and it is the direct consequence of the defects of his qualities. He is capable and energetic. He always thinks things will be best done if he does them himself. Hence the centralization of a camp has been forced upon the police, and the result has been to destroy the force as thief-catchers without converting them into a very effective military organization. The evil effect of the new system, by which the constable has been reduced to a more or less discontented machine, is naturally felt most in the Detective Department, which ought to be the brain of the force. Except for the purpose of dispersing meetings, the police force is breaking down. Those who know the force will declare that there has never been a time since the great strike when the police were so thoroughly out of hand and out of heart. There is no confidence anywhere, but discontent everywhere, and this discontent is felt most keenly at the headquarters of the force – in Scotland-yard itself.[1]

The events of November 1887, when a demonstration of the unemployed was broken up by police and the soldiery, have been covered in detail in Chapter 5. As we have seen 'Bloody Sunday' was twisted by the media and compared to the debacle of 1886 when rioters had attacked property in Pall Mall while police reserves rushed to the Mall to protect Buckingham Palace. At first the firm actions of the police on 'Bloody Sunday' were championed in the press as a victory over the 'dangerous classes' but then, in the pages of the radical press in particular, criticism began to be levelled at the military nature of policing in the capital. When a mysterious, brutal, murderer started to 'rip' prostitutes in the squalid streets of Whitechapel the editor of the *Pall Mall Gazette* spotted an opportunity to exploit the divisions between Warren, the Detective Department and the Home Secretary.

## THE HISTORY OF POLICING IN ENGLAND: A GRADUAL MOVE TOWARDS PROFESSIONALISM

In many ways the criticism of the police reflected an historical ambivalence towards policing in England that had overshadowed the creation and development of professional police forces from the early years of the nineteenth century. In 2000 Robert Reiner wrote that '[w]elcome or unwelcome, protectors, pigs or pariahs, the police are an inevitable fact of modern life'.[2] However, while it might be correct to see professional policing as a fixture of everyday life in the twenty-first century, it is much less clear that it was inevitable at the beginning of the nineteenth. In the last quarter of the eighteenth century, when fear of crime was on the increase, there were regular and forthright complaints about the effectiveness or otherwise of the amateur parish constables and poorly paid watchmen that policed rural and urban England. Some of this criticism was well deserved, but much of it has been taken out of context and exaggerated by early historians of the police. In recent years historians have undertaken detailed studies of policing agents that operated before Sir Robert Peel brought into existence the first professional police force in England in 1829. These have suggested much continuity between the amateurs of the late eighteenth and early nineteenth centuries and the professionals that replaced them.[3]

The creation of professional police forces was overshadowed by concerns about the curtailment of hard-won freedoms in the century following the civil wars between King Charles I and parliament and the 'Glorious Revolution' of 1688 which saw the quiet overthrow of the last Stuart monarch, James II. The notion of a standing army under the control of the monarch was anathema to the English aristocracy and ruling elite. Continental European states had quasi-military police forces that operated both to tackle crime and suppress political discontent. In the atmosphere of the wars against revolutionary and Napoleonic France there was little stomach for creating a police force that might in any way be seen as similar to the spies in uniform that answered to Fouché in Paris. Simply put, the notion of professional policing was altogether too *French*. Policing had traditionally been the preserve of local justices of the peace and was funded by ratepayers. Any suggestion that central government should take over control, or that additional funds should be raised, was firmly rebutted.

Attempts to create a uniform system of police in London in the wake of the chaos of the Gordon Riots were scuppered by the intransigence of the City of London in 1785, which was not prepared to give up control over its own policing networks – with some justification as they appear to have operated quite effectively.[4] In 1792, in response to concerns about the avarice of entrepreneurial JPs in Middlesex, seven police offices were established in the capital, with a small force of thief-takers attached to each. This reform was inspired by the example of Bow Street where Sir John Fielding had been developing a system of detection and patrols with some tacit support from government. However, when Peel eventually submitted his proposals for a professional body of policemen any detective element was notably absent. Once again this reflected the attitudes of Englishmen towards policing: detection was considered to be little more than a system of espionage. Thus, the 'new' police were distinguished not only by their blue swallow-tailed coats and stove-pipe hats, but also by their role. They were there to patrol the streets and by doing so prevent crime and maintain order. They were not thief-takers like their colleagues at Bow Street and it took some time for this situation to change.

The role of the new police brought them into immediate conflict with the working classes of nineteenth-century London. One way of conceptualizing the Victorian police has been to view them as 'domestic missionaries'; as tools of a puritanical middle class bent on dragging the degenerate proletariat up to their standards of decency and morality. This standpoint, which sits in stark contrast to early histories that depicted the police as much needed companions in the war on crime, places the police at the centre of a class war raging across the nineteenth century.[5] That the Victorian police acted as a 'lever of urban discipline' (as Robert Storch has characterized it) is evident in the sorts of activities they performed:[6] patrolling the streets, moving-on traders and dice players and arresting drunks and prostitutes. Policing was concentrated on the poorer, working-class districts of London, in the belief that controlling working-class behaviour would prevent crime in the wealthier areas of the capital: 'policing St. Giles to protect St. James' as it was sometimes called (St Giles was a notoriously poor and criminal area situated where Tottenham Court Road meets Oxford Street in the modern capital). This brought them into direct contact, and indeed conflict, with the inhabitants of working-class districts and those using the streets. Costermongers, or 'costers' (street traders who sold their wares from barrows), were particularly vexed at being told to 'move along' as they tried to eek out a living. Given that the police also broke up the recreational activities of costers – such as illegal dogfights – it is not surprising that punching a policeman (to the cry of 'Give it to the copper!') was a popular pastime. 'To serve out a policeman is the bravest act by which a costermonger may distinguish himself', one proud costermonger told Henry Mayhew.[7]

However, partial views such as Storch's can obfuscate the reality of the situation on the ground and Stephen Inwood's work on the early experiences of the Metropolitan Police has offered a more balanced view of police practice. Inwood demonstrated that while directives were circulated to the police that were aimed at curbing some expressions of working-class culture it is less clear that they were rigorously applied.[8] At an operational level the police appreciated that imposing notions of middle-class morality on working-class districts was fraught with difficulties. In order to police an area effectively the police knew they had to work *with* the community. If the actions of individual or collective policing alienated the broad mass of working people they would be unable to police by consent. The Met simply did not have enough officers or enough power to be 'domestic missionaries' in the way that this role has been envisaged by Storch.[9] As a result a 'softly softly' approach to policing working-class areas developed and the police achieved a level of toleration and respect among the policed communities. Working people were also quick to utilize the police courts, and the police themselves, to help resolve their disputes and prosecute those that offended, assaulted or robbed them, as Jennifer Davis' work on the police courts has shown.[10]

Thus, by the last quarter of the nineteenth century the police in London had at least overcome some of the incipient problems that had dogged their early development as a 'new engine power and authority' on the streets of the capital of Empire.[11] Despite this the *Pall Mall Gazette*'s attack was not entirely unfounded. The police, or at least those that ran the police – Warren and Home Secretary Henderson – were easy targets for press condemnation, as the Ripper apparently killed and mutilated at will. The *Gazette* was not alone in suggesting that the police had got their priorities all wrong, as Figure 8 demonstrates. The *Gazette* complained that:

> Battalion drill avails nothing when the work to be done is the tracking down of a midnight assassin, and the qualities which are admirable enough in holding a position or dispersing a riot are worse than useless when the work to be done demands secrecy, cunning, and endless resource.[12]

'Battalion drill' referred to Warren's apparent preference for seeing his men in uniform and on parade rather than in plainclothes skulking about the streets. This brings us back to the second issue that beset the embryonic police force in

MILITARY DRILL v. POLICE DUTY.

**Figure 8** 'Military drill v. police duty', *Funny Folks*, September 1888.[13]

the nineteenth century: the apparent absence of detection.

As we have seen the early commissioners of the Met shunned the notion of detection as un-English and unwelcome and so the new police followed the model of the old watch and *not* the Bow Street Runners. However, in 1842 the police came under intense pressure to catch the murderer of a woman whose dismembered body was found at a house on Putney Heath, Roehampton. The killer was quickly identified as Daniel Good but it took over a week to finally entrap the killer, who was found almost by accident by a former policeman working for the railways.[14] The garroting panic of 1862 further demonstrated the need for professional thief-takers adept at taking on what were seen as professional thieves emanating from the newly conceptualized 'criminal class'. The Detective Department was established in the wake of the Good murder enquiry and over the second half of the century the negative perception of detection was slowly eroded. The public began to warm to the idea of the detective as characters in popular fiction, such as Dickens' Inspector Bucket in *Bleak House* (based on the real-life Detective Inspector Field), helped to glamorize the role. Bucket was followed by Sergeant Cuff, in Wilkie Collins' *The Moonstone*, before

Sherlock Holmes firmly established the detective in the public psyche in the 1880s. The short stories of Conan Doyle demonstrated the value of detection in the capture of criminals and the solving of crime. The CID, created in 1878, was fully established by the time of the Whitechapel murders, claiming 15,000 arrests each year in London and by 1884 there were 294 police detectives on the Metropolitan force.

## FENIAN DYNAMITARDS: THE METROPOLITAN POLICE AND EARLY IRISH REPUBLICAN TERRORISM IN LONDON

Britain remained reluctant to create a political secret police such as existed in several Continental states, but increasingly pressures began to force moves in that direction. As a result of revolutionary politics in Europe, Britain had become home to political refugees such as Karl Marx and Friedrich Engels. While the press in England boasted that 'it would never happen here' the prospect of revolution and the growing fear that Britain's dominant position in the world was being undermined by foreign competition prompted a limited surveillance of radicals, anarchists, nihilists and socialists, some of whom were to be found among the new immigrant communities of the East End. Even the British Library was approached for a reader's ticket so that certain individuals, such as Marx and his daughter, could be watched. The threat to the Empire did not, however, come from the author of *Das Kapital* or from the black-coated bomb-throwing anarchists satirized by G. K. Chesterton in *The Man who was Thursday*. Britain's threat lay much closer to home in the unresolved and ongoing political time bomb that was Ireland and Irish nationalism.

In December 1884 James Gilbert Cunningham, newly arrived from New York City, took lodgings in Great Prescott Street. He had passed through customs with almost 60 lb. of American-made dynamite. Soon afterwards Henry Burton, taking a similar route as a steerage passenger, also arrived in East London and found digs at 5 Mitre Square, just inside the City and one of the sites of the Whitechapel murders. Unfortunately for Burton, one of the other residents at number 5 was a City policeman, Constable Wilson. Burton and Cunningham were Irish-Americans fully committed to the cause of Irish nationalism. They had come to bring terror to the heart of the Empire by attacking a number of high-profile locations, including the Houses of Parliament.[15]

Burton's role was to co-ordinate the bombings. The first of these, planned for 2 January, was on the underground railway. Joseph Hammond was the guard on the 8.57 train to Hammersmith that left Aldgate at 9.01 p.m., four minutes late.

As it passed the signal outside of Gower Street station on the Metropolitan Line at 9.14 p.m. there was a 'very loud explosion at the fore part of the train', which 'smashed the windows and put out all the lights'.[16] When it came into Gower Street a porter ordered all the passengers off so that the train could be examined for damage. PC Crawford, who was on duty outside Gower Street, heard the explosion and saw a 'flash and a cloud of dust' and hurried down to see what had happened. There he took names and addresses and calmed a screaming woman who had sustained a nosebleed. None of the injuries seemed that serious.

The newspapers carried reports of the 'outrage' in their morning editions; the *Pall Mall Gazette* secured the eyewitness testimony of one of the passengers, a Mr William Smith of Euston Road. Smith told the paper that:

> We had passed King's-cross without anything unusual happening, and were chatting quietly together when we were terrified by a fearful crash like thunder, accompanied by an immense sheet of flame, which seemed to lick the sides of the carriages, and for a moment it seemed as if the tunnel was on fire. To add to the terror of the situation both our lamps went out and we were left in total darkness. Several of the passengers cried out that they were hurt, and some women who were in the next compartment screamed loudly.

He went on to add that 'the force of the concussion threw us all off our seats, and umbrellas, hats and papers were mixed up in terrible confusion'.[17] The explosion also unseated the ticket collector, and was felt above ground by pedestrians, 'while the horses of the omnibuses and other vehicles were so startled by the noise that they were restrained only with great difficulty from running away'.[18] The police arrived and, with the help of Colonel Majende, the Home Office's inspector of explosives, examined the damage. The bomb had done relatively little damage to persons or property. While it had taken out the windows in the carriages and created a small hole in the tunnel wall it had singularly failed to halt the running of the underground for any significant period, nor had it, thankfully, taken any lives or caused serious injury.

Its more immediate effect was to remind English society that a small and desperate band of Irish republicans were determined to take violent direct action in support of their cause. There had been attacks in 1884 at Victoria Station and a number of other London terminals and three 'dynamitards' had blown themselves up in an attack on London Bridge. The blast was not intended to destroy the bridge, but to frighten the government. Sir Edward Jenkinson (assistant under secretary for police and crime in Ireland, and in charge of secret service operations there) then received reliable information that the Houses of Parliament were next on the terrorists' list of targets.[19] In May 1884, Robert Levy and his brother were in Trafalgar Square when they noticed a black bag unattended 'lying under one of the lions . . . facing the National Gallery'. Being naturally curious they examined it. Finding it locked, Robert gave it a kick before his sibling picked it up. This brought it to the attention of the policeman on duty in the square, who took the bag and the boys back to Scotland Yard. There the bag was opened and found to contain explosives: 17½ cakes wrapped separately in papers on which was printed 'Atlas powder A' to be precise.[20] The bag also contained detonators and fuses.

While the attack on Trafalgar Square had been foiled by the inquisitiveness of two teenage boys and the rather crude nature of the explosive device, three other bombs *had* exploded in London that May. One took out the windows at the rear of the Junior Carlton Club injuring five people, while a second exploded outside the home of Sir William Watkin Wynn on St James' Square. The most audacious attack, however, was on the offices of the recently created Special Irish Branch at Scotland Yard.[21] At 9.20 a.m. on 30 May an explosion damaged the buildings at the police headquarters injuring several people and knocking one officer unconscious. The 'enemies of civilisation have been busy this year [1884]', warned one regional newspaper, and they were clearly resuming the 'Dynamite War' in 1885.[22]

The first blow in this war had been struck in 1867 when an explosion at Clerkenwell Prison had shocked the English authorities. The Irish Republican Brotherhood (IRB) had been established in 1858 with the Fenian Brotherhood (FB) (named for the legendary prehistoric Irish army, the Fianna) being founded in New York City in the same year. The Clerkenwell outrage forced the English government to act – not to address the issue of Irish independence – but to tighten up security and create a secret service department to combat the threat posed by Irish terrorism.[23] Sir Robert Anderson, who was later to become involved in the Ripper investigation, was given a key role in counter terrorist measures. Over the next 17 years the Dynamite War unfolded with fundraising in the United States providing the means for a series of attempts on British interests at home and abroad. To counter this, the intelligence agencies tried to cultivate informers and stay one step ahead of the bombers. In Ireland coercive measures were in force, restricting the activities of political radicals; but no such measures were, or could be, applied in Britain or the USA, and both countries had very large Irish populations living among them.

On 6 May 1882, Lord Cavendish (the reluctant chief secretary to Ireland in waiting) and the permanent secretary, Thomas Burke, were assassinated as they walked through Phoenix Park in Dublin. Their killers left black-edged calling cards with a local newspaper office, claiming the murders were the work of the 'Irish Invincibles'.[24] The men of the FB had sworn an oath to 'labor with earnest zeal for the liberation of Ireland from the yoke of England and for the establishment of an independent government on the Irish soil'.[25] The Phoenix Park killings sent a chilling message to the British government and the politics of Ireland were to dominate home affairs throughout the last decades of the nineteenth century. May 1882 also saw an abortive attack on the Lord Mayor's residence at Mansion House in the heart of the City of London, while in June an IRB arms ring was uncovered by the secret service. The year 1883 saw dynamite attacks in Glasgow, London (including an attempt on the offices of *The Times*), attacks on the underground and the discovery of a bomb factory in Birmingham. Several bombers were arrested and Thomas Gallagher and others sentenced to life imprisonment. However, the war was not over, as the attacks in London in 1884 and 1885 confirmed.

It is clear from the work of the late K. R. M. Short that as English society was increasingly threatened by Irish terror tactics the quality and quantity of information that reached the security services was drying up: 'Fenian informers were becoming scarce as anti-English feeling steadily grew along with nationalist and Fenian certainty of eventual success'. The home secretary, Sir William Harcourt, was 'deeply depressed about the situation' as was the 'spymaster', Sir Edward Jenkinson.[26] Both men feared that without good and reliable information the bombers would be able to strike as and when they wished. Their worst fears were soon to be realized.

Despite the close attentions of the City of London police, Cunningham and Burton had managed to explode a bomb on the Metropolitan Line and had built three other devices that they planned to use to send another powerful message to the English ruling elite. On Saturday, 24 January 1885 they struck, choosing two symbolic targets of British rule: the Houses of Parliament and the Tower of London. Two bombers, probably disguised as man and wife, had smuggled their dynamite packages under their clothes and had split up on entering the Palace of Westminster. The female bomber had deposited her device in the crypt where it drew the attention of a couple of visitors. A Miss Davis spotted a parcel close to the first landing. According to the newspaper report on the Monday the parcel was 'about a foot square, a couple of inches thick, and was wrapped up in a piece of brown cloth, not unlike the material used for workmen's jackets'.[27] Miss Davis 'noticed that some steam or smoke was emanating from the bundle, but, unsuspicious of harm, would have passed on. Her brother-in-law, however, had observed the package, and at once cried "This is dynamite, run!"'[28] This brought the on duty policeman, PC Cole, running to the scene. Cole seized the lethal package and ran up the stairs, only for it to explode in his face.

The *Daily News* reported that 'in an instant the scene was one which even those who were there, through the bewildering terror which possessed them, find it impossible to describe. Cole was knocked down and had several ribs broken, and Police-constable Cox, who was close by, was also knocked down, severely shaken, and sustained a contusion on the head'.[29] Cox had run to the sound of the blast, abandoning his position in the lobby thus allowing the second bomber to drop his parcel in the chamber of the House of Commons where it went off a few minutes later causing considerable damage but no fatalities.

Over at the Tower, Cunningham had placed his device behind a screen in the White Tower where thousands of visitors regularly gathered to view the suits of armour and medieval weaponry. The bomb ignited at 2 p.m. just as those at parliament were set off, but apart from the associated terror and confusion there were few injuries. Elizabeth Balaan was knocked unconscious and was taken to the London Hospital on Whitechapel Road, and two boys suffered slight cuts. The *Pall Mall Gazette* reported that '[a]ll the visitors, except the injured were detained and closely questioned. One of these, a young man of twenty-one years, described as an Irish-American, was taken into custody and carried first to Leman-street police-station, and subsequently to Scotland Yard . . . He gave the name of Cunningham, with the aliases Gilbert and Dalton'.[30] One of the bombers was in custody and 'careful police work' soon led to the arrest of Thomas Burton who had been seen in conversation with Cunningham earlier in the month in Whitechapel.[31]

The newspaper reaction was generally, and understandably, one of outrage that the 'dynamitards' had struck again. *The Times* condemned the 'indiscriminate slaughter of holiday makers and working people' (despite the fact that no one had died) and argued that it was 'imperatively necessary to adopt vigorous measures, both offensive and defensive, against an insidious, unscrupulous, and implacable, though, in point of numbers as well as character, a thoroughly contemptible, enemy'.[32] The *Morning Advertiser* was quick to condemn the perpetrators as monsters: 'These dynamitards are in the fullest sense *hostes humani generis* [the 'enemies of mankind'], and should be treated as vermin outside the pale of ordinary law', before reminding their readers that it was the writers of inflammatory pamphlets that were really to blame. 'Englishmen may well ask' it continued, 'How long is this state of things to continue?'[33] In a similar vein the *Daily Chronicle* asked 'What is to be done towards stamping out this horror of horrors? We know the cause – the teaching of a demoralized and seditious press – the revilings [sic] of a villainous and ribald platform – both tolerated to an extent which has produced in our community the superlative degree of crime',[34] while the *Standard* demonstrated its failure to grasp the reality of the situation

Figure 9 The *Graphic's* dramatic illustration of the Fenian attack on the Palace of Westminster, January 1885, from Miss Davies' report.[35]

in Ireland by noting that: 'To the great body of the Irish it cannot, we are sure, be useless to address some words of warning and remonstrance. Let them consider what they have received from England during the last sixteen years, and then ask themselves whether they ought to make it evident to the whole world that they have no sympathy whatever with these atrocious schemes'. This echoed the comments of *Lloyd's Weekly Newspaper* in the wake of the underground attack that it was 'probably of little use to point out once more to their authors the utterly stupid criminality involved in these continued attempts on private property, which re-act on the Irish people as a whole; as is shown by the distrust with which many employers regard Irishmen, and their increased difficulty in obtaining work in many leading firms'.[36] The *Daily Telegraph* again used the bombings to criticize the police and their 'failure to catch even a single dynamitard in the fact', although the arrest of Cunningham would seem to have passed them by on this occasion.[37]

In Austria the *Allgemeine Zeitung* urged caution and a sense of perspective: 'Modern civilization is not to be frightened into fits because at the utmost a thousand madmen wage war against it. Nor will two entire continents place themselves under martial law and dictatorship because a few insane persons have succeeded in ruining some stonework and perhaps causing the death of one or two innocent persons'.[38] The *Warsaw Official Gazette*, perhaps unsurprisingly, called for international solidarity against a 'murderous alliance' of anarchists: 'To that league of destruction a league of defence must be opposed' – an international 'War on Terror' in nineteenth-century language perhaps.[39] One of these 'international anarchists' was asked his opinion on the London bombings: he was scathing. 'Stepniak', supposedly a Russian nihilist, dismissed the bombings as 'Mere baby work; any child could do as much. Stupid, objectless, directed against no particular individual, furthering no great cause'. The *Pall Mall Gazette* added,

> On the whole, £20,000 represents the outside damage done by the three carefully planned explosions about which all the world is talking this morning. No one was killed; about a score of men, women, and children were slightly injured; two policemen have lost their hearing; and that is all. A wretched twopenny halfpenny affair it is to be sure, and one which ought to be most reassuring and even comforting to all those who have watched the progress of the struggle between society and the demons of dynamite . . . [for] what have they done? Altogether they have not [in two years of the bombing campaign] done more damage than £100,000 would make good. They have not killed a creature, blocked a railway, destroyed a building, or in any way checked for a moment the even flow of English life.

It then ridiculed the conservative press for overreacting and calling for clampdowns on political protest and writings.[40]

Cunningham was charged at Bow Street Police Court with causing explosions and another detective who was to feature prominently in the Whitechapel murders, Frederick Abberline, appeared to insist the alleged bomber was detained in custody until his trial.[41] Burton and Cunningham went for trial at the Old Bailey in May 1885 and the court sat in judgement on them for a week before they were both found guilty (the later for the bombing of the Tower and the underground in January, and Burton for planting bombs at Charing Cross and Paddington stations in 1884). The evidence against them was considerable, with an army of expert witnesses and many who could identify the two men as having travelled from the United States to Liverpool. In response Cunningham called two single

Irish women to make statements on his behalf and Burton's legal representative read a prepared statement of denial. They received life sentences. PC Cole became something of a hero, having been hospitalized until late March as a result of his actions in Westminster Hall. The judge, Mr Justice Hawkins, 'called attention to a presentment by the Grand Jury, expressing their strong approval of the conduct of the Police in this case'; this must have been a welcome endorsement of the Met in trying times.[42]

## HEADLESS AND CLUELESS? THE HUNT FOR THE RIPPER

Unfortunately for the force this feeling of goodwill was not to last very long. Within a year of the successful conviction of the two Fenian dynamitards the windows of the Carlton Club on Pall Mall were being smashed and within two years Warren's handling of the demonstration of the unemployed in Trafalgar Square was being roundly condemned in the popular press. Things could have been very different: the *Pall Mall Gazette* identified Warren as a real Victorian boys' own hero – a man cut from the same pattern as Lord Gordon of Khartoum. However, Sir Charles' approach to policing was to concentrate on drill and marching and discipline, and he made no apologies for favouring the uniformed over the plainclothed branch of the force. He clashed notably with his putative boss, the Home Secretary Matthews, and his own subordinate, Assistant Commissioner CID James Monro. Politics played their part here as Monro enjoyed the confidence of the secretary of state while Warren was largely sidelined. At the end of August 1887 the relationship between Warren and Monro had deteriorated to such an extent that the latter resigned his position as head of CID. He was replaced by Sir Robert Anderson, whose role in countering terrorism has already been discussed. However, Anderson was not a well man and went on convalescent leave to Switzerland, something the *Pall Mall Gazette* was quick to highlight in the wake of the 'double event':

> In his [Anderson's] absence the Criminal Investigation Department is delivered over to anarchy plus the incessant interference of Sir Charles Warren. Now Sir Charles Warren is a very able General and a very excellent man, but Sir Charles Warren presiding over the Criminal Investigation Department is like a hen attempting to suckle kittens. He does not know the A B C of the business.[43]

Anderson had been absent from his desk before the death of Mary Nichols opened the official file into the Whitechapel murders and so, in effect, the CID was leaderless in the face of the most difficult inquiry in its short history. Indeed it was this rather than any other failing of the detective department that the paper chose to dwell upon:

> The chief official who is responsible for the detection of the murderer is as invisible to Londoners as the murderer himself. You may seek for Dr. Anderson in Scotland-yard, you may look for him in Whitehall-place, but you will not find him, for he is not there . . . No one grudges him this holiday. But just at present it does strike the uninstructed observer as a trifle off that the chief of London's intelligence department in the battle, the losing battle which the police are waging against crime, should find it possible to be idling in the Alps.[44]

Anderson's absence was being used as a stick with which to beat the home secretary and chief commissioner, however, it is questionable what the titular head of CID would have done differently if he had not been abroad or unwell. What does seem strange from a modern perspective is that he was not relieved of duty and someone else put in command. The problem of the Met would seem to have been one of co-ordination and leadership rather than the incompetence that has so often been alleged.

BLIND-MAN'S BUFF.
[As played by the Police.]
"TURN ROUND THREE TIMES,
AND CATCH WHOM YOU MAY!"

**Figure 10** 'Blind-man's buff', *Punch*, September 1888.[45]

The Ripper investigation has had a great deal of criticism, both from contemporaries and more recent histories as a contemporary cartoon from *Punch* illustrates (Figure 10). However, much of this criticism is unfair given the limited resources available to the police in the 1880s. The late Victorian police force was not as well provisioned with technology as their twenty-first century descendants: no DNA or crime pattern analysis, no offender profiling, no CCTV, no squad cars or mobile phones. Even fingerprinting was not to arrive until the last years of the century and the science of blood typing was yet to be developed. So the notion of forensic science was a distant pipedream for the detectives trailing the Whitechapel murderer. Given their relative infancy of detection techniques the police needed to catch the killer in the act.

Warren appointed Chief Inspector (CI) Donald Swanson to head the investigation while Abberline was brought in to lead the inquiry on the ground, as he was familiar with the area having been stationed there before moving to Scotland Yard.[46] The death of a prostitute was not an unusual event in the East End but violent deaths and murders were far from commonplace in the period and we should again be wary of believing the rhetoric of much of the popular press that was quick to point to the lawlessness and brutality of life in the poorer districts of the capital.

In terms of police procedure, Swanson recorded that a number of initiatives were taken by the police in the wake of the murders. House-to-house inquiries were made and 80,000 pamphlets asking for information were delivered. Common lodging houses in the area were visited and over 2,000 lodgers questioned. The Thames River Police looked into the movements of ships, since several witness statements had suggested that the killer had the look of a sailor (most probably a foreigner from the Portuguese merchant fleets or a 'Laskar'). As a result of their inquiries the police took 80 persons in for further questioning, while 300 other 'suspicious characters' were investigated. Butchers and slaughter-men had fallen under suspicion given their relationship with sharp knives and the cutting up of bodies. Whitechapel had been closely associated with the meat trade for centuries with cattle being driven there from Smithfield Market for slaughter. The large Jewish community was also served by many kosher butchers, or *shochets*. Therefore many butchers and those working in the related trades were interviewed and the 'characters of the men employed [therein] enquired into'. The police also looked into the movement of visitors to the area, such as a group of 'Greek Gipsies', the many foreign street entertainers and the 'Cowboys' and 'Indians' from 'Buffalo' Bill Cody's visiting American exhibition. Much of this was predicated on the notion that an Englishman could not have committed such an atrocious series of crimes.

Many arrests were made, some of them stupid ones. The widening police search in some ways revealed the pressure and desperation the Met faced in trying to prevent further tragedies and catch the murderer. In the aftermath of Annie Chapman's death Edward Quinn had been drinking at a bar near the Woolwich Arsenal. On his way to the bar he had tripped and fallen in the street, bruising and cutting his face and hands. His appearance was such that one of his fellow drinkers accosted him and told him 'I mean to charge you with the Whitechapel murders'. Quinn tried to laugh it off but eventually he was taken to the nearest police station and sent before the magistrate at Woolwich Police Court. There he protested his innocence declaring: 'Me murder a woman! I could not murder a cat', which drew some laughter from the courtroom. Quinn was released, another unfortunate victim of the fervor that surrounded the killings.[47]

Advice came forward from psychics and spiritualists; a relatively new and widely discredited 'science' that attracted those people, like Madame Blavatsky, to the idea that the spirit world could offer answers for the living. But the advances of these 'meddlers' were largely ignored by detectives who were sifting through the growing piles of information and leads relating to the case. One of the more bizarre and disturbing aspects of the Ripper case was the huge number of hoax letters and false leads that were sent to the police via the Central News Agency and the London press. Commissioner Warren looked into the possibility of using bloodhounds but this became a bit of a farce: two dogs were borrowed and underwent some training but it would have been impossible to expect a blood-hound to follow a trail through the streets of East London with all the competing scents and the total failure to preserve the crime scene. It was also suggested that the police should photograph the eyes of the victim. It was believed, by some, that the retinas of dead persons retained the image of the last person they had seen before death – in this case hopefully that would have been the murderer. However bizarre this may seem the home secretary did write to Warren after the 'double event' to ask if it had been attempted – it had not. More sensibly, it is possible that the police may have issued an order to prostitutes, following Catherine Eddowes' death, to stay off the streets or effectively lose police protection. No order has survived in the police file but no murders 'on the street' happened after October – Mary Kelly was killed indoors. Police constables also fitted strips of rubber to their hobnailed boots to reduce the noise; plainclothes detectives prowled the streets and infested the local pubs, and it was suggested that beat bobbies should disguise themselves as women to entrap the killer.

There was an ongoing argument about the value of offering rewards for information with Warren, initially at least, very much against it. The local chairman of the Whitechapel Vigilance Committee, George Lusk, accused the government and police of double standards in not stumping up a reward when they had been quick to do so after Lord Cavendish's murder by Irish republicans years earlier. To many in the East End it seemed that elite lives were given a much higher value than those of the poor 'unfortunates' that serviced the sexual needs and desires of poor and well-to-do male Londoners. Following the murder of Catherine Eddowes on City territory in Mitre Square and a well-attended public meeting where the government and police were loudly criticized, the City of London Police and the lord mayor put up rewards of £500. Warren again told Matthews that a reward was 'of no practical use' before then advocating one of £5,000. Matthews smelt a rat, and in a private letter he complained that: 'Anybody can offer a reward and it is the first idea of ignorant people. But more is expected of the CID. Sir C. W. will not save himself, or put himself right with the public, by merely suggesting that.'[48]

In the eighteenth century rewards were commonplace. Individuals could earn rewards from the successful prosecution of felons for a number of property crimes including highway robbery and horse theft.[49] This had led to corrupt practices and the emergence of blood-money scandals, the last of which had been exposed in 1816 and 1818. Concerns about entrepreneurial policing had been voiced in the debates about the creation of a professional force and the government was understandably reluctant not to return to the practice in the 1880s. However, some individuals – Samuel Montagu MP and George Lusk himself – did offer private rewards for information about the Whitechapel murders.[50] The home secretary himself was clear that offering a reward would be a retrograde step, and he told the House of Commons his reasons for this. The Home Office had frequently offered rewards but had abandoned the practice in 1884 after a conspiracy to conceal a bomb at the German Embassy (and then frame an individual using planted evidence) was exposed. Matthews went on to add, with some justification given the numerous examples of persons being accused in the streets, that while there might be occasions when rewards were necessary (for example, to illicit information about the whereabouts of the murderer if his identity became known):

> In the Whitechapel murders, not only are these conditions wanting at present, but the danger of a false charge is intensified by the excited state of public feeling.[51]

The panic that was induced by the killings and the police's failure to catch the murderer manifested itself in a number of ways and touched areas far beyond the capital. An elderly man walking in an unspecified mining district of England was accosted by a group of 'seven stout collier lads'. They accused him of being 'Jack the Ripper' and demanded he 'come along wi' us' to the nearest police station. In Whitechapel a young chestnut seller reported a bizarre encounter with a man who claimed to know a great deal about the killing of Mary Kelly. The stranger was dressed 'like a gentleman' complete with tall silk hat and a black shiny bag that apparently contained, 'Something the Ladies don't like'.[52] A German visitor walking down the Whitechapel Road was chased by a mob after a woman stared into his face and screamed 'he's Jack the Ripper!' and a plainclothes police officer suffered similar manhandling by local 'roughs' who mistook him for the notorious killer on account of his 'low broad-brim hat of rather singular appearance'.[53] An arrest was made on the Old Kent Road when a man left a bag at a public house that was found to contain a variety of sharp implements including a 'very sharp dagger' and two pairs of 'very curious looking scissors'.[54] Meanwhile even as far away as Glasgow the police were warned to be on their guard at night; 'if they hear any cry of distress, such as "Help," "Murder," or "Police," they are to hasten to the spot at once'. This latter request seems somewhat unnecessary since presumably they might have been expected to undertake that particular task without the need for a circular to remind them.[55]

It should be remembered that aside from the Ripper inquiry the Met still had to continue to perform a great deal of mundane daily tasks. The *Pall Mall Gazette's* concerted attack on the London force included a detailed analysis of police numbers and roles. The Met numbered some 13,315 men in 1888 and 1,500 of these were patrolling the streets in four-hour shifts between 6 a.m. and 10 p.m. before 5,000 night officers came on to relieve them. A further 464 officers were stationed at fixed points throughout the capital during the day. Licensed cabs and other vehicles had to be checked, letters and correspondence read and answered, inquiries into crimes followed up and recorded. The *Pall Mall Gazette* noted that:

> In the course of the twenty-four hours they will take into custody 181 persons, of whom 40 will be drunk and disorderly, 16 simply drunk, 10 will be disorderly persons, 8 will be disorderly prostitutes, while about 4 will be arrested merely as suspicious characters, and 12 as vagrants. One-half of the arrests will be for offences against order, the other half will be criminal. Taking one day with another the police run in every twenty-four hours about 30 thieves, 18 persons guilty of assault, while there are nearly half-a-dozen persons locked up for assaults on the police nearly every day all the year round.[56]

This range of activity is echoed by the records of the Thames Police Court as we saw in the previous chapter. From the surviving ledgers of the court we can see that in September 1888 policemen were bringing in large numbers of drunks, disorderly persons, prostitutes and petty thieves including a number of young boys found guilty of setting off fireworks in the streets. Many of those appearing had been accused of assault – sometimes on the police as a subsidiary to being arrested for drunkenness. The *Pall Mall Gazette* noted that these latter assaults nearly always resulted in convictions and the magistrates at the Thames Police Court fined offenders 10s or sent them to gaol. Overall the paper praised the average bobby on the beat, ending its report on police duties with the comment that 'sufficient has been said to show that they do a very good day's work every twenty-four hours'.[57] *The Graphic* had echoed these sentiments in 1887. Although it acknowledged that within a body of men as large as that of the Metropolitan Police there were bound to be a 'few erring mortals in their midst' there were also 'men of pluck and fibre, doing their duty honestly, valiantly and well'.[58]

Victorian police officers in the capital were largely drawn from the ranks of the working classes, as Haia Shpayer-Makov's important study of the late Victorian force has established.[59] The constituency for police officers was the same as that for the ranks of the army – steady, reliable men who would obey their social superiors and not question orders. The early police commissioners believed that solid agricultural workers would produce the best recruits but the evidence of Shpayer-Makov's study suggests that a broader cross section of working men joined the force, many of them coming from outside of the capital. The work of a London bobby was rather dull and repetitive with an emphasis on beat patrolling over investigation and the commensurate risk of physical violence in the more dangerous areas such as St Giles and the East End. As a result, in the early years of the force many of those who had exchanged jobs as skilled members of the working classes left the Met in their droves. The force was left with 'men from unskilled or semi-skilled backgrounds, for whom the police service was an avenue of upward mobility'.[60] A career in the police represented an opportunity for steady work at a reasonable rate of pay in a period when pay and the availability of the work was subject to the fluctuations of trade and the wider economy. This probably resulted in the police being largely staffed with men of little imagination who were not well suited to the pursuit of a cunning serial murderer. However, they were generally honest, hard-working and physically strong, healthy (an advantage given that in the poorer districts of London illness and malnutrition were commonplace) and taller than average so that they were able to deal with most of the trouble they might encounter on the streets.

Sir Charles Warren's commitment to 'battalion drill' (as the *Pall Mall Gazette* so disparagingly dismissed it) was almost all the training new recruits received. Apart from learning how to obey orders and walk their beat at a steady pace, a new London bobby would have had to have learnt the rest of his trade on the job from his colleagues. In this, as Shpayer-Makov shows, a police culture was disseminated to the new members of the force. As Stephen Inwood's work also demonstrates local policemen therefore learnt how to police their particular areas, regardless, in some respects, of how the upper echelons wished them to operate. Naturally this closeness to the community may have led some to get a little too cosy with the locals they policed and corruption was always possible, on the other hand, however, it probably allowed them to get the information they needed to deal with more serious criminality. The imbedded antipathy towards the police from some sections of East End society was certainly a factor in the failure of the Met to catch the Ripper. In some respects the Victorian police could not win: the middle classes saw policemen as unimaginative 'jobsworths' while the working classes complained that they were indiscriminate in their targets and open to bribes. Many working-class people would have probably resented being lectured by men from their own background while the middle classes expected them to behave as their servants did.

## CONCLUSION

Could the Metropolitan Police have caught the Whitechapel killer? Why did they fail? The answer is complex but I think that history has been a little hard on the police. Serial killers are extremely rare and very hard to track. Most murderers leave clues because they kill those close to them while serial murderers choose strangers. Without the benefits of modern technology and forensic science the Victorian police were severely hamstrung and almost totally reliant upon catching 'Jack' in the act. The nature of the victims meant that the murders occurred in out of the way places where few witnesses were likely to have seen anything. They were also not an organization steeped in the principles of detection, and for this Warren and his predecessors are perhaps culpable. The evolving history of policing in England, and the problematic relationship between the police and the public, meant that detectives were thought of with suspicion for much of the century. The failure of the Ripper inquiry did result in a gradual improvement in policing methods and the resignation of Warren no doubt helped this process. Thereafter the Met had a less military feel to it. One final point is worth considering in the light of the supposed failure to apprehend the murderer. If one believes that the killer was actually a poor immigrant Jew called Kosminsky (or similar) then the notion that the inquiry failed has to be revised. If Paul Begg is correct then the police did capture the Ripper but were unable to persuade an important witness, possibly Israel Schwarz, to give evidence in court. This might be another convenient device to explain why he was never prosecuted but it does have a certain credibility. The suspect was locked up in a mental asylum where he died some years later. So if perhaps the police did have their man, we will probably never know.[61]

# 9

# London's Shadows: The Darker Side of the Victorian Capital

In 1888 London was the capital of the greatest empire the world had ever known. In the opulent thoroughfares of the West End the glittering lamps illuminated the homes of the wealthy and the emporiums that provided the countless luxuries they enjoyed. Robert Cecil, the second marquis of Salisbury led the Conservative government that ruled from 1886 to 1892 and then had the dubious honour of presiding over the debacle of the South African War. At Buckingham Palace the elderly Queen Victoria had celebrated her golden jubilee the previous year. London led the world in transportation: the underground railway was 25 years old in 1888, the Paris metro was still two years away while the New York subway did not begin operating until 1904. London was also a place of entertainment with dozens of theatres and music halls offering an eager public a dazzling array of burlesque, melodramas, spectacular shows and pantomime to cater for all tastes and budgets. If you had the money then late nineteenth-century London had everything one might wish for.

However, there was a dark side to Victorian London. In the shadows lurked all manner of vice and crime, degradation and despair. The late Victorian period had witnessed a gradual rise in criminality after a steady decline from the mid-century. There was a sense that the new police were no longer winning the war on crime and commentators questioned the leadership of the 'boys in blue'. On the streets of the East End the costermongers still grumbled that these 'blue locusts' were more intent on disrupting their recreational habits and interfering with their attempts to scrape together a living than they were in dealing with proper villains.

The wealth of the West was in stark contrast with the poverty of the East as Charles Booth was to discover. Booth was unconvinced by the socialist agitator Hyndeman's claim that poverty was rife in the capital and set out to deploy the new science of social investigation to prove his point. Instead he discovered that the situation was much worse than he had suspected. As armies of reformers, do-gooders, Christian missionaries and journalists swarmed into the alleys and courts of Spitalfields and Whitechapel they could see for themselves the debilitating effects of overcrowding and abject poverty. The term 'unemployment' entered the dictionary in 1888 and has remained a constant measure of economic failure in Britain ever since.

The middle-class charity visitors had differing views of the poor but most, if not all, believed that there were real problems being stored up for society in the future. Many fundamentally believed that poor living conditions, which required families to share cramped accommodation and forced brothers and sisters to sleep together, was corrupting the morals of the working classes. Incest may not have been 'common' as Andrew Mearns had alleged but it was not unheard of. Cholera had been eradicated, largely thanks to John Snow's discoveries in the late 1850s, but mortality rates were still much higher in the East than in the rest of London. With desperate poverty came a retreat from Christianity and missionaries were as keen to minister to the spiritual needs of the people of the East End as they were to the 'savages' of the African continent in the earlier years of the century. What the poor made of all these well-meaning Christian ladies appearing on their doorsteps is hard to judge: some may well have welcomed the attention and the attempts to help, others probably resented the intrusion into their homes. In the words of women like Margaret Tillyard we can hear the prevailing voice of a paternalistic ruling class that believed it had a duty towards those it clearly felt to be its social inferiors.

We can be critical of individuals such as Beatrice Webb and Helen Bosanquet and accuse them of failing to understand that the real problems of nineteenth-century society were based in the economic inequality that powered the wheels of Victorian industry and progress. Simply put, if Victorian Britain was to be the most powerful nation in the world then the capitalist system demanded sacrifices. That so many of these were concentrated in the poorer districts of the capital was an inevitable consequence of years of inequality and neglect. Despite fears that the great unwashed residuum of East London would be seduced by the type of socialist or anarchist revolutionary politics that blighted continental Europe, the worst that the capital experienced was an occupation of Trafalgar Square and a few days of rioting. Paris suffered considerably worse in the dark days of the Commune. London labour was never as well organized as the ruling classes feared and the partial extension of the franchise in 1867 and 1884 had given a semblance of power to working men.

The Ripper murders concentrated attention on the area but it would be wrong to argue that they were responsible for dramatic change or reform. After all, men like Samuel Barnett, the rector of St Jude's, had been working quietly in the district for many years before. The model dwelling movement had been around since mid-century and had been attempting to improve conditions, as had the Cross and Torrens legislation in the last quarter. Reform had been largely ineffective, as much Victorian reform was, because it lacked a powerful body to implement it. The Metropolitan Board of Works was woefully ill-equipped to take on the improvement of centuries of slum building and private profiteering. In 1888 the London County Council was created and arguably it was the investiture of this august body that provided the impetus for real change. That said, the social problems of the East End – exacerbated as they were by waves of overseas immigration in the last 25 years of the century – were not really addressed until after the Second World War and the introduction of social welfare policies by Atlee's Labour government.

The press were also behind the move to improve conditions in the East End of London. Journalists such as Jack London went undercover to expose the worst excesses of doss houses. Much of this rings a little hollow to the modern reader; how much they were keen to promote change and how much they simply wanted to sell newspapers is open to question. Perhaps we should give then the benefit of the doubt and recognize that we are probably guilty of viewing the 'new journalism' of the nineteenth century from the perspective of our own disillusion with the tawdry modern media machine. Men like William Stead were driven by a desire to see real change and if his methods left behind martyrs to his cause like Rebecca Jarrett perhaps that is a small price to pay for ensuring that fewer teenage girls were routinely raped and abused for the gratification of wealthy Victorian gentlemen. Stead's final outing was to see him take a newly launched liner on a fateful voyage across the Atlantic. He died on the *Titanic*, so never got to file the copy.

Stead had chosen to highlight the traffic in young women, a cause that had been taken up earlier without success. Throughout the century, and indeed in our own, the problem of prostitution was discussed and agonized over by politicians, reformers and social purity campaigners. In the 1860s it was the state of the nation's armed forces that worried contemporaries like William Acton. The result was the introduction of unpopular legislation that attempted to control the activities of prostitutes and by implication, all working-class women. The Contagious Diseases Acts were eventually repealed after a long campaign but they reflect the gender inequalities of late Victorian Britain. In a footnote to Josephine Butler's campaign we might reflect that many of the women that became involved in her campaign went on to take their new-found political consciousness into the movement for women's votes. This crude attack on the female body corporeal helped formulate the female body *politic*.

William Stead helped to change the British newspaper industry by presenting the news in a new and exciting way for a growing and more literate population. The *Pall Mall Gazette* and its imitators used headlines and pictures to spice up the news – these have a much more 'modern' feel to them than the staid and solid columns of *The Times*. In the second half of the century newspapers reported more and more crime stories to titillate and frighten their readers in equal measure and we can learn much about contemporary attitudes towards criminality from their pages. The late Victorians were keen to place the blame for most property crime on a mythic 'criminal class' that consisted of a whole host of stereotypes of hardened villains with apelike faces and hunched shoulders. The casual criminal that appeared at the Thames Police Court charged with petty theft or drunkenness could be dismissed as a victim of circumstances or need but the Bill Sykes' of this world were highlighted as belonging to another race. The *Pall Mall Gazette* may have poked fun at the Italian criminologist Cesare Lombroso's study of criminality but the authorities certainly operated a policy of dealing with habitual criminals firmly. The prison system of the late Victorian period was no picnic for those who found themselves within the walls of Pentonville or Holloway.

That many of these felons hailed from the East End was of no surprise to Charles Booth and others. Large parts of Whitechapel and Spitalfields were coloured black on his poverty maps and indentified as the habitat of the criminal and those that would not work. Walter Dew, the policeman that was the first to view Mary Kelly's mutilated body, observed that Whitechapel was an area with a 'reputation for vice and villany unequalled anywhere in the British Isles'.[1] His comments may well have reflected a frustration with the inability of the police to catch the Whitechapel murderer and a desire to shift some of the blame onto the area and its people. Indeed this seems to have been a device employed by several of the newspapers of the period. The killer epitomized all that was rotten in the slums of Whitechapel – a phantom born out of the filth and degradation of Godless communities. From the moment he started killing poor women, 'Jack' became a cultural construction used to serve a multitude of diverse causes. He was a purifying angel, an enlightened reformer and a harbinger of revolution.

The mythologizing of 'Jack' has continued ever since. He has been seen as a decadent milord, an English gentleman preying on poor working-class women who have no value in his notion of society. Alternatively 'Jack' is a medical man, someone who has ripped up the Hippocratic oath as assuredly as he ripped open his victim's bodies. Both myths mirror contemporary fears about a decadent aristocracy and the growth of the medical profession. Lastly, the killer had to be a foreigner because no Englishman could possibly commit such bestial and horrific crimes and have the intelligence to get away with it. After all, with the exception of the 'master criminal' Charlie Peace, the criminal classes of London were poor specimens of humanity and the steady bobbies of the Met would surely have captured 'Jack' had he been one of them.

But to frame the killer as a foreigner – more specifically as an immigrant Jew who had fled persecution in the Russian Empire – fitted contemporary concerns about immigration and religious difference. The Jewish community of the East End suffered abuse in the summer of 1888 as scapegoats were sought and the papers were quick to trot out all the usual rhetoric of anti-Semitism. Men like Arnold White were quite happy to perjure themselves before parliamentary committees if it led to a stoppage of immigrants from Eastern Europe. Much of the prejudice that was aimed at the 'greeners' from the pale was a result of cultural differences of language and religious practice. For others, like the socialist leader Henry Mayers Hyndman, the age old accusation that the immigrants were taking British jobs was used as cover for their own racist opinions. East End Jewry survived the Ripper panic and went on to survive Mosely's Blackshirts. They left the East End in the postwar period as their industriousness earned them better homes in the north of the capital, not because they were chased out by small mindedness and prejudice. The East End has long provided a temporary refuge for foreign immigrants drawn by persecution or a desire to improve their economic situation; now the area is largely settled by Bangladeshi Muslims who are reaping the current hysteria surrounding Islamist terrorism.

As I have hopefully suggested throughout this book the East End itself has been the subject of manipulation to the extent that its identity is hard to define. Geographically we may know where it lies but trying to determine who is an 'Eastender' and what the 'East End' means is unlikely to produce a single, definitive, answer. In walking around the area where the Ripper killed five or more women in 1888 one is struck both by the relative closeness of the sites – and therefore the sense that this is a small area of the capital – and by the dynamic nature of change that continues every year. East London is undergoing rapid development even as I write, with millions of pounds of taxpayers' money being spent in rejuvenating the area ahead of the 2012 Olympics. East London is having a facelift, similar to that of the London Docks in the 1980s and arguably the area around Liverpool Street and Commercial Street in the 1880s. The geography of the East End will be altered to make way for new businesses, new roads, new facilities and new homes. Whether this will ultimately serve the needs of its people is another moot point. The slum clearance of the late Victorian period did little more than displace thousands of poor Londoners, forcing them to room with friends and family locally. Without easy and affordable transport links to their places of work there was little hope that native East Londoners could hope to move out to the leafy suburbs to live alongside the more affluent middle classes.

This study is called *London's Shadows* because it is about those aspects of late Victorian society that so frightened and exercised contemporaries. Poverty, prostitution and crime were the stains on the Imperial map that were not shown in the atlases of the day. Those maps proudly painted large swathes of the world in pink to testify to the grandeur of British Imperial power. Many Victorians would probably have preferred to ignore the fact that this power and wealth was built upon the conquest of inferior peoples and the exploitation of millions of working people. After all to do so was to recognize that something was wrong and, content in their comfortable drawing rooms and gentlemen's clubs, few felt the need to look at the world too closely – especially the world that was just across the metropolis.

Jack the Ripper changed this, if only for a brief period. At the opening of the most recent Ripper movie, *From Hell*, the strapline declares that 'One day men will look back and say that I gave birth to the Twentieth Century'.[2] This is of course is not a quote from the Ripper himself since his identity remains a mystery. It may derive, though, from one of the many letters, Maybrick's diary or from Alan Moore's graphic novel. It is undoubtedly a creation of fiction but it once again serves to remind us that the murders were seen as representative of a changing society. The murders characterize a certain loss of innocence and jar with our images of cheery East End life peopled by chirpy cockney pearly kings and queens. This was far from the reality of the nineteenth-century East End – just as the Queen Vic and Albert Square depict a fantasy of East London today.[3]

The Whitechapel murders continue to fascinate, and inspire countless new documentaries, films and true crime studies every year. They do so because they tap into our inner fears about murder and serial killing – which are out of all proportion to the actual risk we face as individuals. The Ripper crimes were almost unique in the period and even if we have had plenty of serial murderers since then the chances of anyone reading this book falling victim to such a twisted fiend are probably less than your chances of winning the lottery. So is there any value in continuing to search for the murderer of Polly Nichols, Annie Chapman, Elizabeth Stride, Catherine Eddowes and Mary Kelly? After all what are we going to discover? Certainly not the true identity of 'Jack the Ripper', at least not to the satisfaction of everyone with a vested interest in the case. Is there more to understand about the lives of the women that plied their trade on the streets around Flower and Dean Street? When the archives at The Women's Library open the files on hundreds of street prostitutes we might gain a little more detail about their lives and motivations but we have some years to wait. When we do it will probably tell us that most of those walking the streets were poor and living a hand-to-mouth existence. It will tell us that they were often depressed (several women were prosecuted at the Thames Police Court for attempting suicide in the 1880s) and frequently dependent upon alcohol. It will be no surprise to learn that they had failed marriages or abusive partners, that they had been in and out of the workhouse or infirmary and that many of them were chronically ill. This did not make them all victims of the Ripper. Whoever the Ripper was, he was only responsible for the deaths of between five and nine women who are listed in the Metropolitan Police files at The National Archives. Hundreds of poor working-class women prostituted themselves and suffered more mundane deaths than the victims of the Ripper.

If there is a reason to continue to study the events of August to November 1888 then it is to try to understand the reality of the lives of ordinary people living in one of the most depressed corners of the British Empire. We know more about them because of the efforts of contemporary journalists and essayists as well as the more recent writings of local historians and amateur sleuths. History has often been the unseen victim of much of the verbiage written about the case. According to one important historiographical study the historian's 'first duty is [to] accumulate factual knowledge about the past – facts which are verified by applying critical method to the primary sources; those facts will in turn determine how the past should be explained or interpreted'.[4] However, in many of the books written about the Ripper the facts have been treated with scant care and dismissed or ignored when they fail to fit a preferred thesis. An earlier work than John Tosh's noted that the expression 'the facts speak for themselves' is incorrect.[5] The esteemed historian Edward Carr declared that the facts 'speak only when the historian calls on them: it is he who decides to which facts to give the floor, and in what order or context'.[6] Many of the facts of the Ripper case are open to interpretation, still more have been lost or stolen or destroyed. This allows each new interpretation to be presented and so the role of testing has been adopted by the ever-growing band of brothers (and sisters) who maintain the Casebook website and its multitude of message boards. Many of them will undoubtedly pick some holes in my own analysis of the case and indeed the area and period of history.

The past does have lessons to teach us about the present and the study of crime and poverty in the past necessarily chimes with problems in our own period. We are not living in late nineteenth-century Britain. We have a system of welfare that, despite its cracks and creaks, manages to cope with the worst excesses of poverty. The state supports our basic needs by redistributing wealth in a way that our Victorian ancestors would hardly have credited. Many of us take the National Health Service and the Universal State Pension for granted, while grumbling that the former is ineffectual and too costly and that the latter does not provide nearly enough for our aging society. In 1888 neither of these institutions existed, neither did income support or child and unemployment benefits. But before we sit back and congratulate ourselves on the progress we have made we might reflect on Oxfam's calculation that one in five of the British population is still living in poverty. This means that over 13 million of us fall below a set of indicators that measure poverty levels in the UK and elsewhere.[7] Now these can be challenged, as can Seebohm Rowntree's study in York in 1901 and Charles Booth's analysis of London in the 1880s. It remains a fact that we live in an economically unequal society. One of the results of this is that some people will turn to crime as a way of coping with their inability to earn money in any other way. Inequality breeds dissatisfaction and alienation. Some of those who steal and kill do so because they feel little empathy with a society that has seemingly rejected or at best overlooked them. Others steal because they have reached the point at which they cease to care about a society that holds nothing for them so they turn to stimulants such as alcohol and drugs, and fund their addictions through petty crime.

The continual cry of the people of Whitechapel in the midst of the murder panic was that no one cared about the plight of the poorest members of society. If the Ripper had chosen to butcher the wife of a wealthy banker or a member of the Royal Family then rewards would have been offered and the entire effort of the police in the capital directed towards his capture. Churchill was right to highlight the dangers of ignoring the plight of the poor in a society where there was an 'unnatural gap between rich and poor', but despite the efforts of the past 120 years we have still not managed to eradicate this distinction.[8] This is why we must study the past: to make sure that we do not forget why we need to change the future.

# Notes

*Notes to Chapter 1: Creating the 'Myth' of Jack the Ripper*

1  *The Monthly Packet* (1/8/1882)
2  *The Monthly Packet* (1/8/1882)
3  *The Monthly Packet* (1/8/1882)
4  Alexandra Warwick and Martin Willis (eds), *Jack the Ripper: Media, Culture, History*, (Manchester: Manchester University Press, 2007); Alex Werner and Peter Ackroyd, *Jack the Ripper and the East End*, (London: Chatto & Windus, 2008); Lee Perry Curtis, *Jack the Ripper and the London Press*, (New Haven: Yale University Press, 2002)
5  www.casebook.org
6  'Jack the Ripper: Killer Revealed', *Discovery Channel* (October 2010)
7  Christopher Frayling, 'The House that Jack Built', in Warwick and Willis (eds), *Jack the Ripper*, 17
8  Frayling, 'The House that Jack Built', 26
9  Stewart Evans and Paul Gainey, *The Lodger: Arrest and Escape of Jack the Ripper*, (London: Century, 1993)
10  C. E. Purcell and B. A. Arrigo, *The Psychology of Lust Murder: Paraphilia, Sexual Killing, and Serial Homicide*, (California: Academic Press, 2006) 26
11  Inspector Littlechild, quoted in Evans and Gainey, *The Lodger*
12  Tony Williams and Humphrey Price, *Uncle Jack*, (London: Orion, 2005)
13  Robin Odell, 'Jack in the Box', *Journal of the Whitechapel Society*, 2, (June 2005)
14  Stephen Knight, *Jack the Ripper: The Final Solution*, (Chicago: Academy Chicago, 1986); see also Melvyn Fairclough, *The Ripper and the Royals* (London: Duckworth, 1991) which includes a foreword by Joseph Sickert
15  Alan Moore, *From Hell*
16  Jean Overton Fuller, *Sickert and the Ripper Crimes* (Oxford: Mandrake, 2001)
17  For a detailed examination of the 'Ripper' correspondence see Stewart P. Evans and Keith Skinner, *Jack the Ripper: Letters from Hell*, (Stroud: Sutton, 2001)
18  Clive Bloom, 'The Ripper Writing: A Cream of a Nightmare Dream', in Warwick and Willis (eds), *Jack the Ripper*, 92
19  Bloom, 'The Ripper Writing', 105
20  *Punch* (29/9/1888)

*Notes to Chapter 2: Murder and Mayhem in Victorian London: The Whitechapel Murders of 1888 in context*

1  www.oldbaileyonline.org (t18660709–616, trial of Patrick Harrington); *Lloyd's Weekly Newspaper*, (1/7/1866)

2  www.oldbaileyonline.org (t18751122–1, trial of Henry and Thomas George Wainwright)

3  www.oldbaileyonline.org (t18751122–1, trial of Henry and Thomas George Wainwright)

4  *The Bristol Mercury* (1/1/1875)

5  *The Illustrated Police News* (8/10/1892)

6  *The Times* (2/2/1888)

7  *Lloyd's Weekly Newspaper* (8/4/1888)

8  Philip Sugden, *The Complete History of Jack the Ripper* (London: Da Capo Press, 2002), 32

9  *The Illustrated Police News* (14/4/1888)

10  *The Illustrated Police News* (14/4/1888)

11  *Daily News* (16/8/1888)

12  www.oldbaileyonline.org (t18880917–834, trial of Richard Patterson)

13  *Pall Mall Gazette* (3/10/1888)

14  *Birmingham Daily Post* (3/10/1888)

15  *Birmingham Daily Post* (3/10/1888)

16  Catherine E. Purcell and Bruce A. Arrigo, *The Psychology of Lust Murder: Paraphilia, Sexual Killing, and Serial Homicide*, (California: Academic Press, 2006), 1

17  Dr Richard von Krafft-Ebing, *Psychopathia Sexualis with Especial Reference to Contrary Sexual Instinct: A Medico-Legal Study*, (London: F. A. Davis, 1893) translated by C. G. Chaddock

18  Krafft-Ebing, *Psychopathia Sexualis*, 59

19  Purcell and Arrigo, *The Psychology of Lust Murder*, 1

20  Purcell and Arrigo, *The Psychology of Lust Murder*, 6–7

21  Purcell and Arrigo, *The Psychology of Lust Murder*, 21

22  Robert K. Ressler, Ann W. Burgess and John E. Douglas, *Sexual Homicide. Patterns and Motives*, (London: Simon & Schuster, 1993), 123

23  Ressler, Burgess and Douglas, *Sexual Homicide*, 131

24  Gwynn Nettler, *Criminal Careers Volume 2: Killing One Another*, (Ohio: Anderson Publishing, 1982), 131

25  Purcell and Arrigo, *The Psychology of Lust Murder*, 21

26  Krafft-Ebing, *Psychopathia Sexualis*, 66

27  Robert Anderson, 'The lighter side of my official life', *Blackwood's Magazine*, 187 (1910), 356

28  Krafft-Ebing, *Psychopathia Sexualis*, 67
29  Nettler, *Criminal Careers Volume 2*, 131
30  Pieter Spierenburg, *A History of Murder: Personal Violence in Europe from the Middle Ages to the Present*, (Cambridge: Polity, 2008), 193
31  Spierenburg, *A History of Murder*
32  David Canter, *Criminal Shadows: Inside the Mind of the Serial Killer*, (London: HarperCollins, 1994), 98–9
33  MEPO 3/140
34  *The Times* (10/8/1888)
35  Sugden, *Complete History*, 16
36  MEPO 3/140
37  Paul Begg, *Jack the Ripper: The Definitive History*, (London: Longman, 2004), 55
38  Canter, *Criminal Shadows*
39  Begg, *Jack the Ripper*, 55
40  *The Times* (10/8/1888)
41  MEPO 3/140
42  Begg, *Jack the Ripper*, 93
43  Begg, *Jack the Ripper*, 93
44  Begg, *Jack the Ripper*, 93
45  MEPO 3/140
46  MEPO 3/140
47  MEPO 3/140
48  *Northern Echo* (1/9/1888)
49  *The Times* (24/9/1888)
50  Elwyn Jones and John Lloyd, *The Ripper File*, (London: Barker, 1975), 15
51  Begg, *Jack the Ripper*, 151
52  Jones and Lloyd, *The Ripper File*, 20
53  Begg, *Jack the Ripper*, 153
54  *New York Times* (9/9/1888)
55  *New York Times* (9/9/1888)
56  *The Times* (26/9/1888)
57  Jones and Lloyd, *The Ripper File*, 24
58  Sugden, *Complete History*, 91
59  *The Illustrated Police News* (22/9/1888)
60  *The Times* (15/9/1888)
61  *The Times* (15/9/1888)
62  Notably the Zodiac killer in California (who wrote coded messages to the press) and the Yorkshire Ripper case (when a member of the public sent taped 'confessions' to the police) in the last quarter of the twentieth century.
63  *Pall Mall Gazette* (1/10/1888)
64  Jones and Lloyd, *The Ripper File*, 36

65  MEPO 3/141
66  MEPO 3/141
67  MEPO 3/141
68  *Pall Mall Gazette* (1/10/1888)
69  Report of Chief Inspector Swanson on Mitre Square murder, 6 November 1888
70  Begg, *Jack the Ripper*, 189
71  Walter Dew, *I Caught Crippen*, (London: Blackie & Son, 1938), 129
72  Report of Chief Inspector Swanson on Mitre Square murder, 6 November 1888
73  Report of Chief Inspector Swanson on Mitre Square murder 6, November 1888
74  *Pall Mall Gazette* (1/10/1888)
75  *Pall Mall Gazette* (1/10/1888)
76  *Pall Mall Gazette* (3/10/1888)
77  Elizabeth Stride had rented a room from McCarthy at 38 Dorset Street; Fiona Rule, *The Worst Street in London*, (Surrey: Ian Allen, 2009), 129
78  Rule, *The Worst Street in London*, 112
79  Begg, *Jack the Ripper*, 241
80  Dew, *I Caught Crippen*, 148
81  Dew, *I Caught Crippen*, 161
82  *Pall Mall Gazette* (13/11/1888)
83  *Pall Mall Gazette* (13/11/1888)
84  Dew, *I Caught Crippen*, 250
85  MEPO 3/141
86  *The Times* (12/11/1888)
87  *The Times* (12/11/1888)
88  *The Times* (14/11/1888)
89  *The Times* (19/7/1889)
90  MEPO 3/140
91  *The Times* (19/7/1889)
92  MEPO 3/141
93  www.oldbaileyonline.org (t18770507–436, trial of W. Broder)
94  www.oldbaileyonline.org (t18770507–436, trial of W. Broder)
95  www.oldbaileyonline.org (t18770507–436, trial of W. Broder)
96  MEPO 3/141

*Notes to Chapter 3: East Meets West: The Contrasting Nature of Victorian London and the Mixed Community of the East End*

1  Jan Marsh, *Back to the Land. The Pastoral Impulse in Victorian England from 1880 to 1914*, (London: Quartet Books, 1982), 9
2  Colin Matthew, *The Nineteenth Century*, (Oxford: Oxford University Press, 2005), 42

3   Peter Mathias, *The First Industrial Nation. An Economic History of Britain 1700–1914*, (London, Routledge, 1987), 166–7

4   N. McCord, *British History 1815–1906*, (Oxford: Oxford University Press, 1991), 210

5   Marsh, *Back to the Land*, 3

6   *Merry & Wise: An Illustrated Monthly Magazine for Young People* (1/2/1869)

7   *Merry & Wise: An Illustrated Monthly Magazine for Young People* (1/2/1869)

8   *The Juvenile Companion and Sunday School Hive* (1/11/1869)

9   *The Woman's Signal* (2/5/1895)

10  *Fun* (11/4/1874)

11  Bill Hutchings, *The Poetry of William Cowper*, (London: Croom Helm, 1983), 215

12  Marsh, *Back to the Land*, 4

13  P. J. Waller, *Town, City and Nation: England 1850–1914*, (Oxford: Oxford University Press, 1983), 187

14  R. J. Morris and Richard Rodger, *The Victorian City: A Reader in British Urban History 1820–1914*, (London: Longman, 1997), 8

15  James Walvin, *Victorian Values*, (London: Andre Deutsch, 1987), 110

16  David Newsome, *The Victorian World Picture: Perceptions and Introspections in an age of Change*, (London: John Murray, 1997), 185

17  Raymond Williams, *The Country and the City*, (London: Chatto & Windus, 1973), 217

18  P. J. Keating, 'Fact and Fiction in the East End' in H. J. Dyos & Michael Wolff, *The Victorian City: Images and Realities*, Vol. 2 (London: Routledge & Kegan Paul, 1973), 585

19  *The Nineteenth Century* XXIV (1888), 262, quoted in William J. Fishman, *East End 1888*, (London: Gerald Duckworth, 1988), 1

20  Quoted in Robert Mighall, *A Geography of Victorian Gothic Fiction: Mapping History's Nightmares*, (Oxford: Oxford University Press, 1999), 68

21  Quoted in Ian Maclachlan, 'A bloody offal nuisance: the persistence of private slaughter-houses in nineteenth-century London', *Urban History*, 43:2, (2007), 238

22  *The Satirist; or, the Censor of the Times* (12/7/1840)

23  Peter Ackroyd in Alan Palmer, *The East End: Four Centuries of London Life*, (New Jersey: Rutgers University Press, 2000), xi

24  Peter Ackroyd in Alan Palmer, *The East End: Four Centuries of London Life*, (New Jersey: Rutgers University Press, 2000), xi

25  Begg, *Jack the Ripper: The Definitive History*, (London: Longman, 2004), 10

26  Begg, *Jack the Ripper*, 10

27  Palmer, *The East End*, xvii

28  See Angus Calder, *The Myth of the Blitz*, (London: Jonathan Cape, 1990)

29  Keating, 'Fact and Fiction in the East End', 590

30  W. Besant, *All Sorts and Conditions of Men: An Impossible Story*, (London: Chatto & Windus, 1882)

31  Keating, 'Fact and Fiction in the East End', 593

32  Charles Booth, *East London*, (London: Macmillan, 1889), 591–2

33  *The Graphic* (27/8/1887)

34  *Manchester Times* (25/2/1865)

35  *Daily News* (4/1/1873)

36  *The Graphic* (2/5/1885)

37  *Pall Mall Gazette* (19/1/1887)

38  *Pall Mall Gazette* (19/1/1887)

39  *Daily News* (20/1/1887)

40  *Pall Mall Gazette* (21/1/1887)

41  *Pall Mall Gazette* (22/1/1887)

42  Murray Baumgarten, 'Seeing Double: Jews in the Fiction of F. Scott Fitzgerald, Charles Dickens, Anthony Trollope, and George Eliot', in Bryan Cheyette (ed.), *Between 'Race' and Culture: Representations of 'the Jew' in English and American Literature*, (California: Stanford University Press, 1996), 48

43  Fishman, *East End*, 158

44  Baumgarten, 'Seeing Double', 50

45  Fishman, *East End*, 148

46  PP 1888 (303) Report from the Select Committee on Emigration and Immigration (foreigners), 89

47  Oswald Mosely's The British Union of Fascists commonly called 'Blackshirts' because of the militaristic uniform they adopted.

48  A. L. Cohen, 'The Memorable Sunday – October 4th', in Tony Kushner and Nadia Valman (eds), *Fascism and Anti-Fascism in British Society*, (London: Vallentine Mitchell, 2000), 198

49  *Reynolds's Newspaper* (31/7/1887)

50  *Birmingham Daily Post* (22/8/1887)

51  'Arnold White (1848–1925)', *Oxford Dictionary of National Biography*, (www.oxforddnb.com)

52  *Pall Mall Gazette* (9/2/1886)

53  *Pall Mall Gazette* (18/2/1886)

54  *Pall Mall Gazette* (18/3/1886) (26/3/1886)

55  *Pall Mall Gazette* (18/3/1886) (26/3/1886). 'Sweating' was the practice of using outworkers to undertake work in their own homes, reducing the need to supply workshop space for employers and so making manufacture more profitable and circumnavigating the Factory Acts. See James Andrew Schmiechen, 'Sweated Industries and Sweated Labour: A Study of Industrial Disorganization and Worker Attitudes in the London Clothing Trades, 1867–1909', *The Journal of Economic History*, 36:1 (March 1976), 283–6

56  PP 1888 (303), 39

57  David Englander (ed.), *A Documentary History of Jewish Immigrants in Britain, 1840–1920*, (Leicester: Leicester University Press, 1994), 15–16

58  Lloyd P. Gartner, *The Jewish Immigrant in England, 1870–1914*, (London: Simon Publications, 1960), 17

59  Gartner, *The Jewish Immigrant in England*, 40; William J. Fishman, *East End Jewish Radicals, 1875–1914*, (London: Gerald Duckworth, 1975), 30

60  Fishman, *East End*, 131

61  Fishman, *East End*, 133

62  Fishman, *East End*, 132

63  Gartner, *The Jewish Immigrant in England*, 40–1; Fishman, *East End Jewish Radicals*, 28

64  A Ukase was an imperial decree issued by the Russian Tsar

65  Englander (ed.), *A Documentary History*, 22

66  PRO MEPO 2/733, quoted in Englander (ed.), *A Documentary History*, 82

67  PP 1888 (303), 24

68  J. H. Stallard, *London Pauperism amongst Jews and Christians*, (London: 1867), quoted in Englander (ed.), *A Documentary History*, 111

69  Fishman, *East End*, 133

70  *The Lancet* (3/5/1884), quoted in Englander (ed.), *A Documentary History*, 86

71  Quoted in Fishman, *East End*, 157

72  *Pall Mall Gazette* (7/5/1888); Fishman, *East End*, 162

73  *Pall Mall Gazette* (23/2/1886)

74  Quoted in Fishman, *East End*, 173

75  Stephanie L. Barczewski, *Myth and National Identity in Nineteenth-Century Britain*, (Oxford: Oxford University Press, 2000), 143

76  *Manchester Times* (20/10/1888)

77  David Englander, 'Booth's Jews: the presentation of Jews and Judaism in life and labour of the people of London', *Victorian Studies*, 32:4 (Summer 1989), 552

78  Englander, 'Booth's Jews', 552

79  Quoted in Lynn Hollen Lees, *Exiles of Erin: Irish Migrants in Victorian London*, (Manchester: Manchester University Press, 1979)

80  Lees, *Exiles of Erin*, 56

81  H. J. Dyos, 'Railways and housing in Victorian London', *Journal of Transport History*, 2 (1955–1956), 14–18

82  Lees, *Exiles of Erin*, 86

83  Montague Gore, *On the Dwellings of the Poor*, 2nd edition (London: 1851), xiv, quoted in Lees, *Exiles of Erin*, 71

84  Hugh Heinrick, *A Survey of the Irish in England*, Alan O'Day (ed.), (London: Hambledon Press, 1872 and 1990), 2–3

85  Henry Pelling, *Popular Politics and Society in Late Victorian Britain*, (London:

MacMillan, 1968), 32

86    *Lloyd's Weekly Newspaper* (23/1/1881)

87    Colin G. Pooley, 'Segregation or Integration? The Residential Experience of the
      Irish in Mid-Victorian Britain', in R. Swift and S. Gilley (eds), *The Irish in Britain,
      1815–1939*, (London: Pinter Publishers, 1989), 71–2

88    Graham Davis, *The Irish in Britain, 1815–1914*, (Dublin: Gill & Macmillan, 1991),
      116

89    Davis, *The Irish in Britain*, 118

90    Derek Hudson, *Munby: Man of Two Worlds*, (London: John Murray, 1972) quoted
      in Lees, *Exiles of Erin*, 96

91    Hudson, *Munby*, quoted in Lees, *Exiles of Erin*, 96

92    Pelling, *Popular Politics*, 7

93    McCord, *British History*, 371

94    LMA, Thames Police Court Minute book, September 1888

95    *Reynolds's Newspaper* (2/1/1881)

96    *Lloyd's Weekly Newspaper* (14/3/1886)

97    LMA, Thames Police Court Minute book, September 1888

98    www.oldbaileyonline.org (t18881022–976, trial of John Murphy and John Barrett)

99    LMA, Thames Police Court Minute book, September 1888

100   *Reynolds's Newspaper* (11/1/1880)

101   *The Illustrated Police News* (9/1/1886)

102   *The Illustrated Police News* (22/1/1881)

103   *Pall Mall Gazette* (19/10/1888)

104   *Manchester Times* (20/10/1888)

105   Stewart P. Evans and Keith Skinner, *Jack the Ripper: Letters from Hell*, (Stroud:
      Sutton Publishing, 2001), 63

106   *Lloyd's Weekly Newspaper* (21/10/1888). Lusk later reformed the committee after
      a member of the public came forward with funds and it redoubled its efforts after
      Mary Kelly's murder

107   *Lloyd's Weekly Newspaper* (21/10/1888)

108   Ng Kwee Choo, *The Chinese in London*, (Oxford: Oxford University Press, 1968),
      18

109   *Lloyd's Weekly Newspaper* (30/12/1888)

110   *Pall Mall Gazette* (10/2/1912)

111   G. E. Mitton, *Peeps at Great Steamship Lines – The Peninsular and Oriental*,
      (London: A&C Black, 1913), 57–8

112   Palmer, *The East End*, 89

113   Gareth Stedman Jones, 'The "Cockney" and the Nation, 1780–1988', in D. Feldman
      and G. S. Jones (eds), *Metropolis London: Histories and Representations since 1800*,
      (London: Routledge, 1989), 277

114   Jones, 'The "Cockney"', 278

115  Jones, 'The "Cockney"', 288

116  *Tinsley's Magasine* (April 1869), quoted in Jones, 'The "Cockney"', 290

117  *Punch*, (9/3/1878)

118  Quoted in Jones, 'The "Cockney"', 292

119  *Punch* (2/4/1881)

120  Jones, 'The "Cockney"', 313

121  *Aberdeen Weekly Journal* (6/7/1888)

122  *East London Observer* (7/7/1888); *Pall Mall Gazette* (7/7/1888)

123  PP 1888 (361) First report from the Select Committee of the House of Lords on the sweating system; together with the proceedings of the committee, minutes of evidence, and appendix, iii

124  PP 1888 (361), 5

125  PP 1888 (361), 26

126  *Pall Mall Gazette* (1/8/1888)

127  *The Link*, 'White slavery in London' (23/6/1888)

128  Stephen Inwood, *City of Cities: The Birth of Modern London*, (London: Macmillan, 2005), 99

129  *Pall Mall Gazette* (9/7/1888)

130  Inwood, *City of Cities*, 99

131  *Pall Mall Gazette* (16/7/1888)

132  *Reynolds's Newspaper* (17/7/1888)

133  *Reynolds's Newspaper* (22/7/1888)

134  Fishman, *East End*, 103

135  Quoted in Inwood, *City of Cities*, 98

136  *Pall Mall Gazette* (16/7/1888)

137  *Manchester Times* (13/10/1888)

138  Michael Young and Peter Willmott, *Family and Kinship in East London*, (London: Routledge, 1957)

139  Young and Willmott, *Family and Kinship in East London*, 158

*Notes to Chapter 4:  Read All About It! Ripper News and Sensation in Victorian Society*

1  Lee Perry Curtis, *Jack the Ripper and the London Press*, (New Haven: Yale University Press, 2002), 59

2  Alan Lee, 'The Structure, Ownership and Control of the Press, 1855–1914', in G. Boyce, J. Curran and P. Wingate (eds), *Newspaper History: From the 17th Century to the Present Day*, (London: Constable, 1978), 117

3  Curtis, *Jack the Ripper*, 56

4  Curtis, *Jack the Ripper*, 57

5  Curtis, *Jack the Ripper*, 57

6   Richard Williams, 'The Press and Popular Culture, an Historical Perspective', in Boyce, Curran and Wingate (eds), *Newspaper History*, 48

7   'Useful Sunday literature for the masses', *Punch* (22/9/1849)

8   *Pick Me Up!* (6/10/1888)

9   W. T. Stead, 'Government by journalism', *The Contemporary Review*, 49: (May 1886)

10  Stead, 'Government by journalism'

11  Rob Sindall, *Street Violence in the Nineteenth Century*, (Leicester: Leicester University Press, 1990), 32

12  Anthony Smith, 'The long road to objectivity and back', in Boyce, Curran and Wingate (eds), *Newspaper History*, 168

13  Oxford English Dictionary (OED) quoted in Curtis, *Jack the Ripper*, 66

14  Michael Diamond, *Victorian Sensation: Or the Spectacular, the Shocking and the Scandalous in Nineteenth-Century Britain*, (London: Anthem Press, 2004), 219

15  Diamond, *Victorian Sensation*, 232

16  Quoted in Diamond, *Victorian Sensation*, 193

17  *Reynolds's Newspaper* (12/6/1881)

18  *The Illustrated Police News* (4/6/1881)

19  *The Graphic* (11/6/1881)

20  'The latest murder', *Moonshine* (15/11/1890)

21  J. Bondeson, *London Monster: A Sanguinary Tale*, (Philadelphia: University of Pennsylvania Press, 2000)

22  For details of the garrotting panic see J. Davis (1980) and Sindall (1987)

23  Bondeson, *London Monster*

24  Bondeson, *London Monster*, 195

25  P. Haining, *The Legend and Bizarre Crimes of Spring Heeled Jack*, (London: Muller, 1977)

26  Jennifer Davis, 'The London Garrotting Panic of 1862: A Moral Panic and the Creation of a Criminal Class in Mid-Victorian England', in Gatrell V. A. C., B. Lenman and G. Parker (eds), *Crime and the Law. The Social History of Crime in Western Europe since 1500*

27  Stanley Cohen, *Folk Devils and Moral Panics. The Creation of the Mods and Rockers*, (London: MacGibbon & Kee, 1972)

28  See Davis, 'The London Garrotting Panic'; Peter King, 'Newspaper reporting and attitudes to crime and justice in late-eighteenth- and early-nineteenth-century London', *Continuity & Change*, 22 (2007), 73–112; and Robert Sindall, 'The London garotting panics of 1856 and 1862', *Social History*

*Notes to Chapter 5:* The Bitter Cry of Outcast London: *Poverty, Charity and the Fear of Revolution*

1 Rev Andrew Mearns, *The Bitter Cry of Outcast London: An Inquiry into the Condition of the Abject Poor*, (London: 1883)

2 MEPO 2/181 Letter to CW regarding the homeless in TS from Cavanagh (29/7/1887)

3 MEPO 2/181 (23/7/1887)

4 *Morning Post* (24/8/1887)

5 *Notes and Proceedings* (30/8/1887)

6 MEPO 2/181 Report from A division in response to the *Notes and Proceedings* article (1/9/1887)

7 H. J. Goldsmid, *Dottings of a Dosser: Being the Revelations of the Inner Life of Low London Lodging Houses*, (London: T. Fisher Unwin, 1886), 73–4

8 *The Bitter Cry of Outcast London* was probably authored by the Rev William Carnall Preston, a former newspaper editor. Mearns was the researcher and was helped in this by another clergyman, the Rev James Munro.

9 Mearns, *The Bitter Cry of Outcast London*

10 H. Bosanquet, *Rich and Poor*, (London: Macmillan, 1898), 138

11 S. B. Saul, *The Myth of the Great Depression 1873–1896*, (London: Macmillan, 1972)

12 Mearns, *The Bitter Cry of Outcast London*

13 G. Darley, 'Octavia Hill (1838–1912)', *Oxford Dictionary of National Biography*, www.oxforddnb.com (accessed 10/3/09)

14 Darley, 'Octavia Hill', 2

15 Quoted in W. Thomson Hill, *Octavia Hill. Pioneer of the National Trust and Housing Reformer*, (London: Hutchinson, 1956), 59

16 O. Hill, *Homes of the London Poor*, (London: Macmillan, 1883), 21–2

17 Stephen Inwood, *City of Cities: The Birth of Modern London*, (London: Macmillan, 2005), 40

18 PP 1884–85 [C.4402] [C.4402-I] [C.4402-II] First report of Her Majesty's commissioners for inquiring into the housing of the working classes, 4

19 Alan Palmer, *The East End: Four Centuries of London Life*, (New Jersey: Rutgers University Press, 2000), 81; G. Steadman Jones, *Outcast London: A Study in the Realationship between Classes in Victorian Society*, (london: Oxford University Press, 1971), 188

20 Stedman Jones, *Outcast London*, 205; A. Yelling, *Slums and Slum Clearance in Victorian London*, (London: Routledge, 1986), 28

21 PP 1884–85, 12

22 PP 1884–85, 163

23 A. Davin, *Growing Up Poor: Home, School and Street in London 1870–1914*, (London: Rivers Oram Press, 1996)

24  J. White, *Rothschild Buildings. Life in an East End Tenement Block 1887–1920*, (London: Routledge & Kegan Paul, 1980), 62

25  Yelling, *Slums*, 34

26  A. S. Wohl, *The Eternal Slum*, (London: Edward Arnold, 1977), 22–3

27  Wohl, *The Eternal Slum*, 23

28  PP 1884–85, 21

29  Yelling, *Slums*, 28

30  White, *Rothschild Buildings*, 131

31  S. Merrett, *State Housing in Britain*, (London: Routledge & Kegan Paul, 1979), 30

32  *The Times* (2/3/1861)

33  Gus Elen song quoted in E. Hopkins, *A Social History of the English Working Classes, 1815–1945*, (London: Hodder & Stoughton, 1979), 116–17

34  PP 1884–85

35  J. White, 'Jewish Landlords, Jewish Tenants: An Aspect of Class Struggle Within the Jewish East End', in A. Newman (ed.), *The Jewish East End, 1840–1939*, (London: Jewish Historical Society of England, 1981), 207

36  Mearns, *The Bitter Cry of Outcast London*

37  Stedman Jones, *Outcast London*

38  Wohl, *The Eternal Slum*, 26

39  Andrew Mearns, *The Bitter Cry of Outcast London*, A. S. Wohl (ed.), 34

40  Charles Booth, quoted in Davin, *Growing Up Poor*, 31

41  Lyrics by Collins and F.W. Leigh

42  *The Times* (22/2/1884)

43  Davin, *Growing Up Poor*, 46 – see tables 3.1 and 3.2

44  White, *Rothschild Buildings*

45  White, *Rothschild Buildings*, 51

46  R. Samuel, *East End Underworld. Chapters in the Life of Arthur Harding*, (London: History Workshop Series, 1981)

47  In December 2008 the Conservative leader, David Cameron, declared that: 'the biggest challenge facing Britain today is mending our broken society', *Daily Telegraph* (16/12/2008)

48  White, *Rothschild Buildings*

49  White, *Rothschild Buildings*

50  P. Malpass, 'Continuity and change in philanthropic housing organisations: The Octavia Hill Housing Trust and the Guinness Trust', *London Journal*, 24:1 (1999), 45

51  Quoted in John N. Tarn, *Five Per Cent Philanthropy: An Account of Housing in Urban Areas between 1840 and 1914*, (Cambridge: Cambridge University Press, 1973), 22

52  Richard Rodger, *Housing in Urban Britain 1780–1914*, (Basingstoke: Palgrave, 1989), 45

53 Tarn, *Five Per Cent Philanthropy*, 18
54 S. Martin Gaskell, *Model Housing. From the Great Exhibition to the Festival of Britain*, (London and New York: Mansell, 1987), 30
55 Gaskell, *Model Housing*, 30
56 Gaskell, *Model Housing*, 32
57 Tarn, *Five Per Cent Philanthropy*, 46
58 Wohl, *The Eternal Slum*, 160
59 Wohl, *The Eternal Slum*, 144
60 M. J. Daunton, *House and Home in the Victorian City: Working-Class Housing 1850–1914*, (London: Edward Arnold, 1983), 192
61 Wohl, *The Eternal Slum*, 155
62 Wohl, *The Eternal Slum*, 146
63 Wohl, *The Eternal Slum*, 164
64 Daunton, *House and Home in the Victorian City*, 192, 194
65 J. London, *The People of the Abyss*, (London: Macmillan, 1903), 128
66 Goldsmid, *Dottings of a Dosser*
67 Inwood, *City of Cities*, 42
68 London, *People of the Abyss*, 129
69 Goldsmid, *Dottings of a Dosser*, 28; London, *People of the Abyss*, 129
70 Goldsmid, *Dottings of a Dosser*, 10
71 Goldsmid, *Dottings of a Dosser*, 27–8
72 For the history of the Poor Law and the workhouse see (among others) S. Webb and B. Webb, *English Poor Law History* (London: Longmans, 1927–29); J. R. Poynter, *Society and Pauperism*, (London: Routledge & Kegan Paul, 1969); M. E. Rose, *English Poor Law, 1780–1930* (Newton Abbot: David & Charles, 1971); Elizabeth T. Hurren, *Protesting about Pauperism: Poverty, Politics and Poor Relief in Late-Victorian England, 1870–1900*, (London: Royal Historical Society, 2007)
73 NA MEPO 2 correspondence 82559 (letter dated 16 November 1887)
74 M. Brodie, 'Artisans and dossers: the 1886 West End riots and the East End casual poor', *London Journal*, 24:2 (1999), 34
75 Jerry White, *London in the Nineteenth Century: 'A Human Awful Wonder of God'*, (London: Vintage, 2008), 374–6
76 PP 1886 *Report of a Committee to Inquire and Report as to the Origin and Character of the Disturbances which took place in the Metropolis on Monday, the 8th of February and as to the conduct of the Police Authorities in relation therein*
77 PP 1886 *Report of a Committee*, v
78 PP 1886 *Report of a Committee*, 64–5
79 *Pall Mall Gazette* (9/2/1886)
80 *Pall Mall Gazette* (9/2/1886)
81 *Pall Mall Gazette* (9/2/1886)
82 *Pall Mall Gazette* (9/2/1886)

83   White, *London in the Nineteenth Century*, 374

84   Stedman Jones, *Outcast London*, 343; E. Hobsbawm, 'The Aristocracy of Labour Reconsidered', in *Worlds of Labour: Further Studies in the History of Labour*, (London: Weidenfeld & Nicolson, 1984), 244

85   Brodie, 'Artisans and dossers', 47–8

86   Stedman Jones, *Outcast London*, 213

87   PP 1886 *Report of a Committee*, x

88   'The unemployed and the police', *Moonshine* (29/10/1887)

89   J. Harris, 'Bosanquet, Helen (1860–1925)', *Oxford Dictionary of National Biography*, www.oxforddnb.com (accessed 10/3/2009)

90   J. Davis, 'Webb, Beatrice (1858–1943)', *Oxford Dictionary of National Biography*, www.oxforddnb.com (accessed 10/3/2009), 1

91   J. Fido, 'The Charity Organisation Society and Social Casework in London 1869–1900', in A. P. Donajgrodski (ed.), *Social Control in Nineteenth-Century Britain*, (London: Crook Helm, 1977), 207

92   G. R. Searle, *A New England? Peace and War 1886–1918*, (Oxford: Oxford University Press, 2004), 194

93   B. Potter, 'A lady's view of unemployment in the east', *Pall Mall Gazette* (18/2/86)

94   Davis, 'Webb, Beatrice', 6

95   A. M. McBriar, *An Edwardian Mixed Doubles. The Bosanquets versus the Webbs: A Study in British Social Policy, 1890–1929*, (Oxford: Oxford University Press, 1987)

96   McBriar, *An Edwardian Mixed Doubles*, 372

97   H. Dendy, 'The Industrial Residuum', in B. Bosanquet (ed.), *Aspects of the Social Problem, by various writers*, (London: Macmillan, 1895), 102

98   J. Lewis, *Women and Social Action in Victorian and Edwardian England*, (California: Stanford University Press, 1991), 155

99   Mearns, *The Bitter Cry of Outcast London*, 26

100  G. Finlayson, *Citizen, State, and Social Welfare in Britain 1830–1990*, (Oxford: Oxford University Press, 1994), 157

101  Helen Bosanquet, *Rich and Poor*, (London: Macmillan, 1898), 119

102  Bosanquet, *Rich and Poor*, 138

103  Bosanquet, *Rich and Poor*, 102

104  Lewis, *Women and Social Action*, 180

105  'The real starver of the poor.–John Bull vainly endeavours to relieve the distress', *Fun* (9/11/1887)

106  Harris, 'Bosanquet, Helen', 1

107  McBriar, *An Edwardian Mixed Doubles*, 118

108  Kathleen Callanan Martin, *Hard and Unreal Advice: Mothers, Social Science and the Victorian Poverty Experts*, (Basingstoke: Palgrave, 2008)

109  C. S. Loch, 'Manufacturing a new pauperism', *The Nineteenth Century*, 37:218 (April 1895), 698–9

110   Finlayson, *Citizen, State, and Social*, 171

111   White, *London in the Nineteenth Century*, 377

112   Quoted in W. F. Lee, 'Demonstrations of Militant Reconstructionists in Metropolitan London, 1880–1914', unpublished PhD (University of New Mexico: 1976), 87

113   V. Bailey, 'The Metropolitan Police, the Home Office and the Threat of Outcast London', in V. Bailey (ed.), *Policing and Punishment in Nineteenth-Century Britain*, (London: Croom Helm, 1981)

114   *Reynolds's Newspaper* (13/11/1887)

115   White, *London in the Nineteenth Century*, 378

116   'Remember Trafalgar Square!', words by Frederick Halliwell, music by Russell Lewis, (London, British Library)

117   *Pall Mall Gazette* (14/11/1887)

118   *Daily Chronicle, Daily Telegraph, The Times, Standard* (all 14/11/1887)

119   Linnell's death calls to mind the death of Mr Tomlinson following a possible assault by a policeman controlling the crowds at the G20 demonstration, April 2009

120   Lee, 'Demonstrations', 97–8

121   Finlayson, *Citizen, State, and Social Welfare*, 114

122   Lee, 'Demonstrations', 149

123   W. Churchill, *Liberalism and the Social Problem*, (London: Hodder & Stoughton, 1909), 363

*Notes to Chapter 6: City of Dreadful Delights: Vice, Prostitution and Victorian Society*

1   Steven Marcus, *The Other Victorians: A Study of Sexuality and Pornography in Mid Nineteenth Century England*, (New York: Basic, 1964)

2   Matthew Sweet, *Inventing the Victorians: What We Know About Them and Why We're Wrong*, (New York: St Martin's, 2001)

3   E. M. Sigsworth and T. J. Wyke, 'A Study of Victorian Prostitution and Venereal Disease', in Martha Vicinus, *Suffer and be Still: Women in the Victorian Age*, (Bloomington: Indiana University Press, 1972)

4   Sigsworth and Wyke, 'A Study of Victorian Prostitution', 87

5   Christopher Frayling, 'The House that Jack Built', in Alexandra Warwick & Martin Willis (eds), *Jack the Ripper: Media, Culture, History*, (Manchester: Manchester University Press, 2007), 16

6   Seth Koven, *Slumming: Sexual and Social Politics in Victorian London*, (New Jersey: Princeton University Press, 2004), 4

7   Henry Mayhew, *London, Labour and the London Poor*, (London: Charles Griffin, 1861)

8  Mayhew, *London, Labour and the London Poor*, 32

9  Henry Mayhew, *London Labour and the London Poor: Volume Four, Those that will not Work*, (London: 1861), published as *London's Underworld in the Victorian Period*, (New York: Dover Publications, 2005), 7

10  Mayhew, *London Underworld in the Victorian Period*, 24

11  Mayhew, *London Underworld in the Victorian Period*, 24

12  Paula Bartley, *Prostitution. Prevention and Reform in England, 1860–1914*, (London: Routledge, 2000), 10

13  Clive Emsley, *Crime and Society in England, 1750–1900*, (London: Longman, 1997), 154

14  Tony Henderson, *Disorderly Women in Eighteenth-Century London: Prostitution and Its Control in the Metropolis, 1730–1830*, (London: Longman, 1999); Drew D. Gray, *Crime, Prosecution and Social Relations*, (Basingstoke: Palgrave Macmillan, 2009)

15  Jeffrey Weeks, *Sex, Politics and Society: The Regulation of Sexuality since 1800*, (London: Longman, 1981) (2nd edition), 85

16  Frank Mort, *Dangerous Sexualities: Medico-Moral Politics in England since 1830*, (London: Routledge & Kegan Paul, 1987), 65

17  Mort, *Dangerous Sexualities*, 67

18  Mayhew, *London Underworld in the Victorian Period*, 26

19  F. Smith, 'The Contagious Diseases Acts reconsidered', in *Social History of Medicine* 3:2 (1990), 197

20  Weeks, *Sex, Politics and Society*, 86

21  Lucy Bland, *Banishing the Beast: Sexuality and the Early Feminists*, (New York: The New Press, 1995), 98

22  Mort, *Dangerous Sexualities*, 87

23  Weeks, *Sex, Politics and Society*, 87

24  Weeks, *Sex, Politics and Society*, 90

25  The registers are held by the LMA, in the series PS/TH/A/01/001–472; the register for most of 1888 is no. 12

26  PS/TH/A/01/012, 9/8/1888 and 9/10/1888

27  Weeks, *Sex, Politics and Society*, 89

28  *Pall Mall Gazette* (4/7/1885)

29  *Pall Mall Gazette* (6/7/1885)

30  Alfred S. Dyer, *The European Slave Trade in English Girls. A Narrative of Facts*, (London: Dyer Brothers, 1880)

31  Deborah Gorham, 'The "Maiden Tribute of Modern Babylon" re-examined: child prostitution and the idea of childhood in late-Victorian England', *Victorian Studies*, 21:3 (Spring 1978), 359

32  Alison Plowden, *The Case of Eliza Armstrong, 'A Child of 13 bought for £5'*, (London: BBC publications, 1974)

33  *Lloyd's Weekly Newspaper* (16/8/1885)

34  www.oldbaileyonline.org (t18851019–1031, case of Rebecca Jarrett, William Thomas Stead, Sampson Jacques, William Bramwell Booth, Elizabeth Combe, 19 October 1885)

35  *Pall Mall Gazette* (11/11/1885)

36  *Pall Mall Gazette* (11/11/1885)

37  *Pall Mall Gazette* (11/11/1885)

38  Trevor Fisher, *Prostitution and the Victorians*, (Stroud: Sutton, 1997), 134–5

39  Gorham, 'The "Maiden Tribute of Modern Babylon" re-examined', 355

40  Mayhew, *London Underworld in the Victorian Period*, 104

41  Mayhew, *London Underworld in the Victorian Period*, 107

42  Judith R. Walkowitz, *Prostitution and Victorian Society: Women, Class, and the State*, (Cambridge: Cambridge University Press, 1980), 21.

43  Walkowitz, *Prostitution and Victorian Society*, 19

44  William Acton, *Prostitution Considered in Its Moral, Social and Sanitary Aspects: in London and Other Large Cities*, (London, 1870)

45  Walkowitz, *Prostitution and Victorian Society*, 14

46  Walkowitz, *Prostitution and Victorian Society*, 14

47  Bartley, *Prostitution*, 10

48  Neal Stubbings Shelden, *The Victims of Jack the Ripper*, (Chestertown: Inklings Press, 2007)

49  Sheldon, *The Victims of Jack the Ripper*, 43

50  Walter Dew, *I Caught Crippen*, (London: Blackie & Son, 1938), 86

51  Sheldon, *The Victims of Jack the Ripper*

52  Sheldon, *The Victims of Jack the Ripper*

*Notes to Chapter 7:  Crime and the Criminal Class in Late Victorian London*

1  Martin J. Wiener, *Reconstructing the Criminal. Culture, Law, and Policy in England, 1830–1914*, (Cambridge: Cambridge University Press, 1994), 228

2  Henry Mayhew, *London Labour and the London Poor: Volume Four, Those that will not Work*, (London: 1861), published as *London's Underworld in the Victorian Period*, (New York: Dover Publications, 2005), 109

3  Henry Maudsley, *Body and Mind*, (London: Macmillan, 1873), quoted in Wiener, *Reconstructing the Criminal*, 230

4  Andrew Barrett and Christopher Harrison (eds), *Crime and punishment in England: a sourcebook*, (London: UCL, 1999)

5  James Greenwood, *The Seven Curses of London*, (London: Stanley Rivers, 1869), 92

6  Greenwood, *Seven Curses of London*, 57

7  Quoted in Wiener, *Reconstructing the Criminal*, 233

8   Cesare Lombroso, *The Criminal Man*, translated by Mary Gibson and Nicole Hahn Rafter, (Durham, NC: Duke University Press, 2006)

9   Gibson and Hahn Rafter, Introduction, in Lombroso, *The Criminal Man*, 8

10  Lombroso, *Criminal Man*, 53

11  J. Redding Ware, *Before the Bench. Sketches of Police Court Life*, (London: c.1890), 25

12  *Pall Mall Gazette* (25/10/1881)

13  *Glasgow Herald* (5/7/1884)

14  *Pall Mall Gazette* (10/10/1887)

15  *Pall Mall Gazette* (11/9/1889)

16  Havelock Ellis, *The Criminal*, (London: 1890)

17  'Whitechapel, 1888', *Punch* (13/10/1888)

18  David Garland, *Punishment and Modern Society: A Study in Social Theory*, (Oxford: Clarendon Press, 1991), 146

19  See Jennifer Davis, 'A poor man's system of justice'

20  *The Graphic* (27/8/1887)

21  These are held by the LMA under the catalogue prefix PS/TH/A and are open to general consultation.

22  J. Davis, 'Prosecutions and Their Context. The Use of the Criminal Law in Later Nineteenth-Century London', in D. Hay and F. Snyder, *Policing and Prosecution in Britain 1750–1850*, (Oxford: Clarendon, 1989), 403

23  *Pall Mall Gazette* (13/8/1887)

24  *The Graphic* (27/8/1887)

25  Redding Ware, *Before the Bench*, 29

26  Redding Ware, *Before the Bench*, 29

27  Redding Ware, *Before the Bench*, 29

28  *The Illustrated Police News* (7/5/1887)

29  *The Illustrated Police News* (28/5/1887)

30  *The Illustrated Police News* (29/1/1887)

31  Refer to Peter King, 'Summary justice and social relations in eighteenth-century England', *Past and Present*, (May 2004); Gwenda Morgan and Peter Rushton, 'The magistrate, the community and the maintenance of an orderly society in eighteenth-century England', *Historical Research*, 76:191 (2003); Drew D. Gray, *Crime, Prosecution and Social Relations: The Summary Courts of the City of London in the Late Eighteenth Century* (Basingstoke: Palgrave Macmillan, 2009); Robert B. Shoemaker, *Prosecution and Punishment: Petty Crime and the Law in London and Rural Middlesex, c.1660–1725*, (Cambridge: Cambridge University Press, 1991); Bruce Smith, 'Circumventing the Jury: Petty Crime and Summary Jurisdiction in London and New York City, 1790–1855' (PhD diss., Yale University, 1996)

32  *The Illustrated Police News* (1/1/1887)

33  V. A. C. Gatrell, 'The Decline of Theft and Violence in Victorian and Edwardian

England', in V. A. C. Gatrell *et al., Crime and the Law. The Social History of Crime in Western Europe since 1500,* (London: Europa, 1980), 285

34  *The Illustrated Police News* (17/9/1887)

35  Police Code Book 1870 Northampton Record Office

36  *The Illustrated Police News* (12/3/1887)

37  *The Graphic* (27/8/1887)

38  Davis, 'Prosecutions and Their Context', 411

39  See Drew D. Gray, *Crime, Prosecution and Social Relations,* (Basingstoke: Palgrave Macmillan, 2009), for the use of this strategy by City of London justices in the late eighteenth century.

40  *Lloyd's Weekly Newspaper* (7/8/1887)

41  *The Illustrated Police News* (26/3/1887)

42  *Pall Mall Gazette* (29/4/1887)

43  *Pall Mall Gazette* (18/10/1887)

44  *The Graphic* (20/8/1887)

45  www.oldbaileyonline.org

46  www.oldbaileyonline.org

47  'Other' includes grave robbing, possessing navy stores and attempting to create mutiny on the high seas.

48  Clive Emsley, *Crime and Society in England, 1750–1900,* (London: Longman, 1997), 22

49  www.oldbaileyonline.org (t18880730–720, trial of Weston Montacute, [30/7/1888])

50  www.oldbaileyonline.org (t18890204–253, trial of Peter Wallace [4/2/1889] and t18880917–882, trial of Alfred Stewart [17/9/1888])

51  www.oldbaileyonline.org (t18880528–578, trial of Margaretta Becker, [28/5/1888] and t18880917–879, trial of William John Milne [17/9/1888])

52  www.oldbaileyonline.org

53  www.oldbaileyonline.org

54  www.oldbaileyonline.org (t18800803–499, trial of James Keightley, Hannah Keightley, Sarah Bennett, Richard William Wood, Mary Martha Wood, Benjamin Charles Norris [3/8/1880])

55  www.oldbaileyonline.org (t18800803–499, trial of James Keightley *et al.*)

56  www.oldbaileyonline.org (t18810238–386, trial of Thomas Butler [27/3/1881])

57  www.oldbaileyonline.org (t18830625–654, trial of Henry Morris [25/6/1883])

58  www.oldbaileyonline.org (t18860913–887, trial of Dennis Bryan, [13/9/1886])

59  www.oldbaileyonline.org (t18880130–287, trial of Henry Burrows [30/1/1888])

60  www.oldbaileyonline.org (t18880130–266, trial of Jane Ward [30/1/1888])

61  www.oldbaileyonline.org (t18880702–672, trial of George Cullen [2/7/1888])

62  *Reynolds's Newspaper* (21/8/1881)

63  *Punch* (19/2/1881)

64   *Funny Folks* (8/10/1881)

65   *Moonshine* (London, England), Saturday, January 14, 1888

66   J. A. Sharpe, *Dick Turpin: The Myth of the English Highwayman*, (London: Profile, 2005)

67   *Pall Mall Gazette* (31/8/1887). The *Gazette* recorded Dudley's name as Webbers for some unknown reason. www.oldbaileyonline.org (t18870912–999, trial of James Flewitt [12/9/1899])

68   www.oldbaileyonline.org (t18990306–235, trial of James Flewett [6/3/1899])

69   www.oldbaileyonline.org (t18880130–256, trial of John Kaylor and Thomas McCarthy [30/1/1888])

70   www.oldbaileyonline.org (t18880730–734, trial of James Elliot [30/7/1888])

71   www.oldbaileyonline.org [t18870627–713, trial of William Warner [27/6/1887])

72   Gatrell, 'Crime, authority and the policeman-state', 244

73   Emsley, *Crime and Society in England, 1750–1900*, (London: Longman, 2005), 278

74   Philip Priestley, *Victorian Prison Lives: English Prison Biography, 1830–1914*, (London and New York: Methuen, 1985), 12

75   James Monro, Assistant Commissioner of the Police of the Metropolis, *A Report of the History of the Department of the Metropolitan Police known as the Convict Supervision Office: Detailing System and Showing Results and Effects Generally on the Habitual Criminal Population*, (London: 1886), 4–6

76   Monro, *A Report*, 10

77   Norval Morris and David Rothman (eds), *The Oxford History of the Prison: The Practice of Punishment in Western Society*, (New York: Oxford University Press, 1998)

78   Michael Ignatieff, *A Just Measure of Pain: Penitentiaries in the Industrial Revolution, 1780–1850*, (London: Macmillan, 1978)

79   Quoted in Priestley, *Victorian Prison Lives*, 132–3

80   Priestley, *Victorian Prison Lives*, 124–31

81   Sir Edmund Du Cane, *The Punishment and Prevention of Crime*, (London: MacMillan, 1885), quoted in Priestley, *Victorian Prison Lives*, 194

82   Sir Edmund Du Cane, *The Punishment and Prevention of Crime*, (London: MacMillan, 1885), quoted in Priestley, *Victorian Prison Lives*, 195

83   Howard Association, *Defects in the Criminal Administration and Penal Legislation of Great Britain and Ireland with Remedial Suggestions*, (1872), quoted in Priestley, *Victorian Prison Lives*, 157

84   Quoted in Priestley, *Victorian Prison Lives*, 43

85   Quoted in Priestley, *Victorian Prison Lives*, 229

86   Michel Foucault, *Discipline and Punish: The Birth of the Prison*, (London: Penguin, 1991)

87   Priestley, *Victorian Prison Lives*, 229

88   Morris and Rothman (eds), *The Oxford History of the Prison*

*Notes to Chapter 8: Watching the Detectives: The Police and the Hunt for Jack the Ripper*

1  *Pall Mall Gazette* (1/10/1888)

2  R. Reiner, *The Politics of the Police*, (Oxford: Oxford University Press, 2000) (3rd edition), 15

3  See D. Gray, *Crime, Prosecution and Social Relations*, (Basingstoke: Palgrave Macmillan, 2009); A. Harris, *Policing the City. Crime and Legal Authority in London, 1780–1840*, (Columbus: Ohio State University Press, 2004); R. Paley "'An imperfect, inadequate and wretched system"? Policing London before Peel', *Criminal Justice History*, 10 (1989), 95–130; E. Reynolds, *Before the Bobbies: The Night Watch and Police Reform in Metropolitan London, 1720–1830*, (Basingstoke: Palgrave Macmillan, 1998); for a definitive history of the Police see C. Emsley, *The English Police. A Political and Social History*, (London: Longman, 1991)

4  Gray, *Crime, Prosecution and Social Relations*

5  R. Storch, 'The plague of the blue locusts: police reform and popular resistance in Northern England, 1840–57', *International Review of Social History*, 20:1 (1975), 61–91

6  Storch, 'The plague of the blue locusts'

7  D. Taylor, *The New Police in Nineteenth-Century England. Crime, Conflict and Control*, (Manchester: Manchester University Press, 1997), 105

8  S. Inwood, 'Policing London's morals: the Metropolitan Police and popular culture, 1829–1850', *The London Journal*, 15:2 (1990), 129–46

9  R. Storch, 'The policeman as domestic missionary: urban discipline and popular culture in northern England, 1850–1880', *Journal of Social History*, 9:4 (1976), 481–509

10  J. Davis, 'A poor man's system of justice: the London police courts in the second half of the nineteenth century', *Historical Journal*, 27:2 (1984), 309–35

11  D. Phillips, '"A New Engine Power and Authority": The Institutionalization of Law-Enforcement in England 1780–1830', in V. A. C. Gatrell, Bruce Lenman and Geoffrey Parker, *Crime and the Law: The Social History of Crime in Western Europe Since 1500*, (London: Europa, 1980)

12  *Pall Mall Gazette* (1/10/1888)

13  'Military drill v. police duty', *Funny Folks* (15/9/1888)

14  *Freeman's Journal and Daily Commercial Advertiser* (19/4/1842)

15  K. R. M. Short, *The Dynamite Wars: Irish-American Bombers in Victorian Britain*, (Dublin: Gill and Macmillan, 1979), 205

16  www.oldbaileyonline.org, (t18850420–532, trial of Harry Burton and James George Gilbert)

17  *Pall Mall Gazette* (3/1/1885)

18  *Pall Mall Gazette* (3/1/1885); *Daily News* (3/1/1885)

19   Short, *The Dynamite Wars*, 200

20   www.oldbaileyonline.org (t18850420–532, trial of Burton and Gilbert)

21   Short, *The Dynamite Wars*, 184

22   *Hull Packet and East Riding Times* (2/1/1885)

23   Short, *The Dynamite Wars*, 13–15

24   Short, *The Dynamite Wars*, 75

25   A pledge by Timothy O'Sullivan to work for the liberation of Ireland as a member of the Fenian Brotherhood, undated, Baltimore, Maryland, Fenian Brotherhood Collection, www.aladin.wrlc.org/gsdl/collect/fenian/fenian.shtml (accessed 16/4/09)

26   Short, *The Dynamite Wars*, 202

27   *Daily News* (26/1/1885)

28   *Daily News* (26/1/1885)

29   *Daily News* (26/1/1885)

30   *Pall Mall Gazette* (26/1/1885)

31   Short, *The Dynamite Wars*, 208

32   'The dynamite explosions in London', *The Graphic* (1/31/1885)

33   *The Times* (26/1/1885)

34   *Morning Advertiser* (26/1/1885)

35   *Daily Chronicle* (26/1/1885)

36   *Standard* (26/1/11885); *Lloyd's Weekly Newspaper* (4/1/1885)

37   *Daily Telegraph* (26/1/1885)

38   *Pall Mall Gazette* (26/1/1885)

39   *Pall Mall Gazette* (26/1/1885)

40   *Pall Mall Gazette* (26/1/1885)

41   *Daily News* (27/1/1885)

42   www.oldbaileyonline.org (t18850420–532, trial of Burton and Gilbert)

43   *Pall Mall Gazette* (1/10/1888)

44   *Pall Mall Gazette* (1/10/1888)

45   'Blind-man's buff', *Punch* (22/9/1888)

46   Donald Rumbelow, *The Complete Jack the Ripper* (London: Weidenfeld & Nicolson, 1987), 71

47   *The Times* (18/9/1888)

48   P. Begg, *Jack the Ripper: The Definitive History* (London: Longman, 2004), 203

49   J. Beattie, *Crime and the Courts in England, 1660–1800*, (New Jersey: Princeton University Press, 1986), 50–2

50   Rumbelow, *The Complete Jack the Ripper*, 73

51   *The Times* (13/11/1888)

52   *The Times* (15/10/1888); (10/11/1888)

53   *The Times* (15/11/1888)

54   *The Times* (15/11/1888)

55  *The Times* (12/11/1888)

56  *Pall Mall Gazette* (1/10/1888)

57  *Pall Mall Gazette* (1/10/1888)

58  *The Graphic* (27/8/1887)

59  Haia Shpayer-Makov, *The Making of a Policeman: A Social History of a Labour Force in Metropolitan London, 1829–1914*, (Aldershot: Ashgate, 2002)

60  Wilbur R. Miller, 'Review', *Crime, History & Society*, 8:2 (2004)

61  Begg, *Jack the Ripper*

*Notes to Chapter 9:  London's Shadows: The Darker Side of the Victorian Capital*

1  Walter Dew, *I Caught Crippen* (London: Blackie & Son, 1938), 85

2  Albert Hughes and Allen Hughes, *From Hell*, (Los Angeles: Twentieth Century Fox Film Corporation, 2001) (DVD)

3  *Eastenders* is the BBC's long running soap set in the fictional Albert Square where the Queen Vic pub is the focus of the local community.

4  John Tosh, *The Pursuit of History: Aims, Methods and New Directions in the Study of Modern History*, (London: Longman, 1991) (2nd edition), 132

5  E. H. Carr, *What is History?* (London: Penguin, 1964), 11

6  Carr, *What is History?*, 11

7  www.oxfam.org.uk

8  W. Churchill, *Liberalism and the Social Problem*, (London: Hodder & Stoughton, 1909), 363

# Bibliography

## PRIMARY SOURCES AND PRINTED WORKS BEFORE 1950

William Acton, *Prostitution Considered in Its Moral, Social and Sanitary Aspects in London and Other Large Cities*, (London: 1870)

Robert Anderson, 'The lighter side of my official life', *Blackwood's Magazine*, 187 (1910)

W. Besant, *All Sorts and Conditions of Men: An Impossible Story*, (London: Chatto & Windus, 1882)

Charles Booth, *East London*, (London: Macmillan, 1889)

B. Bosanquet (ed.), *Aspects of the Social Problem, by Various Writers*, (London: Macmillan, 1895)

H. Bosanquet, *Rich and Poor*, (London: Macmillan, 1898)

Walter Dew, *I Caught Crippen*, (London: Blackie & Son, 1938)

Alfred S. Dyer, *The European Slave Trade in English Girls. A Narrative of Facts*, (London: Dyer Brothers, 1880)

W. Churchill, *Liberalism and the Social Problem*, (London: Hodder & Stoughton, 1909)

Havelock Ellis, *The Criminal*, (London: 1890)

H. J. Goldsmid, *Dottings of a Dosser: Being the Revelations of the Inner Life of Low London Lodging Houses*, (London: T. Fisher Unwin, 1886)

James Greenwood, *The Seven Curses of London*, (London: Stanley Rivers, 1869)

O. Hill, *Homes of the London Poor*, (London: Macmillan, 1883)

Dr R. von Krafft-Ebing, *Psychopathia Sexualis with Especial Reference to Contrary Sexual Instinct: A Medico-Legal Study*, translated by C. G. Chaddock, (London: F. A. Davis, 1893)

J. London, *People of the Abyss*, (London, 1903)

C. S. Loch, 'Manufacturing a new pauperism', *The Nineteenth Century*, 37:218 (April 1895)

Cesare Lombroso, *The Criminal Man*, translated by Mary Gibson and Nicole Hahn Rafter, (Durham, NC: Duke University Press, 2006)

J. London, *The People of the Abyss*, (London: Macmillan, 1903)

Henry Mayhew, *London, Labour and the London Poor*, (London: Charles Griffin, 1861)

Rev Andrew Mearns, *The Bitter Cry of Outcast London: An Inquiry into the Condition of the Abject Poor*, (London: 1883)

G. E. Mitton, *Peeps at Great Steamship Lines – The Peninsular and Oriental*, (London: Black, 1913)

James Monro, Assistant Commissioner of the Police of the Metropolis, *A Report of the History of the Department of the Metropolitan Police known as the Convict Supervision Office: Detailing System and Showing Results and Effects Generally on The Habitual Criminal Population*, (London: 1886)

J. Redding Ware, *Before the Bench. Sketches of Police Court Life*, (London: c.1890)

W. T. Stead, 'Government by journalism', *The Contemporary Review*, 49: May (1886)

S. Webb and B. Webb, *English Poor Law History*, (London: Longmans, 1927–29)

## NEWSPAPERS AND PERIODICALS

*Aberdeen Weekly Journal*
*Birmingham Daily Post*
*The Bristol Mercury*
*Daily Chronicle*
*Daily News*
*Daily Telegraph*
*East London Observer*
*Freeman's Journal and Daily Commercial Advertiser*
*Fun*
*Funny Folks*
*Glasgow Herald*
*The Graphic*
*Hull Packet and East Riding Times*
*The Illustrated Police News*
*The Juvenile Companion and Sunday School Hive*
*The Lancet*
*The Link*
*Lloyd's Weekly Newspaper*
*Manchester Times*
*Merry & Wise: An Illustrated Monthly Magazine for Young People,*
*The Monthly Packet*
*Morning Advertiser*
*Morning Post*
*Northern Echo*
*Notes and Proceedings*
*Pall Mall Gazette*
*Pick Me Up!*

*Punch*
*Reynolds's Newspaper*
*The Satirist; or, the Censor of the Times*
*The Spectator*
*Standard*
*The Times*
*The Woman's Signal*

## ARCHIVAL SOURCES

LMA, Thames Police Court Minute book, September 1888

Parliamentary papers
PP 1884–85 [C.4402] [C.4402-I] [C.4402-II] First report of Her Majesty's
  commissioners for inquiring into the housing of the working classes
PP 1886 *Report of a Committee to Inquire and Report as to the Origin and Character of*
  *the Disturbances which took place in the Metropolis on Monday, the 8th of February*
  *and as to the conduct of the Police Authorities in relation therein*
PP 1888 (303) Report from the Select Committee on emigration and Immigration
  (foreigners)
PP 1888 (361) First report from the Select Committee of the House of Lords on
  the sweating system; together with the proceedings of the committee, minutes of
  evidence, and appendix

National Archives
MEPO 2/181
MEPO 2/733
MEPO 3/140

## SECONDARY SOURCES

V. Bailey (ed.), *Policing and Punishment in Nineteenth-Century Britain*, (London:
  Croom Helm, 1981)
V. Bailey, 'The fabrication of deviance: "dangerous classes" and "criminal classes" in
  Victorian England', in Rule J. and Malcolmson R. (eds), *Protest and Survival. The*
  *Historical Experience. Essays for E.P. Thompson*, (London: Merlin Press, 1993)
Stephanie L. Barczewski, *Myth and National Identity in Nineteenth-Century Britain*,
  (Oxford: Oxford University Press, 2000)
Andrew Barrett and Christopher Harrison (eds), *Crime and Punishment in England: a*
  *sourcebook*, (London: UCL 1999)

Paula Bartley, *Prostitution. Prevention and Reform in England, 1860–1914*, (London: Routledge, 2000)

J. Beattie, *Crime and the Courts in England, 1660–1800*, (New Jersey: Princeton University Press, 1986)

Paul Begg, *Jack the Ripper: The Definitive History*, (London: Longman, 2004)

Lucy Bland, *Banishing the Beast: Sexuality and the Early Feminists*, (New York: New Press, 1995)

Jan Bondeson, *The London Monster: A Sanguinary Tale*, (Philadelphia: University of Pennsylvania Press, 2000)

G. Boyce, J. Curran and P. Wingate (eds), *Newspaper History: From the 17th Century to the Present Day*, (London: Constable, 1978)

M. Brodie, 'Artisans and dossers: the 1886 West End riots and the East End casual poor', *London Journal*, 24:2 (1999)

Angus Calder, *The Myth of the Blitz*, (London: Jonathan Cape, 1990)

David Canter, *Criminal Shadows: Inside the Mind of the Serial Killer*, (London: HarperCollins, 1994)

E. H. Carr, *What is History?* (London: Penguin, 1964)

Bryan Cheyette (ed.), *Between 'Race' and Culture: Representations of 'the Jew' in English and American Literature*, (California: Stanford University Press, 1996)

Alexander Chisholm, *The News from Whitechapel: Jack the Ripper in the* Daily Telegraph, (London: McFarland, 2002)

Ng Kwee Choo, *The Chinese in London*, (Oxford: Oxford University Press, 1968)

Stanley Cohen, *Folk Devils and Moral Panics. The Creation of the Mods and Rockers*, (London: MacGibbon, 1972)

Patricia Cornwell, *Portrait of a Killer – Jack the Ripper: Case Closed*, (London: Little, Brown, 2002)

Lee Perry Curtis, *Jack the Ripper and the London Press*, (New Haven: Yale University Press, 2002)

M. J. Daunton, *House and Home in the Victorian City: Working-Class Housing 1850–1914*, (London: Edward Arnold, 1983)

A. Davin, *Growing Up Poor: Home, School and Street in London 1870–1914*, (London: Rivers Oram, 1996)

Graham Davis, *The Irish in Britain, 1815–1914*, (Dublin: Gill & Macmillan, 1991)

J. Davis, 'The London garotting panic of 1862: a moral panic and the creation of a criminal class in mid-Victorian England', in Gatrell, V. *et al.* (eds) *Crime and Law, The Social History of Crime in Western Europe since 1500* (London: Europa, 1980)

J. Davis, 'A poor man's system of justice: the London police courts in the second half of the nineteenth century', *Historical Journal*, 27:2 (1984)

Michael Diamond, *Victorian Sensation: Or the Spectacular, the Shocking and the Scandalous in Nineteenth-Century Britain*, (London: Anthem Press, 2004)

A. P. Donajgrodski (ed.), *Social Control in Nineteenth-Century Britain*, (London: Crook Helm, 1977)

H. J. Dyos and Michael Wolff, *The Victorian City: Images and Realities volume 2*, (London: Routledge & Kegan Paul, 1973)

H. J. Dyos, 'Railways and housing in Victorian London', *Journal of Transport History*, 2 (1955–1956)

Clive Emsley, *Crime and Society in England, 1750–1900*, (London: Longman, 1997)

C. Emsley, *The English Police. A Political and Social History*, (London: Longman, 1991)

David Englander (ed.), *A Documentary History of Jewish Immigrants in Britain, 1840–1920*, (Leicester: Leicester University Press, 1994)

David Englander, 'Booth's Jews: the presentation of Jews and Judaism in life and labour of the people of London', *Victorian Studies* (Summer 1989)

Stewart Evans and Paul Gainey, *The Lodger: The Arrest and Escape of Jack the Ripper*, (London: Century, 1993)

Stewart P. Evans and Keith Skinner, *Jack the Ripper: Letters from Hell*, (Stroud: Sutton, 2001)

Melvyn Fairclough, *The Ripper and the Royals*, (London: Duckworth, 1992)

D. Feldman and G. S. Jones (eds), *Metropolis London: Histories and Representations since 1800*, (London: Routledge, 1989)

Martin Fido, *The Crimes, Detection and Death of Jack the Ripper*, (London: Weidenfeld & Nicolson, 1987)

G. Finlayson, *Citizen, State, and Social Welfare in Britain 1830–1990*, (Oxford: Oxford University Press, 1994)

Trevor Fisher, *Prostitution and the Victorians*, (Stroud: Sutton, 1997)

William J. Fishman, *East End 1888*, (London: Gerald Duckworth, 1988)

Michel Foucault, *Discipline and Punish: The Birth of the Prison*, (London: Penguin, 1991)

Jean Overton Fuller, *Sickert and the Ripper Crimes*, (Oxford: Mandrake, 2001)

David Garland, *Punishment and Modern Society: A Study in Social Theory*, (Oxford: Clarendon Press, 1991)

Lloyd P. Gartner, *The Jewish Immigrant in England, 1870–1914*, (London: Simon Publications, 1960)

S. Martin Gaskell, *Model Housing. From the Great Exhibition to the Festival of Britain*, (London and New York: Mansell, 1987)

V. A. C. Gatrell, B. Lenman and G. Parker (eds), *Crime and the Law. The Social History of Crime in Western Europe since 1500*, (London: Europa, 1980)

V. A. C. Gatrell, 'Crime, authority and the policeman-state', in F. M. L. Thompson (ed.), *The Cambridge Social History of Britain 1750–1950*, 3, *Social agencies and institutions*, (London: Cambridge University Press, 1990)

Deborah Gorham, 'The "Maiden Tribute of Modern Babylon" re-examined: child prostitution and the idea of childhood in Late-Victorian England', *Victorian Studies*, 21:3 Spring (1978)

D. Gray, *Crime, Prosecution and Social Relations: The Summary Courts of the City of London in the Late Eighteenth Century*, (Basingstoke: Palgrave Macmillan, 2009)

P. Haining, *The Legend and Bizarre Crimes of Spring Heeled Jack*, (London: Muller, 1977)

D. Hay and F. Snyder (eds), *Policing and Prosecution in Britain 1750–1850*, (Oxford: Clarendon, 1989)

Hugh Heinrick, *A Survey of the Irish in England*, Alan O'Day (ed.), (London: Hambledon Press, 1872 and 1990)

Tony Henderson, *Disorderly Women in Eighteenth-Century London: Prostitution and Its Control in the Metropolis, 1730–1830*, (London: Longman, 1999)

W. Thomson Hill, *Octavia Hill. Pioneer of the National Trust and Housing Reformer*, (London: Hutchinson, 1956)

E. Hobsbawm, 'The Aristocracy of Labour Reconsidered', in *Worlds of Labour: Further Studies in the History of Labour*, (London: Weidenfeld & Nicolson, 1984)

E. Hopkins, *A Social History of the English Working Classes, 1815–1945*, (London: Hodder & Stoughton, 1979)

Albert Hughes and Allen Hughes, *From Hell*, (Los Angeles: Twentieth Century Fox Film Corporation, 2001) (DVD)

Elizabeth T. Hurren, *Protesting about Pauperism: Poverty, Politics and Poor Relief in Late-Victorian England, 1870–1900*, (London: Royal Historical Society, 2007)

Bill Hutchings, *The Poetry of William Cowper*, (London: Croom Helm, 1983)

Michael Ignatieff, *A Just Measure of Pain: Penitentiaries in the Industrial Revolution, 1780–1850*, (London: Macmillan, 1978)

Stephen Inwood, *City of Cities: The Birth of Modern London*, (London: Macmillan, 2005)

Stephen Inwood, *A History of London*, (London: Pan Macmillan, 2000)

S. Inwood, 'Policing London's morals : the Metropolitan Police and popular culture, 1829–1850', *The London Journal*, 15:2 (1990)

Elwyn Jones and John Lloyd, *The Ripper File* (London: Barker, 1975)

Peter King, 'Newspaper reporting and attitudes to crime and justice in late-eighteenth- and early-ninteenth-century London', *Continuity & Change*, 22 (2007)

Seth Koven, *Slumming: Sexual and Social Politics in Victorian London*, (New Jersey: Princeton University Press, 2004)

Tony Kushner and Nadia Valman (eds), *Fascism and Anti-Fascism in British* Society, (London: Vallentine Mitchell, 2000)

W. F. Lee, 'Demonstrations of Militant Reconstructionists in Metropolitan London, 1880–1914', Unpublished PhD (University of New Mexico: 1976)

Lynn Hollen Lees, *Exiles of Erin: Irish Migrants in Victorian London*, (Manchester: Manchester University Press, 1979)

J. Lewis, *Women and Social Action in Victorian and Edwardian England*, (California: Stanford University Press, 1991)

A. M. McBriar, *An Edwardian Mixed Doubles. The Bosanquets versus the Webbs: A Study in British Social Policy, 1890–1929*, (Oxford: Oxford University Press, 1987)

N. McCord, *British History 1815–1906*, (Oxford: Oxford University Press, 1991)

Ian Maclachlan, 'A bloody offal nuisance: the persistence of private slaughter-houses in nineteenth-century London', *Urban History*, 43:2 (2007)

P. Malpass, 'Continuity and change in philanthropic housing organisations: the Octavia Hill Housing Trust and the Guinness Trust', *London Journal*, 24:1 (1999)

Steven Marcus, *The Other Victorians: A Study of Sexuality and Pornography in Mid Nineteenth Century England*, (New York: Basic Books, 1964)

Jan Marsh, *Back to the Land. The Pastoral Impulse in Victorian England from 1880 to 1914*, (London: Quartet Books, 1982)

Kathleen Callanan Martin, *Hard and Unreal Advice: Mothers, Social Science and the Victorian Poverty Experts*, (Basingstoke: Palgrave 2008)

Peter Mathias, *The First Industrial Nation. An Economic History of Britain 1700–1914*, (London: Routledge, 1987)

Colin Matthew, *The Nineteenth Century*, (Oxford: Oxford University Press, 2005)

S. Merrett, *State Housing in Britain*, (London: Routledge & Kegan Paul, 1979)

Robert Mighall, *A Geography of Victorian Gothic Fiction: Mapping History's Nightmares*, (Oxford: Oxford University Press, 1999)

Wilbur R. Miller, 'Review', *Crime, History & Society*, 8:2 (2004)

Alan Moore and Eddie Campbell, *From Hell*, (Cross Cut, 2008)

Norval Morris and David Rothman (eds), *The Oxford History of the Prison: The Practice of Punishment in Western Society*, (New York: Oxford University Press 1998)

R. J. Morris and Richard Rodger, *The Victorian City: A Reader in British Urban History 1820–1914*, (London: Longman, 1997)

Frank Mort, *Dangerous Sexualities: Medico-Moral Politics in England Since 1830*, (London: Routledge & Kegan Paul, 1987)

Gwynn Nettler, *Criminal Careers Volume 2: Killing One Another*, (Ohio: Anderson Publishing, 1982)

A. Newman (ed.), *The Jewish East End, 1840–1939*, (London: Jewish Historical Society of England, 1981)

David Newsome, *The Victorian World Picture: Perceptions and Introspections in an Age of Change*, (London: John Murray, 1997)

Robin Odell, 'Jack in the Box', *Journal of the Whitechapel Society*, 2 (June 2005)

R. Paley '"An imperfect, inadequate and wretched system"? Policing London before Peel', *Criminal Justice History*, 10 (1989), 95–130

Alan Palmer, *The East End: Four Centuries of London Life*, (New Jersey: Rutgers University Press, 2000)

Henry Pelling, *Popular Politics and Society in Late Victorian Britain*, (London: MacMillan, 1968)

Alison Plowden, *The Case of Eliza Armstrong, 'A Child of 13 bought for £5'*, (London: BBC Publications, 1974)

J. R. Poynter, *Society and Pauperism*, (London: Routledge & Kegan Paul, 1969)

Philip Priestley, *Victorian Prison Lives: English Prison Biography, 1830–1914*, (London and New York: Methuen, 1985)

Catherine E. Purcell and Bruce A. Arrigo, *The Psychology of Lust Murder: Paraphilia, Sexual Killing, and Serial Homicide*, (California: Academic Press, 2006)

R. Reiner, *The Politics of the Police*, (Oxford: Oxford University Press, 2000) (3rd edition)

Robert K. Ressler, Ann W. Burgess and John E. Douglas, *Sexual Homicide. Patterns and Motives*, (London: Simon & Schuster, 1993)

E. Reynolds, *Before the Bobbies: The Night Watch and Police Reform in Metropolitan London, 1720–1830*, (Basingstoke: Palgrave Macmillan, 1998)

Richard Rodger, *Housing in Urban Britain 1780–1914*, (Basingstoke: Palgrave, 1989)

M. E. Rose, *English Poor Law, 1780–1930* (1971)

Fiona Rule, *The Worst Street in London*, (Surrey: Ian Allen, 2009)

Donald Rumbelow, *The Complete Jack the Ripper*, (London: Weidenfeld & Nicolson, 1987)

R. Samuel, *East End Underworld. Chapters in the Life of Arthur Harding*, (London: History Workshop Series, 1981)

S. B. Saul, *The Myth of the Great Depression 1873–1896*, (London: Macmillan, 1972)

G. R. Searle, *A New England? Peace and War 1886–1918*, (Oxford: Oxford University Press, 2004)

J. A. Sharpe, *Dick Turpin: The Myth of the English Highwayman*, (London: Profile, 2005)

Haia Shpayer-Makov, *The Making of a Policeman: A Social History of a Labour Force in Metropolitan London, 1829–1914*, (Aldershot: Ashgate, 2002)

Neal Stubbings Shelden, *The Victims of Jack the Ripper*, (Chestertown: Inklings Press, 2007)

K. R. M. Short, *The Dynamite Wars: Irish-American Bombers in Victorian Britain*, (Dublin: Gill & Macmillan, 1979)

Rob Sindall, *Street Violence in the Nineteenth Century* (Leicester: Leicester University Press, 1990)

Robert Sindall, 'The London garotting panics of 1856 and 1862', *Social History*, 12:3 (October 1987)

F. Smith, 'The Contagious Diseases Acts reconsidered', in *Social History of Medicine* 3, (1990)

Pieter Spierenburg, *A History of Murder: Personal Violence in Europe from the Middle Ages to the Present*, (Cambridge: Polity, 2008)

G. Stedman Jones, *Outcast London: A Study in the Relationship between Classes in Victorian Society*, (London: Oxford University Press, 1971)

R. Storch, 'The policeman as domestic missionary: urban discipline and popular culture in northern England, 1850–1880', *Journal of Social History*, 9:4 (1976)

R. Storch, 'The plague of the blue locusts: police reform and popular resistance in Northern England, 1840–57', *International Review of Social History*, 20:1 (1975)

P. Sugden, *The Complete History of Jack the Ripper*, (London: Da Capo Press, 2002)

Matthew Sweet, *Inventing the Victorians: What We Know about Them and Why We're Wrong*, (New York: St Martin's, 2001)

R. Swift and S. Gilley (eds), *The Irish in Britain, 1815–1939*, (London: Pinter Publishers, 1989)

John. N Tarn, *Five Per Cent Philanthropy: An Account of Housing in Urban Areas between 1840 and 1914*, (Cambridge: Cambridge University Press, 1973)

D. Taylor, *The New Police in Nineteenth-Century England. Crime, Conflict and Control*, (Manchester: Manchester University Press, 1997)

John Tosh, *The Pursuit of History: Aims, Methods and New Directions in the Study of Modern History*, (London: Longman, 1991) (2nd edition)

James Tully, *The Secret of Prisoner 1167. Was this Man Jack the Ripper?* (London: Robinson, 1997)

Martha Vicinus, *Suffer and be Still: Women in the Victorian Age*, (Bloomington: Indiana University Press, 1972)

Judith R. Walkowitz, *City of Dreadful Delight: Narratives of Sexual Danger in Late-Victorian London*, (Chicago: University of Chicago Press, 1992)

Judith R. Walkowitz, 'Jack the Ripper and the Myth of Male Violence'. *Feminist Studies*, 8:3 (1982)

Judith R. Walkowitz, *Prostitution and Victorian Society: Women, Class, and the State*, (Cambridge: Cambridge University Press, 1980)

P. J. Waller, *Town, City and Nation: England 1850–1914* (Oxford: Oxford University Press, 1983)

James Walvin, *Victorian Values*, (London: Andre Deutsch, 1987)

Alexandra Warwick and Martin Willis (eds), *Jack the Ripper: Media, Culture, History*, (Manchester: Manchester University Press, 2007)

Jeffrey Weeks, *Sex, Politics and Society: The Regulation of Sexuality since 1800*, (London: Longman, 1981) (2nd edition)

Alex Werner and Peter Ackroyd, *Jack the Ripper and the East End*, (London: Chatto & Windus, 2008)

Martin J. Wiener, *Reconstructing the Criminal. Culture, Law, and Policy in England, 1830–1914*, (Cambridge: Cambridge University Press, 1994),

Jerry White, *London in the Nineteenth Century: 'A Human Awful Wonder of God'*, (London: Vintage, 2008)

J. White, *Rothschild Buildings. Life in an East End Tenement Block 1887–1920*,

(London: Routledge & Kegan Paul, 1980)

A. S. Wohl, *The Eternal Slum*, (London: Edward Arnold, 1977)

Raymond Williams, *The Country and the City*, (London: Chatto & Windus, 1973)

Tony Williams and Humphrey Price, *Uncle Jack*, (London: Orion, 2005)

A. Yelling, *Slums and Slum Clearance in Victorian London*, (London: Routledge, 1986)

Michael Young and Peter Willmott, *Family and Kinship in East London*, (London: Routledge, 1957)


ELECTRONIC RESOURCES

www.casebook.org

www.oldbaileyonline.org

*Oxford Dictionary of National Biography* (www.oxforddnb.com)

# Index